Inside Urban Charter Schools

INSIDE URBAN CHARTER SCHOOLS

Promising Practices and Strategies in Five High-Performing Schools

KATHERINE K. MERSETH

with

KRISTY COOPER, JOHN ROBERTS, MARA CASEY TIEKEN,
JON VALANT, AND CHRIS WYNNE

HARVARD EDUCATION PRESS
CAMBRIDGE, MASSACHUSETTS

The contents of this book were developed under a grant from the U.S. Department of Education (Award 84.282N). However, those contents do not necessarily represent the policy of the Department of Education, and you should not assume endorsement by the Federal government.

Library of Congress Control Number 2008942555

Paperback ISBN 978-1-934742-10-5
Library Edition ISBN 978-1-934742-11-2

Published by Harvard Education Press,
an imprint of the Harvard Education Publishing Group

Harvard Education Press
8 Story Street
Cambridge, MA 02138

Cover Design: Perry Lubin

The typefaces used in this book are Minion Pro for text and Futura Condensed for display.

Contents

Acknowledgments

We are indebted to the administrators, teachers, students, and parents of the five charter schools that are the focus of this study. These schools are the Academy of the Pacific Rim Charter Public School, Boston Collegiate Charter School, Community Day Charter Public School, MATCH Charter Public High School, and Roxbury Preparatory Charter School. Administrators and teachers took time away from their challenging jobs to open their hearts and minds to our research team, responding to questions and requests for data without hesitation. Parents offered valuable insights into their children's experiences. Students welcomed us into their schools, and their parents spoke with sincerity and emotion about the importance of these schools in the lives of their families. We wish specifically to recognize the school liaisons at each site: Will Austin, Mary Chance, Catherine Egan, Piel Hollingsworth, Dana Lehman, Josh Phillips, Tara Small, and Kathleen Sullivan.

We wish to thank members of each school's administrative team for their detailed input and specific comments on the school cases (chapters 1–5). The cross-school chapters and the conclusion (chapters 6–11) reflect the support and perspective of the entire research team, in collaboration with the primary authors. Without the extraordinary cooperation and willingness of all these individuals to participate in this study, the book would not exist.

Many other individuals contributed in significant and important ways as well. We thank Matt Eskin, Kenneth Wang, and Christian Wilkens for their participation on the research team in its beginning stages; their assistance included research design, data collection, and data analysis. Harvard Graduate School of Education student colleagues Ben Castleman, Amy Fowler, Megin Charner-Laird, and Carla Shalaby made additional contributions.

Through frequent and lengthy conversations, Harvard faculty colleagues and other professionals offered thoughtful advice and important perspectives to consider and explore. For this, we gratefully acknowledge Stacey Childress, Richard Elmore, Bob Fogel, Ronnie Fuchs, Deborah Garson, Patricia Albjerg

Graham, Monica Higgins, Susan Moore Johnson, Dan Koretz, Stig Leschly, Lois Lowry, Gale Merseth, Paul Reville, Nan Stone, and Judith Uhl.

Judith Wasserman provided essential administrative support to the research team and patiently compiled references for the work. We received additional editorial input from a review panel convened by the Massachusetts Charter Public School Association (MCPSA); from Caroline Chauncey and other members of the Harvard Education Publishing Group; from project evaluators Andrew Churchill and Sharon Rallis; and from Cynthia Snow, director of dissemination at the MCPSA.

Members of our families contributed in myriad ways to the completion of this work, including Katherine and Andrew Merseth, Jack and Peggy Roberts, Linda Rollins, Sandy and Donald Tieken, and Ivy Valant.

This book was funded by a grant from the U.S. Department of Education, award 84.282N. It is part of a larger project, Keeping the Promise: The Massachusetts Charter School Dissemination and Replication Project, designed by the MCPSA. The contents of this book do not necessarily represent the policy of the U.S. Department of Education, nor do they represent endorsement by the federal government or MCSPA.

Any errors in the book are the responsibility of Katherine Merseth and members of the research team.

Foreword

In this nation and in the Commonwealth of Massachusetts, we are in a time of serious and thoughtful reexamination of our educational goals and strategies. For roughly a decade and a half, we have been deeply engaged in a powerful education reform movement, yet the results, while showing some promise, are still disappointing. Notwithstanding our high standards and impressive commitment to reach them, educational achievement and socioeconomic status still closely correlate. On average, our education system is still, even after major reforms, most effective at reproducing the existing social order. Despite heroic efforts all across the country and outstanding achievements here in Massachusetts, profound achievement gaps of various kinds persist.

As policy leaders grapple with the reality of the gap between our aspirations and our performance, we continue to be animated by the quest to create better learning conditions so that all students can achieve at high levels and be prepared for success in an internationally competitive, twenty-first century, democratic society. We have struggled to achieve the goals of equity and excellence for a long time in U.S. public education.

Frustration at the mainstream education system's seeming inability to reform itself sufficiently to achieve society's explicit new objective for our schools—"all students achieving at high levels"—has bred renewed interest in reforming education from the outside.

The charter school movement, born in the late 1980s and a source of great hope for the nearly two decades since then, continues to grow gradually. Charter schools now account for a scant 2 percent of all children enrolled in the nation's public schools. Coupled with the slow pace of charter adoption are questions about performance. As is widely recognized in the field of education, there is conflicting evidence about the success of the students in these schools. Proponents and opponents of charter schools rage angry, spirited battles wielding contradictory datasets.

Notwithstanding these charter "wars," reformers, educators, parents, and students continue to find inspiration in the idea of individually chartered, autonomous schools. At the same time, the very existence of charter schools places constructive, competitive pressure on the mainstream system—a largely insulated quasi-monopoly—to improve.

Charter schools were originally conceived as a moderate, market-based solution to contemporary education problems. Less radical than a voucher system, charter schools remained inside the public system and were subject to public regulation, yet they were freed from the control of school district bureaucracies. The theory runs something like this: mainstream public school systems are generally large-scale, highly bureaucratic, monopolistic, and ineffective means of educating children to high standards. Mainstream schools are often insensitive and unresponsive to client needs. Autonomous, independent, client-centered public schools, freed from local bureaucracies, could provide real choices for families and excellent models for public education while putting competitive pressure on the mainstream system to reform itself.

At their inception, charters were offered as the answer to the question of how to close the achievement gaps in this country. The standards movement that was developed simultaneously and was also a strategy for achieving educational equity involved a parallel and generally complementary set of reforms. In order for charters to be properly regulated and evaluated, a set of standards for judging student learning against school performance was needed. The architecture of standards-based reform created the framework for the operation of both mainstream and charter schools. On average, however, neither the standards nor charter strategies, in spite of notable exceptions, has been very successful in closing those achievement gaps.

Many feel that the jury is still out on the success of charter schools, while others feel that charters have already demonstrated superior educational value. Regardless of these arguments, the experience of charter schools thus far has unequivocally demonstrated at least one truth about this new form of governance: changing governance by issuing a charter has, in itself, no inherent impact on improving educational performance. Charters, it turns out, are like time and money in education: it's how you use them that really makes the difference between effective and ineffective performance.

This book describes a handful of truly exceptional schools—schools that happen to be charter schools. These schools are beating the odds and achieving remarkable success with children who often fail in mainstream, public schools. The school portraits in this book raise two important questions: "What are the lessons to be learned from the experience of these schools?" and "What should be done, in policy or practice, in response to these lessons?"

Those of us who make educational policy should be attentive to the lessons from these schools and eager to build on their successes. If we are, we will do what we often ask teachers to do but seldom practice ourselves: data-based decisionmaking.

This challenge seems relatively simple and straightforward, but on closer examination it is not so simple. The data are complex and subject to various interpretations. Moreover, as the authors note, the sample of schools is neither representative of all charter schools nor statistically random. These facts complicate the analysis.

These schools may simply be a collection of exceptional schools. Some might argue that they are exceptional *because* they are charter schools, but the authors of this volume do not take that view. Setting aside for the moment the governance structure that is shared by these schools, we see several common features of educational practice that appear to contribute to the superior performance and learning that characterizes these schools.

All five schools appear to value highly the people who are part of their learning community, especially students, teachers, and families. Each school in its own way sets high expectations for all members of its community and personalizes their strategies for achieving those high expectations. Each of these schools takes itself seriously as a distinct community with particular norms and values, and each spends considerable time and energy acclimating new members of the community to its particular culture. All of these schools view time as a critical resource and routinely dedicate significantly more time to learning than mainstream schools. All of these schools are relatively small, compared to their mainstream counterparts.

Are these qualities of educational practice found in good schools everywhere, irrespective of the particular form of governance, or are they qualities unique to charter schools? If they are not unique to charter schools, is it fair to say that these qualities are more likely to be found in charter schools than in mainstream schools? Alternatively, is there something about being a small school or devoting extra time to instruction that gives rise to the practices that are associated with higher levels of student learning?

This book eloquently describes how some highly commendable educators have used the autonomy and self-determination inherent in a charter. What is of greatest interest is how policymakers might create the conditions of policy and practice necessary to "scale-up" these reforms so that more students might enjoy the substantial benefits of schools like these. In Massachusetts, just over 2.5 percent of our students enjoy access to charter schools and not all these schools are exemplary. At the same time, some indeterminate number of students enjoy access to mainstream schools with varying degrees of autonomy, from schools operating under site-based management to Boston's Pilot Schools. Overall, however, the numbers are tiny. The movement to spread autonomous, teacher-led schools has stalled.

The stalemate has been largely political: The mainstream system is threatened by, resentful of, and, in the opinion of many, financially depleted by the existence of charter schools. Charters feel stymied and stunted by the opposition they have encountered to their well-intentioned entrepreneurial efforts to educate children. The Massachusetts Legislature has been caught for years in the crossfire between advocates of a moratorium on charter schools and proponents of expanded charter school authorization.

If autonomous schools are good for children—and lots of parents seem to think so, as evidenced by the lengthy waiting lists for many charters—then children are losing out as a result of this stalemate. On the other hand, the evidence is inconclusive that charters, per se, are beneficial for students in terms of accelerating learning. Remarkably, the distribution of achievement across and within many charter schools looks a lot like the pattern of distribution in mainstream schools. So, what are we to conclude?

My own conviction is that smaller, at least semiautonomous, teacher-led, extended-time schools will produce success at greater rates than, for example, our typical comprehensive urban high schools. If this is the case, the onus should be on policymakers to invent the ways and means to overcome or bypass the current political deadlock and use the lessons of successful charters to reach more children—ideally, to infiltrate the mainstream system with the kinds of practices described in this book.

The division in our field over the status of charter schools has been destructive because, to the public, the education sector appears to be a house divided not over the interests of children, but over the interests of adults. Charters have been with us in Massachusetts for well over a decade and in other states for close to two decades. It's time to decide where we are going with charters and how this structure or the principles that animate them can best serve the interests of all our children.

I believe that the political stalemate on charters, the tension between proponents and opponents, will continue to frustrate all but modest expansion efforts for the foreseeable future. It is important that we have a healthy, thriving charter sector to provide more choices to families, to allow for greater differentiation in the delivery of educational services, and to put healthy competitive pressure on the mainstream system. However, the principles that animated charter reform should rapidly be made available to far more students. I conclude that we should move with a sense of urgency to incorporate the charter school characteristics identified in this book into mainstream schools.

One of the most salient characteristics of effective charters concerns leadership. The charters described in this book are indigenously led by faculty and administration while being governed by their own boards of directors. Such leadership conveys a critical element in the charter formula: ownership—not ownership by a distant bureaucracy but by the school community itself. With this ownership comes an enhanced sense of leadership, responsibility, and motivation that typically affects all members of the school community. This sense of ownership appears necessary but not sufficient to guarantee a successful school.

This sense of ownership is a palpable quality in effective schools of all kinds, mainstream, charter, and independent. One can usually sense this spirit of responsibility within moments of entering such a school. Teachers feel they own the quality of students' work, while students feel obligated to be successful individually and as a school community.

In any effective school, the kind of motivation that derives from the responsibility of ownership tends to drive school improvement at all levels. Teachers have the opportunity to work continuously to perfect their instructional practice. Students and teachers are typically willing to work longer hours to achieve their goals. Teachers are able to abandon mass-production techniques for interacting with students and can develop individualized, differentiated treatment. High expectations are pervasive and tend to eliminate barriers to achievement. Every student counts, and a relentless effort is mounted to ensure that every student achieves proficiency. Students will say "there's no place to hide," while teachers will do whatever it takes for as long as it takes to help their students achieve success.

Recently, I talked with a veteran teacher in one of the state's largest comprehensive high schools. She complained that reformers often overlook what she sees as the most conspicuously missing ingredients in student achievement: student motivation and effort. Charters, through the mechanism of choice and, in the best cases, through the application of intense, individualized faculty-student engagement, seek to address motivational issues that reformers ignore at their peril. In the high-performing schools described in this book, students are usually highly motivated and regularly apply the kind of effort that is a prerequisite for learning.

These optimum conditions of teaching and learning can be found in the best schools no matter what their form of governance. Schools with high levels of expectation, ownership, and achievement exist in public school systems, in charter schools, and in the independent and parochial school sectors. The question readers should ask as they contemplate the compelling portraits presented in this volume is what they and all of us need to do, in policy and in practice, to make the successes enjoyed by these schools the rule and not the exception.

Paul Reville
Secretary of Education
Commonwealth of Massachusetts

Introduction

Massachusetts public schools are a study in contrasts, with a striking range of accomplishments, disappointments, and opportunities. This range of contrasts is even more striking when one looks at their geographic proximity. Consider the following.

In 2006–07, MATCH Charter School notched its the fourth consecutive school year in which every graduating senior received an acceptance letter from a four-year college. Its performance on the Massachusetts Comprehensive Assessment System (MCAS) ranked among the best in the state: all of its tenth graders scored advanced or proficient in math, and 83 percent scored equally well in language arts. With a population that includes 96 percent students of color and 70 percent of students live at or below the poverty level, MATCH has achieved exemplary results. It has received accolades as one of the country's top one hundred public high schools by *U.S. News & World Report.*

Just a short distance away, a Boston public high school that is about the same size as MATCH and has about 80 percent students of color achieves MCAS scores that are consistently among the lowest in Massachusetts. In 2006-07, just 17 percent of its students scored at proficient or advanced levels on tenth-grade English language arts and 15 percent scored at proficient or advanced levels in mathematics. In the 2006-07 school year, this district high school reported an annual adjusted dropout rate of 18 percent, while MATCH reported a dropout rate of just under 2 percent.[1] Additionally, 60 percent of MATCH students who enroll as ninth graders graduate from the school in four years, while just 44 percent of the students who enroll at this Boston high school as ninth graders graduate in the same amount of time. Self-reported postgraduation plans indicate that fewer than 40 percent of the students in this district high school intend to attend four-year colleges.

Do these two schools have different kids in terms of race, ethnicity, or class? Not really. Kids from different parts of the city? No. Maybe it's that one is a charter school and the other is a traditional public school? Well, no. Consider this.

Another Boston charter school, Roxbury Prep, educates 100 percent students of color. In 2007, 86 percent of their seventh graders scored at proficient or advanced levels in English language arts and 72 percent did so in mathematics. Yet, less than a mile away, another charter school that has been in existence longer than Roxbury Prep earned seventh-grade MCAS scores of 54 percent proficient or advanced in English language arts and 32 percent proficient or advanced in mathematics.

Are the differences between these two schools any greater than the first two? Not really; in fact, the differences are fewer, in that both are charter schools established by the Massachusetts Education Reform Act of 1993. So, what gives?

Some may attribute these test-score differences to chance or blind luck. After all, with nearly two thousand public schools in Massachusetts, it is a statistical certainty that some schools will outperform others. Yet, upon closer examination, a much more complex picture emerges. This book aims to make this complex picture comprehensible to readers by exploring the intricate workings of five consistently high-performing charter schools in urban areas in Massachusetts—four in Boston and one in Lawrence. These schools, while unique in important ways, also share several common practices and approaches to educating children that may hold important keys to providing a first-rate public education for all students, whether in traditional public, charter, private, or parochial schools.

This book offers an opportunity for readers to examine, with a thoroughness often unseen in charter school literature (Gill, Timpane, Ross, Brewer, & Booker, 2007), the inner workings of these institutions and to consider what makes these schools tick. Like fine Swiss watches, these schools operate on multiple levels. On the outside, a watch seems to effortlessly produce the intended outcome: accurate timekeeping. Swiss watch designs may differ, but once the face of a timepiece is removed, a symphony of wheels, dials, gears, levers, and springs appears, each part working in harmony with the others to achieve the intended outcome. And so it is with the charter schools featured in this book. The organization of these schools, like the inner workings of a Swiss watch, is strikingly coordinated and coherent. Within these schools, every person, program, system, structure, and decision has a special role and works in concert toward the fulfillment of clear, widely embraced goals related to academic achievement. The unrelenting passion and commitment of a school's many stakeholders fuel this process, but it is the thoughtful coordination of all of the school's activities—its *coherence* with regard to purpose, people, and planning—that channels the passion and commitment into consistently outstanding results.

Charter Schools

The charter schools featured in this book, like the other four thousand charter schools across the country, are similar to traditional public schools in several regards: they receive government funds to operate, they may not engage in religious instruction, and they are open to all interested students. These schools are state-level entities created by state legislatures and therefore subject to state-level performance requirements, state curricular frameworks, and the federal requirements outlined under the No Child Left Behind Act of 2001 (NCLB). The similarities they have to traditional public schools stimulate a quest to determine which elements of these schools are transferable to all schools.

At the same time, however, charters have several characteristics that distinguish them from traditional public schools. For example, a group of private individuals may open and govern a charter school, in contrast to traditional schools, which are typically governed by a publicly elected board or by individuals appointed by an elected official. Another distinguishing characteristic of charters is that the leaders of these organizations may be individuals with little or no formal training or experience in education. In effect, many charter school founders are nonprofit entrepreneurs who are indirectly accountable to the taxpaying public through the state-level authorizing agency (in this case, the Massachusetts Department of Education). Finally, and perhaps most important, these are schools of choice: parents, students, teachers, and administrators all exercise personal choice in agreeing to attend and work in these schools

This book examines five Massachusetts charter schools that met selection criteria determined by the Massachusetts Charter Public School Association. The criteria were:

- Being located in a Massachusetts district that falls within the top 10 percent of state districts with the highest proportions of children in poverty (according to 2003 U.S. Census figures)
- Significantly outscoring the local district in which the school is located on the state assessment system—the MCAS—in both aggregate scores and the low-income subgroup
- Achieving adequate yearly progress status in 2006 (as defined by NCLB)
- Having received at least one successful charter renewal from the Massachusetts Department of Education

Although these measures are somewhat arbitrary and would result in a different sample of "successful schools" had they been taken in different years,[2] these selection criteria identified five "high-performing" charter schools in the Commonwealth of Massachusetts. They are:

- Academy of the Pacific Rim (in Boston)
- Boston Collegiate Charter School (in Boston)
- Community Day Charter Public School (in Lawrence)
- MATCH Charter Public High School (in Boston)
- Roxbury Preparatory Charter School (in Boston)

Demographic information for these schools, as well as other important data, including grade levels and per-pupil expenditures, follow in tables I.1 and I.2 and figures I.1 through I.5.

Methodology

After receiving the names of the schools selected for the study, the authors spent eighteen months, from January 2007 to June 2008, conducting over ninety interviews with school personnel, observing for more than fifty days in the schools and in nearly 140 classrooms, speaking with parents in focus groups, examining documents and state reports, and reflecting as a team—and with others—about the findings. This work is unique in its depth and qualitative research design. A detailed description of the study's methodology is available in appendix I.A.

Context for This Work

To place the findings of this book in an appropriate context, it is important to address briefly some of the most compelling, frequently cited concerns about charter schools. For example, several researchers argue that charter schools enjoy unfair advantages over traditional public schools with their sometimes smaller special education, low-income, and English-language learner populations (Carnoy, Jacobsen, Mishel, & Rothstein, 2005; Rothstein, 2004; UCLA Charter School Study, 1998; Zollers & Ramanathan, 1998).

Indeed, there is some truth to these arguments. Tables I.1 and I.2 show that most of these schools do have slightly lower percentages of special education and low-income students than the districts in which they are located, with larger discrepancies in non-native English speakers. Other differences, such as the influence of parental choice, may be more difficult to quantify; perhaps charter schools attract unusually motivated children and families, eager

TABLE I.1
Demographic Data for the Boston (Mass.) Public Schools
and the Study Schools Located in Boston

School	Academy of the Pacific Rim (Boston)	Boston Collegiate Charter School (Boston)	MATCH Charter Public High School (Boston)	Roxbury Preparatory Charter School (Boston)	All Boston Public Schools
Founded	1997	1998	2000	1999	N/A
Grades	5–12	5–12	9–12	6–8	N/A
Total enrollment	472	412	222	198	N/A
Race/Ethnicity	57% African American; 23% White; 16% Hispanic; 3% Asian; 1% multiracial, non-Hispanic	64% White; 27% African American; 6% Hispanic; 2% Asian; 1% multiracial, non-Hispanic	62% African American; 30% Hispanic; 4% White; 2% Asian; 2% multi-racial, non-Hispanic	61% African American; 33% Hispanic; 2% Native American; 5% multiracial, non-Hispanic	39% African American; 37% Hispanic; 13% White; 9% Asian; 2% multiracial, non-Hispanic
Free/reduced-price lunch (low-income)	52%	42%	71%	70%	71%
Special education	13%	17%	11%	12%	20%
First language not English	12%	4%	14%	27%	38%
Limited English proficient	1%	0%	0%	1%	19%
Per-pupil expenditures (2006-07)	$13,464	$11,356	$16,643	$14,879	$16,467*

Note: All figures are from the 2007-08 school year unless otherwise noted.

*http://finance1.doe.mass.edu/schfin/statistics/function_3yr_detail.aspx?ID=035

TABLE I.2

**Demographic Data for the Lawrence (Mass.) Public Schools
and the Study Schools Located in Lawrence**

School	Community Day Charter Public School (Lawrence)	All Lawrence Public Schools
Founded	1995	N/A
Grades	K–8	N/A
Total enrollment	330	N/A
Race/Ethnicity	87% Hispanic; 9% White; 2% African American; 1% Asian; 1% multiracial, non-Hispanic	88% Hispanic; 7% White; 3% Asian; 2% African-American
Free/reduced-price lunch (low-income)	64%	83%
Special education	18%	19%
First language not English	80%	82%
Limited English proficient	29%	24%
Per-pupil expenditures	$13,917 (2006-07)	$12,039* (FY07)

Note: All figures are from the 2007-08 school year unless otherwise noted.

*http://finance1.doe.mass.edu/schfin/statistics/function_3yr_detail.aspx?ID=149

teachers, and engaged parents. Finally, choice opens some doors and closes others. Since these particular schools seek to provide their graduates with a choice of secondary school or college, a reasonable question to consider is whether these goals subtly exclude certain students who are not interested in higher education.

At the same time, however, these charter schools must overcome some inherent disadvantages. For example, tables I.1 and I.2 show that three out of the five schools in this study spend considerably less money per pupil than their local districts; certainly some of this money is lost in the need to acquire

FIGURE I.1   Student Demographics by Race

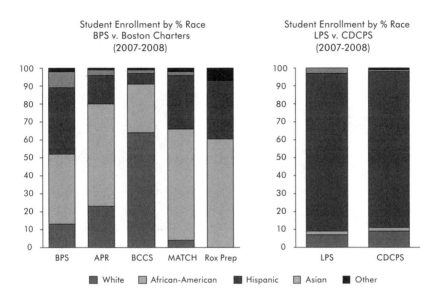

Student Enrollment by % Race
BPS v. Boston Charters
(2007-2008)

Student Enrollment by % Race
LPS v. CDCPS
(2007-2008)

■ White   ■ African-American   ■ Hispanic   ■ Asian   ■ Other

Source: Massachusetts Department of Education

FIGURE I.2   Student Demographics: Boston Public Schools vs. Boston Charters

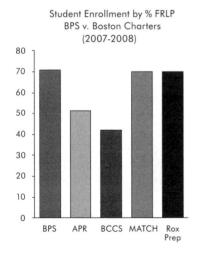

Student Enrollment by % FRLP
BPS v. Boston Charters
(2007-2008)

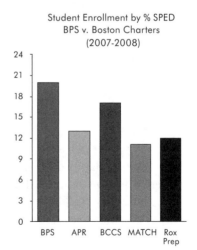

Student Enrollment by % SPED
BPS v. Boston Charters
(2007-2008)

Source: Massachusetts Department of Education

FIGURE I.3   Student Demographics: Lawrence Public Schools vs. Community Day

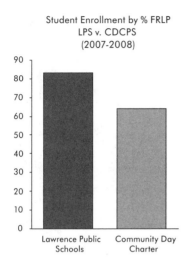

Student Enrollment by % FRLP
LPS v. CDCPS
(2007-2008)

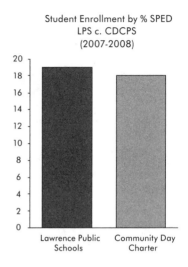

Student Enrollment by % SPED
LPS c. CDCPS
(2007-2008)

Source: Massachusetts Department of Education

FIGURE I.4   Student Demographics: Boston Public Schools vs. Boston Charters

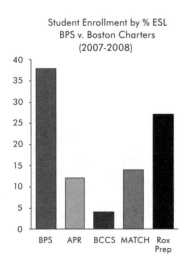

Student Enrollment by % ESL
BPS v. Boston Charters
(2007-2008)

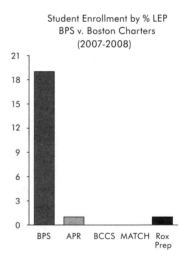

Student Enrollment by % LEP
BPS v. Boston Charters
(2007-2008)

Source: Massachusetts Department of Education

FIGURE I.5   Student Demographics: Lawrence Public Schools vs. Community Day

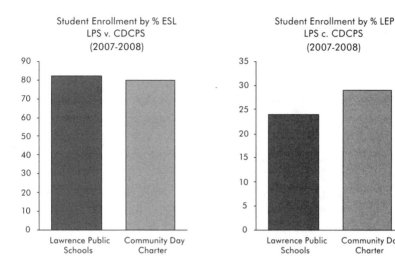

Source: Massachusetts Department of Education

support for facilities not provided by the state. The extent to which these differences influence test scores is impossible to establish with certainty, yet the performance gaps between these schools and their local districts—and many similarly constituted charter schools—are so vast and consistent that these "advantages" are unlikely to fully account for their impressive results. There must be something these schools are doing that merits documentation and replication.

Passionate arguments for and against charter schooling have created a contentious—and unfortunate—context for this book. While not ignoring this debate altogether, the authors wish to largely sidestep ideological positions and exchanges. Therefore, rather than defending or condemning charter schools or charter school policy, the book offers rich qualitative findings that often are lacking in ideological conversations about charter schools. The results of this research offer those interested in school reform a nuanced and careful analysis of the factors that likely contribute to the outstanding academic performance of these five schools. Clearly, generalizations beyond these five schools are beyond the scope of the qualitative data in this book. Nevertheless, the authors believe many important aspects of these schools will inform anyone interested in improving the condition of K–12 education.

Book Structure

The book has four parts: this overview of the work and the charter school debate; a series of ethnographic case studies of each of the five schools; a collection of cross-case chapters that examine common elements across the schools; and a conclusion that raises questions for charter school advocates and detractors alike.

Specific details about each chapter follow:

- Introduction—Provides an introduction to the purpose and content of the book.
- Chapters 1–5: School Profiles—Offer qualitative case studies of each school, bringing the schools and their cultures alive for the reader, introducing a variety of practices in context, and conveying the deliberate coherence and purposefulness of these organizations. Each portrait begins with a descriptive account of life at one school and concludes with an analysis of several factors identified by school personnel as most responsible for the school's success.
- Chapter 6: Theoretical Framework—Provides a unique conceptual framework for the analysis of the school practices by reviewing the effective schools literature and the literature of successful nonprofit organizations. The chapter links these two literatures and delves into research that legitimizes the work of these schools. The chapter frames several themes that catalyze the key elements of success in these schools.
- Chapters 7–10: Cross-Case Chapters—Organize the practices of these five schools into four categories of practice that contribute to success: culture, mission, people, structures, and systems. These elements are integral and unique to the coherent operation of these schools.
- Chapter 11: Stepping Back and Looking Forward—Explores next steps for these charter schools and for the movement at large. The chapter considers several tensions inherent in these schools, and indeed in all schools, and the likely need to focus on instruction to achieve results at the next level.

Cultures of Coherence: Purpose, People, and Planning

These five schools are not without challenges, blemishes, or shortcomings, yet each has repeatedly demonstrated its ability to produce impressive MCAS results with students who normally would attend schools in a high-need urban district. Each has also expressed an eagerness to share its insights with other school leaders, academics, and policymakers in hopes of improving the opportunities students will have beyond their own school walls. Whether one applies elements of systems theory (e.g., Deming, 2000), the advice of management gurus (e.g., Collins, 2005; Drucker, 1990), or concepts of organizational congruence (Tushman & O'Reilly, 2002; Nadler & Tushman, 1980), a central element of high-performing organizations that is evident in these charter schools is the power of coherence. Within these schools, the intense focus on the purpose of their work, the dedication and coordination of people within the organization, and the detailed attention to planning all operate in a coherent fashion at every level. Little stands alone, aloof, or separate. The Oliver Wyman Group (2003), while talking about nonprofits, may as well have been describing these five schools when they stated:

> The organization's performance rests upon the alignment of each of the components—the work, people, structure, and culture—with all of the others. *The tighter the fit—or put another way, the greater the congruence—the higher the performance.* (italics added, p. 9)

The first step in understanding the operation of these schools requires a detailed glimpse into the classrooms and corridors of the school buildings. The next five chapters present the schools one by one in order to give the reader a taste of the life inside each one, and to begin dissecting the organizational elements that make each school a unique educational institution—one whose students are prepared to achieve strong standardized test results.

CHAPTER ONE

COMMUNITY DAY CHARTER PUBLIC SCHOOL

Intimacy in a Data-Driven School

Early in the Morning

The stone building casts an impressive shadow onto Hampshire Street, dwarfing the short line of cars that wait patiently in front. A tall turret studded with large red stones flanks one side of the front steps, and a curved archway nearly hides the structure's front door. A small child clambers up the steps, lunchbox in hand and backpack bouncing, and he disappears into the unlikely home of Community Day's Early Learning Center (ELC).

Community Day Charter Public School serves children in the city of Lawrence, Massachusetts, an old mill town about forty-five minutes north of Boston. Once home to a number of bustling textile mills, the city fell onto hard times with the post–World War II decline of the textile industry. Now these old factories and warehouses sit abandoned and useless alongside the Merrimack River, as seagulls circle empty parking lots and silent, trash-lined streets. Today the city's residents are primarily Latino, due to an influx of Puerto Rican and Dominican immigrants; nearly one-quarter live below the poverty line (U.S. Census Bureau, 2006).

The stately Early Learning Center building, which houses a two-year kindergarten program and a first-grade class, seems out of place among the run-down triplexes and graying apartment buildings surrounding it. Two teachers roam between the cars and buses pulled close to the sidewalk, waving cars

The primary author for this chapter is Mara Casey Tieken.

13

forward, greeting children, exchanging hellos with parents, and watching students make their way up the steps. Some parents accompany their children to the edge of the walkway, bending for a goodbye kiss before the children climb the steps alone. At the top of the steps, the heavy door opens to bright colors, child-sized chairs, cheerful voices, and breakfast.

Students are also arriving at the Lower and Upper schools, located a couple of miles away on Community Day's Prospect Street campus. Cars turn off the potholed street to slowly climb the driveway up steep Prospect Hill, edging to a stop in front of a low building with a short set of concrete steps and simple double door. The building's narrow stained-glass windows reveal its previous role as a school run by an order of Venerini nuns; now it holds Community Day's Lower School. Just beyond the Lower School is the Upper School, a four-story mansion with a precarious perch atop the hill.

In the morning, all students on this campus wait together for the day to begin. Students file in to the Lower School after shaking hands with the head of the Upper School or one of the school's long-time teachers as they alight from their car or bus. The younger, Lower School students sit according to class on the gym floor, occupying themselves by looking over their poster projects or books, chattering in small clusters, or just leaning sleepily against their backpacks. The head of the Lower School stands watch among these small clusters, checking names against the roster on his clipboard. The older, Upper School students, nearly as tall as the teachers they talk with, gather on the school's increasingly crowded front porch.

These spaces grow noisy with students until a little after 8 AM, when the Lower School children—second, third, fourth, and fifth graders—begin filing to their classrooms and the Upper School students march across the parking lot and enter the old mansion. These sixth, seventh, and eighth graders chat quietly as they hang backpacks on hooks, take out homework papers, check in with teachers, and arrange their pencils and books in their desks. By 8:20 AM, the head of the Upper School expects that only the sound of pencils on paper will fill the classrooms as the students settle into the day's academics.

Busy Groups in Tiny Spaces

The Upper School is a labyrinth of rickety staircases, narrow hallways, and small rooms. A quiet calm pervades the space from the front office through the brightly decorated hallways to the individual classrooms. These classrooms, which often have stray reminders of their previous life as a kitchen or bedroom, are decorated with brightly colored student projects, and the walls of

COMMUNITY DAY CHARTER PUBLIC SCHOOL
A Commonwealth Charter School, Founded in 1995

Number of Students and Grade Levels
330 Students in Grades K–8

Race/Ethnicity	*Subgroups*
87% Hispanic	18% Special Education
9% White	64% Low Income
2% African American	80% First Language Not English
1% Asian	29% Limited English Proficient
1% Multiracial, Non-Hispanic	

Source: Massachusetts Department of Education

the eighth-grade classrooms display a calendar highlighting high school application deadlines. Just before a period begins, students grouped by grade level in the sixth grade and by subject area in the seventh and eighth grades fill the classrooms, and they automatically begin work on the "Do-Now" exercise written on the whiteboard. They may remain in this room to hear a lecture or work alone or in pairs on an assignment. However, the students often break into small instructional groups, which are determined according to academic performance data generated by the in-house data manager. These groups, ranging in size from just one or two students to ten or twelve, troop off to work with an instructor in one of the school's tiny nooks.

Across the parking lot at the Lower School, every conceivable inch of space is filled. This building is more school-like in both appearance and affect than the Upper School, with its small gymnasium and cafeteria, large classrooms lining a wide hallway, classroom guinea pigs, and noise echoing through the building. These classrooms hold self-contained classes of second, third, fourth, and fifth graders and two teachers in each one. These teachers also make frequent use of instructional groupings. Thus, it is typical to find a cluster of six or seven students and an adult huddled over reading textbooks in a corner of the gym or at the end of the hall, sitting below the pegs holding guitars used during the Friday music program. One cannot help but notice the sheer number of adults—in classrooms and working with small groups of students—who work within this limited space.

Although its building is vastly different from either the long schoolhouse of the Lower School or the tall mansion of the Upper School, the Early Learning Center is just as economical in its use of space. The cavernous rooms of this former public library are cordoned off by carpeted partitions into small classrooms, short hallways, and a tiny eating area; a small kitchen, bathrooms, and narrow office occupy a cramped corner of the ground floor; a grand curved staircase, carefully navigated by these small students, leads to the two first-grade classrooms on the second floor. Small cubbies with tiny backpacks line the entrance of each kindergarten or first-grade classroom, and juice-boxes sit atop low shelves in a checkerboard arrangement, each waiting to be claimed by its owner during snack time. Colorful displays of laminated calendars and schedules cover the walls, accompanied by the uniform alphabets of the kindergarten's Success for All curriculum. Among these displays are photographs of students and arrangements of their carefully crafted artwork. Students sit in groups at tables, or they gather on the floor to work more closely with a particular teacher—two per classroom, supported by various assistants and special education staff—or engage in a less-supervised activity.

If you wind through the basement of the ELC—past the newly renovated, remarkably cheerful kindergarten classroom housed in the depths of the building, along a narrow corridor, and through a nondescript door at the end of the hall—you will find yourself suddenly in the bright offices of The Community Group, the nonprofit responsible for the birth of Community Day Charter Public School.

In the Beginning

The presence of Community Day's executive director is felt, if not seen, throughout all three school buildings. This elegant woman, whose soft voice belies the strength of her convictions, has directed the school throughout its existence. The school was founded thirteen years ago under her leadership, and under her direction it has weathered the storm of the standards and accountability movement. The school has changed little, she explains, since its beginning days:

> Based on [the] knowledge that we had garnered from working in our daycare programs, we were not happy with the quality of education being offered in the city. We were dealing with low-income people; we knew they

didn't have a lot of alternatives. . . . They had no real choices. They could not afford even the Catholic schools sometimes; generally, their tuitions were too high.

So our idea was to provide an alternative and a choice that was different from what was being offered, but was public education. We began by just running an ad in the paper and [we] got a thick, Oriental rug. We rented a room somewhere, we put a potted plastic plant in a basket . . . because we want[ed] to look credible, [and] we asked, "What do you want?" and people poured into that little room and they opened their hearts to us and told us what they wanted. Mainly what they wanted was a good education where their kids would learn and where their kids would . . . have an opportunity. . . . It was amazing, the people that came to us.

So you could call it market research. . . . We went out to market and we asked people who had no choice, "What do you want?" as if they had money to spend, and then brought them actually into the founding group as a parents advisory board and worked real closely with them in the beginning to deliver what we were hearing.

Armed with this "market research," a dedicated group of invested parents and staff members then wrote a charter and developed a mission statement:

> Our mission is to provide a kindergarten through grade eight school that will draw upon our considerable experience in working together as a community to develop and implement a curriculum that discovers and supports the special characteristics and unique learning styles of each student. We will engage that student in meaningful learning experiences for the purposes of clearly stated goals in the areas of understandings, knowledge, skills, habits and social competencies. The curriculum will be embedded in the reality of city life and will reinforce the positive aspects of our city: its culture, art and economy, its working class history and strong work ethic. Our philosophy is informed by an understanding that learning takes place in the context of family and that family must be supported in ways that make learning for the child possible.

And, years later, this mission still guides the work of the school.

The Business of Learning

Twenty-three students are gathered on the corner carpet in one of the first-grade classrooms. They sit cross-legged, all facing the wall with the calendar. They've just completed their Do-Now—tracing their handprint, a task quickly accomplished by all students—and have been asked to finish the sentence, "My favorite color is . . ."—a more difficult assignment for some. After the teachers have reminded students how to find a color's name on the crayon's wrapper and taken the lunch count, and after the good-morning greeting rituals have been completed, the students' attention turns to the calendar. One teacher leads them through a practiced routine that includes naming "yesterday," "today," and "tomorrow," noting the day's weather, counting the day of school, determining the next shape in a pattern, and—perhaps most important—recognizing who has lost a tooth. Most of these short activities are facilitated by the student of the day, handpicked by the previous student of the day. He carries out his duties unabashedly, confidently posing these questions to his classmates and then choosing respondents and listening to their answers, rephrasing his queries in complete questions when prompted by the teacher. The exchanges are quick, deliberate, routine but engaging—and most students sit quietly and listen. He returns to his spot on the floor, tucking his legs underneath him, and the teacher picks up a copy of *Stuart Little*, a book that the entire school—kindergarten through eighth grade—is currently reading. Teachers hope that conversations about the book will continue at home among siblings, but for these first graders, the story is tough; by the chapter's end, squirming is widespread. But the students gamely—and for the most part correctly—answer the comprehension questions the teacher poses, and a few offer their thoughts on whether Stuart's dilemma will be solved. And then, with a recitation of the Pledge of Allegiance and a rousing round of "It's a Grand Old Flag," morning meeting is over and the day is underway.

Instruction has also begun on the Prospect Hill campus. At the Lower School, each classroom door opens into a flurry of noise and activity. A third-grade class is midway through a 90-minute reading period. The Do-Now long finished, twenty-five children are busy in five clusters throughout the room. A teacher sits on the floor with one group, all with reading textbooks spread on their laps. The students take turns reading short passages from the story; between readings, the teacher asks them to recap the story's action or explain the meaning of a word. In the far corner of the room, the coteacher is using magnetic letters to teach word endings and letter sounds; under her direction, students take turns rearranging the letters to construct new words. A third group of students are reading silently at their desks. The final two groups of children are gathered around clustered desks. Each has several stacks of word cards, from which they are to isolate synonym and antonym pairs. They must then complete a worksheet assessing the same skill. Each group appears to have a couple of hard workers and a few less assiduous students. Two students speed through the worksheet; one spits out a rapid answer and they both jot it on the line. While this pair quickly finishes, another student in the group plays with a pencil sharpener in his desk, and two girls alternate between recording answers on their worksheets and whispering secrets about their classmates. Occasionally the teacher on the floor scans the classroom, requesting that these students get back on task.

In the room next door, the second-grade class is working on a writing lesson. The teacher stands before her students, who are seated at desks arranged in traditional rows. She struggles to capture the attention of these twenty-four young minds; as she explains the structure of a narrative, eyes wander and hands explore inside desks. After lecturing for several minutes, she asks students to name stories with heroes. Some students shoot hands into the air, while others simply shout their responses. When her question doesn't receive the hoped-for response, the teacher gives her own answer. The group's attention falters even more as one student begins to scrape his desk against the floor, and the teacher's repeated "Excuse me" fails to refocus the class.

Across the hall in a fifth-grade mathematics class, half the students are gathered in pairs working to find the lowest common multiple of groups of numbers. The partners work eagerly and strategically—in one pair, a student calls the numbers from the worksheet while the other punches them into a calculator; another pair is engaged in long lists of addition on the papers' margins, occasionally looking over one another's shoulders to check the accuracy of their calculations. A teacher sits at an empty student desk in the middle of the classroom, where struggling students can approach him to be reminded of strategies for finding multiples. The coteacher in this class has the other half of the students—those whose math skills are less advanced—in a room down the hall, where they are completing a problem set involving simple fractions. Next door, a fourth-grade class is working with the science teacher, the only subject-area teacher in grades four through six. An energetic woman who pushes her teaching supplies on an overflowing cart, she has divided the class into five groups, each one responsible for recording facts about a particular biome on a chart. Next, she reassembles the groups so that each contains a representative from every biome and they can share information with their classmates. This reorganization is a little chaotic, and some students have been more thorough in their research than others. The slightly exasperated teacher visits each group to redirect their attention to the chart and, by the period's end, after a flurry of dictated information and hurried copying, the groups have completed their charts.

At the other end of the parking lot, the quiet atmosphere that began the day at the Upper School continues. In one of the sixth-grade classrooms, the Do-

Now—a series of computations, completed individually and checked against an answer key by one of the students—makes a smooth transition into the math lesson. Today's instructional time is dedicated to reviewing last week's test. Students who earned poor scores received their tests the day before, with instructions to have them signed by parents and to rework their incorrect problems as homework. Two teachers—one of the sixth-grade coteachers and the Upper School's generalist teacher (who floats between classrooms to provide additional instructional support and also serve as an in-house substitute teacher)—take these lower-performing students from the classroom. They split into two groups, and one group retreats to the parlor to work through each problem that the students missed, taking turns reworking the problems on a whiteboard. Students who performed well—about half the class—remain in the room with the sixth-grade coteacher responsible for leading math instruction. This teacher passes back their tests, announcing their grades and ribbing students with lower than expected scores, and then they quickly revisit challenging test items. New answers are called out, and the teacher swiftly demonstrates answers on the board—the pace is fast and the atmosphere casual, despite a number of references to the upcoming MCAS.

Down the hall in a seventh-grade social studies class, the Do-Now asks students to evaluate their soon-due research projects against the rubric that will eventually determine grades—a broad rubric that includes the three project elements, "written report," "display," and "evidence of research." The teacher stands watch as students turn in these rubrics, occasionally questioning a student about his or her self-assessment.

On the whiteboard in a neighboring eighth-grade science class a teacher has written, "Aim: Students will be able to explain factors that cause climate change." These eleven students' Do-Now exercise is to evaluate a nearly complete project—a brochure explaining climate change—against a rubric that includes the six dimensions of "neatness," "creativity," "vocabulary," "content," "class work," and "accountability." Students who feel comfortable with their self-assessed scores are permitted to turn in their projects early. The students then complete a guided reading worksheet, an activity introduced with reminders from the teacher regarding the classroom procedures for completing such work; for example, they may work alone or in pairs, or they should consult their textbooks for answers. Most students pair off: one student may read a passage aloud while another distills the question's answer. The teacher walks from pair to pair, looking over shoulders to point out answers that need to be reconsidered, responding to students' questions, or making students' misconceptions evident with a gentle, "Do we have palm trees here in Massachusetts?"

Finally, in the middle of ongoing lessons, books and binders are temporarily abandoned, classroom basketballs are located, and one of the sixth-grade classes troops through a narrow hallway and out to recess. Recess takes place on the parking lot separating the Lower and Upper schools, a crowded blacktop ringed with cars. With a teacher looking on, four girls occupy the corners of a four-square grid painted on the parking lot's surface, and a handful of students chatter as they wait in line for their turns at kickball. Another group of students, joined by the other sixth-grade teacher, plays a cramped game of basketball on the other corner of the small blacktop, careful not to let the ball escape down the steep hill. Absent ringing bells, crowded hallways, and large hordes of jostled students, even recess at the Upper School seems calm.

A Long Day Ends

A little before 4 PM, three yellow school buses pull out from the Early Learning Center, where the school day has just ended. About fifteen ELC students will remain in extended care until 5:45 PM; for the sixty children on the buses—some wriggling with extra energy, others leaning against their backpacks in exhaustion—the slow two-mile trek through Lawrence to the Prospect Street campus begins. The Lower School is undergoing a mass reorganization—bus groups are gathering, violin club members grab their instruments and file to the cafeteria, walkers assemble on the porch. Teachers head outside to supervise dismissal or remain inside to tidy room supplies or herd students into afterschool club locations. And, for the first time all day, noise echoes through the stairwells and hallways of the Upper School. Students mill about classroom doors, filling backpacks and talking loudly, waiting to be dismissed into bus lines outside. As buses leave and walkers begin the long climb down Prospect Hill, members of the Afternoon MCAS Preparation Club begin their tutorials. The basketball team settles down for a 90-minute study hall, supervised by their coach, before climbing aboard a bus to make their late afternoon practice at a local gymnasium. For most, the activity of the day is far from over.

ELEMENTS OF SUCCESS

"It's family." The school's small size, the many siblings in the student body, or the number of adults found in the buildings—all may contribute to the family-like atmosphere of Community Day. The persistent comparisons to "family" heard around the school could have other sources, sources that speak to deliberate philosophical and cultural aspects of the school. Regardless of the source, faculty and parents do not dispute the school's close-knit, intimate atmosphere or its focus on individual children. These two themes—maintaining a culture of intimacy and providing consistent individual attention—define life within the school, making Community Day like "family."

A Culture of Intimacy:
"This is home for us"

A school's culture can be an elusive concept, one notoriously difficult to define or describe. At Community Day, however, school culture is routinely characterized by parents, teachers, and administrators with one word—intimate. This theme is most clearly articulated by parents, as they describe feeling welcome within the school's space. Intimacy is also present within the professional relationships of teaching staff, evidenced by the coteaching model, the team-oriented approach to instructional and curricular matters, and the expected presence of administrators in classrooms. And perhaps most important, intimacy defines the relationships between teachers and students, nurturing relationships that go beyond academic achievement.

"Small climate," "intimate," "a little team" . . . these are the words parents use to describe Community Day. In many schools, parents' comfort level is an afterthought or even ignored, but among nine parents gathered to talk about Community Day, satisfaction with the school's tight-knit culture is high.[1] For these parents, this culture is one of the school's most defining features. As one parent remarked, "It seems everybody knows what's going on at their school. And when you go to talk to somebody, they don't say, 'Who's your kid?' They just know who you are." Another parent continued, "So I think that's where some of the uniqueness of the school comes in . . . even the children know me. As soon as I walk in, [someone says,] 'Victor, your father's here.' You know?" This feeling of belonging, of being welcome and known, was highlighted again and again by parents. One related a story to illustrate her point:

> This morning when I dropped the kids off, my youngest said, "Mommy, I want you to see my sticker chart." So I walked right on in, and the teacher said, "Yup, he knows where it is." And [it] felt like I was home—just walk[ing] in, you know, felt like I was getting a tour of his bedroom or something, not so formal.

Several parent groups may help to foster this feeling of belonging. According to the school's annual report, the Parent Advisory Board (PAB) "giv[es] parents an active and influential voice in the governance of the school." A number of parents describe the PAB as a place to raise concerns or provide counsel to the school's governing board. One recently problematic issue—bus routes that could compromise the safety of young students—was resolved when the PAB brought the issue to the board's attention. Another parent group, the Association of Parents in Action, is more informal and conducts its meetings entirely in Spanish. This group meets over dinner on the last Friday of every month for workshops that address topics of education and schooling. They bring in speakers to explain standardized test scores or how to help a child with homework—another way for parents to feel that they belong to the Community Day family.

Also crucial to maintaining this level of intimacy is deliberate and regular communication between school and home. This communication is consistent: school news and events are related through newsletters and calendars (written in both English and Spanish) that appear so frequently that one parent joked, "I had to buy an extra refrigerator." An administrator also links this communication to the feeling of comfort, even ownership, that parents experience at Community Day:

> Heads of school pick up the phone and talk directly to parents. You don't have to go through, you know, ten steps. You can come into our school any time, and ... parents call it "our school"; they use the possessive pronoun when they talk about the school, which is what [the founding members] wanted.

Another administrator adds, "During our parent interviews [conducted when a student is accepted via the lottery], ... we let them know, if you have a problem, you need to call us because we're going to be calling you. And I think that back and forth makes them feel comfortable."

Such intimacy extends beyond the comfort parents feel within the school and into the professional culture of the school itself. It is notable that teachers seem called to this work precisely for the same sense of belonging described by parents. "You know when you walk into a school and you just have that feeling?" one teacher shares. "I knew this was a place where I just felt like I could be a part of something." An administrator notes that teachers "who have stayed year after year ... know that this is where they need to be. And that's how we all feel. This is home for us."

The professional relationships among staff members institutionalize this intimacy. Beginning with the moment of hiring, collaboration among teachers is expected: "If there was an issue, it wasn't my issue; it was *our* issue, from the point I first got here," a teacher turned administrator notes. From kindergarten to sixth grade, teachers coteach a group of students. In seventh and eighth grade, the classes are organized by subject area. Although teachers usually divide responsibilities for "leading" particular subjects, planning is collaborative: "[We are] really collaborating on what we're doing, and make sure that all of the lessons in the room are working on themes that kind of intertwine, or the material that I'm doing will help build the material that she's about to cover." This kind of collaboration is strategic. For example, in each of the younger classrooms, one of the teachers speaks Spanish, serving as a resource to students still learning to speak, read, and write English and to help communicate with parents. Collaboration also extends beyond the basic coteaching model to include special education teachers; the biweekly instructional team meetings dedicated to discussing the progress of every child become a time for "discussion and maybe even . . . argument" among the general and special education teachers on how to best meet the special education students' needs.

This close-knit collegiality encompasses administrators, as well. Heads of school—one for each school—are an obvious presence in classrooms, sometimes stopping by to simply check in, other times to offer more particular guidance or instructional advice, and occasionally to actually teach a lesson. As an administrator explains:

> One of the things I'm famous for saying [during hiring interviews] is, "If you want to exist on an island, if you want to walk up to your room and shut the door and have a world unto yourself, this is not the place for you. If you want to come and be a part of a team in all aspects, if you understand that the head of school goes into your room, not to check up on you or to spy but to be an integral part of what's happening in here, and you crave that, this is the place for you."

Professional intimacy between teachers and administrators is an expectation, rather than an exception.

In a school known for high MCAS scores and for sending its graduates to highly competitive private high schools, it would be reasonable to imagine that relationships between students and teachers are pressured, narrowly focused, or superficial. However, the staff members of Community Day stress that the school's high expectations and focus on performance do not preclude the creation of a safe, caring space for students. Indeed, the staff seems to strike a balance between pushing students and nurturing children. Teachers describe a kind and gentle classroom space, "a safety net in our own room." The school's atmosphere is "orderly, quiet, calmed down, and relaxed," a parent notes—not a frenzied push for higher scores. And within this environment, relationships between teachers and students can grow. An administrator describes the last day of school: "The buses pulled out and the kids were all crying. [One student] was moving to Alaska, and this big guy was out there and he was crying because it was his last day and I thought, 'There really is something kind of magical between our relationships that have been formed here.'"

Like many of those interviewed, one teacher, an athletic director, describes relationships with students as "tight . . . very close." He explains how the school cultivates these relationships:

> I think it starts in the morning. . . . We greet the kids. We're out there saying, "Hello, how is your day?" . . . And then, just being with them eight hours a day you get to know their personalities, you get to know their quirks, you get to know *them*. . . . The fact we're such a small school, . . . it's really easy for us to talk . . . just because of the size of the place. And I'm lucky because I get to play with them after [school], too. . . . It's great for the kids to see [teachers] in a different light.

Thus, deliberate practices and the school's small size and long day create an environment in which warm relationships and an intimate atmosphere can flourish.

Focus on the Individual Child:
"There is not a student who is going to fall through the cracks"

The nurturing relationships shared by students and staff are hardly accidental. Indeed, such relationships need a foundation that allows for genuine caring. At Community Day, this foundation is the attention given to students as individuals—a priority highlighted in a mission centered on "develop[ing] and implement[ing] a curriculum that discovers and supports the special characteristics and unique learning styles of every student."

Fulfilling this mission begins the moment a student steps from the school bus or climbs from the car. Parents and staff alike underscore the importance of this morning ritual, citing its role in personalizing the school experience—for both students and parents. One parent explains, "There's a whole team of people waiting to shake their hand when they show up and [to say,] 'Have a great day and good luck today.'" Another parent describes it "like the Welcome Wagon." A head of school notes that

> our parents actually pull up to our sidewalk, and our teachers open the door, say good morning to the parents, say good morning to the children, and then [the children] walk into the building. When they walk into the building, I'm either in the hallway or helping with breakfast and I say good morning to those children once again. . . . [Then] they say good morning to the person who's checking them off for breakfast.

This individual attention continues throughout the day. It often occurs in casual encounters between students and teachers, facilitated by ample planning time and a cooperative teaching model. As one teacher describes, "[If] I notice that somebody looks a little off, if I'm not the one doing the lesson, I'll go over and have a little conversation. [Or we talk] at lunch time, because we eat lunch with the kids, at recess, . . . at cleanup time at the end of the day. So there are plenty of opportunities for those kind of casual, 'What's going on?' conversations."

These continuous casual interactions are made possible by a small student body, a relatively stable staff, and a student-teacher ratio of eleven to one. But it is also an intentional, pedagogical goal, as one teacher describes:

> My own philosophy, and the school's, is [that] it's definitely about the individual child. . . . If you want them to meet those standards, you have to figure out, how am I going to get this student to that place, understanding this concept, or getting this concept? . . . I cannot do the same thing for every student. I have to twist it, I have to turn it, I have to figure out, how am I going to reach this one and how am I going to reach that one?

The individual attention thus goes beyond the morning routine or informal interactions. Teachers are well aware of a student's academic proficiencies and difficulties, as a parent notes: "They know their weaknesses, they know their strengths, and the school focuses on that. They help them where they're weak . . . and they try to make it into a strength."

Faculty members express their concern about students' weaknesses and explain the school's desire to address any academic gaps. They often describe these weaknesses as opportunities, experiences, and advantages that these students may not encounter outside of school. They feel that some of their students face adversity, including "language deficiencies," as one teacher noted, or being "lost between the two worlds, the two languages," according to another teacher. One administrator explains:

A lot of our students don't come in with the basic awareness of phonemics. . . . In fifth, sixth, seventh, and eighth grade I'm still filling these gaps of reading and vocabulary and comprehension. . . . They're not going to have someone there to help them with homework. They're not necessarily going to have a computer at home to do work. So it's . . . not using it as an excuse, but understanding the level of where our students are at.

For this administrator, "being aware of the population" means providing essential skills that children can receive at school, rather than at home or in the community. Another administrator draws these same parallels:

Particularly when you're working with city kids, . . . you're compensating for what they don't get at home or didn't get in the early years. . . . [The head of the Early Learning Center] knows every child, every parent in the program . . . and the same with the other heads of school. So there's an intimacy that's needed when you're dealing with some of the dysfunction and addictions and just family problems that our kids have in the city here.

A strong focus on the individual child enables teachers to recognize areas of difficulty and then customize instruction in a number of ways, chief among them being instructional groups within a classroom. Consistent benchmark testing reveals students' actual skill levels and identifies academic gaps, as one administrator explains:

In our well-educated, middle-class ways, we make assumptions about where kids are. . . . So this assessment, even at an early age, helps us say, "Wait a minute, you know, they're not where you think they are. Take them back a couple of steps so that everybody can make progress."

This testing data then informs the construction of groups and facilitates differentiation of instruction. With a team of coteachers in every classroom from kindergarten to sixth grade, often supplemented by a special education instructor or curriculum specialist, the school has the human resources available to create small instructional groups. These groups then target specific missing skills and provide additional scaffolding in problem areas, integrating a child's experiences "with what these students need academically and guaranteeing that we're going to reach every single learner." Another teacher explains that teachers feel that group work "meets the needs because we can really zero in on their issues and their problems and identify kids that aren't getting it." Even with this attention to missing skills and experiences, most staff members feel "they're a group of kids that are as smart as any group. They didn't start out at the race line with everybody; they're way behind it for the most part. So . . .

our team is working as hard as they can . . . to get them up closer to the front of the line."

With a faculty so strongly motivated to provide personal instruction and attention, individualization is a priority among staff members. One teacher even described applying to work at Community Day because "they really cared individually for the students because they knew the students well, . . . they knew what the individual students' needs were. . . ." At this school, stakeholders say, it is about knowing—and then caring for—individuals.

The Coordinated Use of Data: "We know where our students are"

Tucked in a corner of the third floor of the Upper School is a tiny stairwell. The staircase is steep and narrow, barely wide enough to accommodate its occasional climber. At the top is a door, and through the door is a room, nestled under the eaves of the old mansion. Neat stacks of three-ring binders cover every surface and books line the walls; it almost seems as though the contents of the binders and books actually support the mansion's roof. In the center of the room is a desk, covered with tidy piles of papers that trace the academic achievement of a particular student or class.

Entering the office of Community Day's data manager is a little like removing the face of a watch: under the simple, familiar surface lies a mechanized network of gears working continuously to make the machine run. In fact, with Community Day's intimacy, it is easy to forget that this school is, in some respects, a highly effective, very organized enterprise, fueled by a coordinated and intricate system—the use of student data.

If personal attention defines school culture, a number of schoolwide systems make this individualization operate. Teachers enter the school year armed with a detailed curriculum map. This map includes a curriculum developed by a team during the summer, which is based on school standards that add a level of detail to the state-provided standards, and on the "Blue Binders"—pages and pages of data marking the educational performance of their past classes and incoming students. A number of teachers cite these maps as being crucial to the success of the school. They ensure comprehensive coverage of state standards, provide momentum to start the school year, and allow for coordination and reteaching of challenging concepts from year to year. But the Blue Binders are also the bibles of Community Day, for they expose whether these curricular maps and their executions are working. These binders do more than simply house student data—it is the detail, the presentation, and the use of these data that makes them of critical importance.

Teachers are first presented with their three-ring Blue Binders during the weeklong August in-service. Each binder contains two years' worth of grade-level MCAS scores (but does not include data from the previous spring test administration because they are not yet available). Because Massachusetts is one of the few states that provides question-level performance data, Community Day's data manager is able to let teachers know how the curriculum at this school did for two years, in terms of how the kids answered every single question. By each October, the spring MCAS test results are in and, during the Columbus Day in-service, the binders are updated with everything about how each student did who took it the previous year, and about the entire grade as well. In addition, the data manager includes the most up-to-date version of the state standards. Thus, within a binder, a teacher can find the grade-level standards that shape curricula, two years of class test scores that reflect his or her effectiveness in teaching this material, and data revealing the individual academic performances of his or her current class. At Community Day, teachers say, "We know where our students are."

Community Day teachers also have a clear idea of where they want their students to be. Although the state does not generate data that reflect a student's growth over time, the manager personally computes this information and adds it to the binders. He also includes yearly target MCAS scores for each student, MCAS goals that build toward subject-area proficiency in a certain span of years. He explains: "We've made up a report . . . [that] shows this time when they took the test, the time they took the test before. It shows what their difference was, and what we set up is a series of goals."[2] These goals are not inflexible, the manager is quick to note, but are rather guidelines to promote student progress over a series of years. But the goals are important, as the school's founder notes: "One of the things that is . . . integral to our entire operation . . . is goal-setting and measuring whether we're getting to those goals."

Finally, beyond student data, class-level information, and target goals, the Blue Binders contain a rich compendium of resources that allows teachers to become familiar with the MCAS. The binders detail the logistics of administering the MCAS, including guidelines for English-language learners and students with disabilities. According to the data manager, there is a list of "every reading selection that's ever been on that MCAS, with author and title and stuff, just so teachers can get a sense of what to expect." Another spreadsheet lists the words that appear in math and science questions and the frequency with which they occur, because, according to the data manager, "sometimes the word constructions are really screwy in these questions and particularly for kids whose second language is English."

This kind of information—simple spreadsheets, clear-cut goals, links between scores, questions, and standards—underscore the real value of the Blue Binders. For teachers, the binders are a source of usable data that demystifies the test and the numbers it generates. The data manager understands that "what [teachers] want to know is how [their] teaching technique worked overall." Thus he makes the information digestible, from something as simple as color-coding the subject areas and presenting the standards in "a nice, easy fashion" to using an algorithm that illustrates the school's performance on each question relative to the state's performance in order to reveal the school's "weakest standards." The use of the data drives the content of the Blue Binders. The data manager emphasizes that "the only reason for it is for a teacher to use it in their classroom." Conversations with administrators inform what data to include and how to present this information. One head of school explains:

> Before school ends, or in the summer sometimes, [the data manager] will sit down with all three heads of school and say to us, "What was in the binder that you liked? What was in the binder that you didn't like? What do you need to see more of?" Again, we're constantly changing those binders, so that's important to us, that [the data manager] will put in there what our teachers need and what they're going to use. If they're not going to use it, then there's no sense in [including] it.

While the MCAS data in the Blue Binders may be the most obvious example of data use at Community Day, it is not the only source of data. For testing data to truly drive instructional decisions, they must be more sensitive and more comprehensive than the annual numbers provided by the MCAS. Community Day has therefore developed a comprehensive set of benchmark assessments that give teachers an intermediate measure of student learning. These assessments, based on the fine-grained school standards, are created in house. Teams of teachers, meeting over the summer (they are compensated for their time), draw on recent MCAS questions, items from other state assessments, and material developed by other test-prep organizations (including EduSoft, Princeton Review, and ExamView) to generate subject-area tests that teachers administer throughout the year. The benchmark assessments are given four or five times a year at the Lower and Upper schools.[3] Teachers then use these data to measure progress toward the classwide Action Plan—specific teaching objectives relating to grade-level standards—and note which students may need extra instructional attention in order to meet these standards: As one teacher points out, these tests are "good because [they] show us where the weaknesses are." They discuss the results during team meetings and place students in appropriate instructional groups, consulting special education staff if necessary. The beauty of these assessments, according to many teachers, is the immediate diagnostic information they offer. One of the teachers responsible for the development of the exams explains:

> We can get the tests back and the grades back to the teachers with the results, and they can use [these results] in their classroom in twenty-four hours. So it really does affect groupings, it does affect reteaching, and so forth. So in that sense, we like to control it because we know it's going into the tests, we know that it's good material, we know that it's actually going to be used the proper way.

Thus, just as the Blue Binders make yearly MCAS data relevant for instruction and instructional goal-setting, the driving force behind the benchmark assessment is its day-to-day usefulness in the classroom.

Parents also benefit from the massive amount of data collected about their children's academic performance. Teachers write Personal Education Goals (PEGs) for each child at the beginning of the year, using data from the student's Blue Binder to document the student's strengths and weaknesses and develop a "learning plan" that outlines progression to the yearly MCAS goals. Using a staff-development day, teachers update these PEGs with data from benchmark assessments, and the PEGs are issued three times a year as a kind of report card. This highly detailed report card describes the student's learning goals, documents their progress toward these goals, and then delineates the steps that teachers, parents, *and* the student will take to support their learning plan. One parent describes the personalization of the PEG:

> What a report card. [It gives not only] . . . the opportunity to see, . . . 'Okay, this is the grade you got,' but . . . *why*. And this is what they need to focus on, it's all there in writing: Here are the goals for your child, here are the goals for you as a parent, and here are the goals for us as teachers for the next semester.

This highly detailed, highly mechanized system seems to work. Indeed, it is this structured process of data presentation that a number of teachers and administrators cite as the reason for the school's high MCAS scores. When asked how they achieve these scores, one teacher explains:

> I think that [it]'s a lot of test prep. I think it's knowing the test and knowing what skills our kids need to be successful. That's really a lot of it, having past test questions and data that's been received. . . . It's just knowing what the kids need, being prepared, and getting the resources to give them

what they need. [If] the teachers know that open response is difficult for the school, they really tackle it in the summer and they come up with a handbook on strategies for open response, or . . . whatever it happens to be. I think that our school really analyzes their results and the questions and constantly looks at them. . . . They're prepared for the new questions that come on the test, and the kids are prepared too.

* * * * *

Thirteen years ago, a group of educators and parents sat down to write a school's founding mission. They imagined it would be a small school, a school that would serve Lawrence, a school dedicated to providing focused instruction for individual children. And "that's still ultimately the mission," a teacher explains. "Taking the kids where they are, take them as far as you can, hold them to high standards, . . . just really nurture them and care for them, but at the same time, expect them to perform." Mechanized yet personal, performance driven yet intimate, Community Day remains dedicated to this mission.

CHAPTER TWO

ROXBURY PREPARATORY CHARTER SCHOOL

Planning and Executing for Achievement

The stir of pages turning is the only sound in an otherwise silent room, as students of color wearing khaki pants and blue shirts digest their books and breakfasts. Binders and elbows compete with napkins and milk cartons for desk space. Most students face forward in their respective rows; holding copies of *The Kite Runner* and *To Be a Slave,* two prop their backs against an alphabetized word wall, underneath tags that read "ebullient," "exemplary," and "expedient." Other tags bear words like "scholarship," "dignity," and "peace." Students' names are written just below the tags, the phrase "I'm on it" just above.

The teacher sitting at the front of the room raises eyebrows and digests pages of her own. Listed on the board behind her are the "Do-Now" exercise, daily agenda, and homework for the upcoming math class, along with the goal of the day: "Aim—Students will write equations into standard form without fractions." The teacher looks up briefly, scans the room, and resumes her reading. A bell rings, and students dispose of their napkins and milk cartons as a second teacher enters, leaving her supply cart by the doorway, and sprays blue liquid on the overhead projector plate. She scrubs with an index finger as students return to their desks and are then dismissed one row at a time by the first teacher. The silent room empties as the second teacher removes a stack of Do-Nows from her cart and waits by the door for her soon-to-enter math class. Then the work begins:

The primary author for this chapter is Chris Wynne.

8:05   The class enters in a silent, single-file line, and the math teacher greets each student with a Do-Now sheet, a smile, and "Hello."

8:06   All students are seated and working silently on the Do Now, with last night's homework on their desks. The math teacher draws an isosceles triangle on the board, labels the sides X, X, and X + 8, and then circulates between rows, collecting homework and whispering some brief pointers to a few students.

8:11:57 The math teacher returns to the front of the room, looks down at her wristwatch, and says "Three, two, one, *go!*" The "Mad Minute" begins with a split-second *WHOOSH* of papers turning over, followed by a staccato frenzy of scribbling pencils as students calculate the arithmetic problems on the back side of their Do-Now sheets.

8:12:57 The math teacher looks at her wristwatch and says, "Three, two, one, pencils down, trade papers." All pencils are dropped and papers *WHOOSH* between neighboring students.

8:13:05 The math teacher reads the first row of answers to the problems the students have completed: 14, 10, 13, 11, 18, 12, 12 . . .

8:13:11 A student reads the answers to each of the next six rows, and papers *WHOOSH* back to their owners.

8:13:47 Students read aloud their total number correct, in alphabetical order and without prompting. The teacher records their scores.

8:14:07 The teacher asks students if any of the Do-Now problems looked familiar.

Most students nod and raise their hands. The teacher calls on a student who explains that the Do-Now problems were reruns of certain problems from last week's test. "That's right," she confirms. "We somehow missed these problems as a group, and the rest of the year builds on them. Plus, these problems will keep showing up, so we need to be ready for them the next time around. Let's look at number one—what do you think was a common mistake here?" Hands fly up again, and the first volunteer guesses that many students forgot to label all three sides and therefore combined like terms incorrectly. Heads nod in agreement. The math teacher concurs, then asks students to volunteer their answers and records the first one on the board. Pausing, she smiles and waits for more. "Take a risk if you're not sure," she encourages. "The majority doesn't always rule." A few more students share their answers, and these, too, are recorded.

Next door, an English teacher resumes the unfinished conversation from yesterday.

ROXBURY PREPARATORY CHARTER SCHOOL
A Commonwealth Charter School, Founded in 1999

Number of Students and Grade Levels
198 Students in Grades 6–8

Race/Ethnicity	*Subgroups*
61% African American	12% Special Education
33% Hispanic	70% Low Income
2% Native American	27% First Language Not English
5% Multiracial, Non-Hispanic	27% First Language Not English
	1% Limited English Proficient

Source: Massachusetts Department of Education

"Steinbeck and race. Was he a racist? Not a racist? What do you think?" One student says yes, because he used the word "Negro" in his essay *Atque Vale.* Another student downplays Steinbeck's word choice because times were different and because Steinbeck actually characterized the Black community as dignified and composed.

"But in doing so, is Steinbeck making a generalization?" the English teacher inquires.

One student says yes, and suggests that perhaps Steinbeck really *was* racist precisely *because* he made the generalization that no Black person would ever spit on another human being. Waving hands fan the air as the English teacher counters, "But did Steinbeck intend that statement to be *negative*?"

"I think he's *still* racist because he was talking about the *whole* race," a student concludes.

Rubbing his chin, the English teacher then inquires whether it would be fair to make positive generalizations about Roxbury Prep students.

Students exchange looks as a volunteer speculates that such generalizations might be unfair if they made everyone sound exactly the same.

"Can a positive [generalization] be as harmful as a negative one?"

The English teacher allows his question to linger and then tips his hand. "We may not come to consensus about this today, or about Steinbeck in general. And I'm not going to tell you what he was thinking because I'm not him and I don't know. But what I do want is, as you read *Of Mice and Men*, to think about race and what you think Steinbeck's purpose was as he developed his characters." The English teacher informs students that they have eight minutes of class time to begin their reading. Students may read to each other in pairs or read independently, and he will be available for questions. "Be interactive," he instructs, "and be productive."

Students read aloud, most of them in pairs, as the English teacher makes his rounds. He bends, twists, and crouches as students flag him down.

The bell rings, and classroom doors begin to open. Single-file lines of students emerge, turn sharply to the left or right, and remain silent as they hug the walls of the narrow hallway, where waiting staff members smile or stare. One teacher pulls a student out of line and instructs him to tuck in his shirt. Another teacher is wearing a Viking helmet. The lines file down the hall toward the multipurpose room, where Community Meeting takes place every Friday at 12:15 PM. A few students grin and make eye contact with each other, while others eye wall hangings along the way—eighth graders have composed written promises to lead by example; science classes have modeled elements with beads and pipe cleaners; the Word of the Week is "pretentious." A student receives a demerit for talking. One classroom door remains closed, as a teacher with a hoarse yet booming voice ends her lesson: "Don't worry, K'Shawn—it takes a strong man to stand alone," and then, "Who needs an Altoid?— some of you sure do," as students burst into laughter. The laughter ceases on cue as the teacher opens the door and her line silently joins the others.

Inside the multipurpose room, an eighth grader shuffles papers at a small wooden podium facing rows of small blue chairs that are filling with students. Some teachers sit, others stand to the side as a staff member introduces the eighth grader as master of ceremonies. Her peers greet her with thunderous applause and join staff members who loudly cheer, *"positive leaders"* between five purposeful claps. The eighth grader summons various students and staff members to the podium to share the latest goings-on. Ms. Johnson is excited by the election year and starting an Important Events and Debate Club. Ms. Roberts congratulates the most productive students from a recent school fundraiser. Ms. Smith plugs Denzel Washington's new movie, *The Great Debaters,* and offers three social justice "Creed Deeds" to students who attend. Mr. Thompson complements the boys' and girls' basketball teams for maintaining good grades and behavior while winning their first two games . . .

POSITIVE LEADERS (clap, clap, clap-clap-clap)
POSITIVE LEADERS (clap, clap, clap-clap-clap)

Next, a few students step up and read sentences that include the new Word of the Week—"fervent." The audience greets this word fervently, with open palms that flutter in silent applause. Another group of students awards the teacher in the Viking helmet the Harriet Tubman Award for demonstrating pride, dignity, and good humor in his classroom, not to mention giving students the occasional ride home. Finally, there is a skit that a student has written about the Spirit Stick being stolen, complete with a mock court case and three witnesses. It turns out that the Spirit Stick was simply misplaced, and this week it is awarded to a scholarly, peaceful, and invested seventh grader who has staved off winter doldrums with his positive attitude and inquisitive nature. He will be the master of ceremonies next week. The seventh grader is greeted by fervent, nonsilent applause, and the "positive leaders" cheer resumes. The meeting closes with an inspirational quote on Black History Month, and the first rows of students are dismissed.

In near silence, students empty one row at a time and return to their homerooms in an almost-perfect line. Staff members smile or stare. The teacher with the hoarse yet booming voice, eight months pregnant, again mobilizes her class as she draws her clipboard to her chest. Taped to the back of the clipboard is a message: "READ AS THOUGH YOUR LIFE DEPENDS ON IT, BECAUSE IT DOES."

That is a Friday at Roxbury Preparatory Charter School—business as usual, followed by a warm yet strict celebration of committed scholarship and jobs well done. Students are dismissed at 1:20 PM so staff members can get together to discuss better ways to serve them. Located in Roxbury, Massachusetts, Roxbury Prep serves approximately two hundred students in grades six, seven, and eight. The admissions process consists of a random lottery held in March, during which time administrators publicly draw the names of 75 incoming sixth graders from a pool of about 150 interested candidates. Most students live in single-parent households in the nearby communities of Dorchester, Roxbury, and Mattapan, and are academically below grade level when they enroll. Most qualify for free or reduced-price lunch, and, currently, all are students of color.

Roxbury Prep, which was founded in 1999 by codirectors John King and Evan Rudall, has had a change of leadership, but its mission and philosophy have remained consistent: prepare students to enter, succeed in, and graduate from college by challenging them academically, emphasizing the importance of character and community responsibility, and providing a structured and well-supported learning environment. Most students demonstrate substantial improvement on a variety of internal and external assessments, including the math and English language arts test portions of the Massachusetts Comprehensive Assessment System (MCAS). For example, of Roxbury Prep's thirty-five eighth graders in the class of 2006 who took the fourth-grade math MCAS test while attending other schools, 42 percent failed the test in fourth grade, but none of those students failed in the eighth grade. Moreover, although only 19 percent of those students scored advanced or proficient in the fourth grade, 94 percent scored at those levels in the eighth grade. Improvements like these help students gain admission into private college-preparatory high schools or to matriculate at public high schools that have explicit college-preparatory missions. The high school graduation rate among Roxbury Prep's first two graduating classes (2002 and 2003) was 89 percent.

These outcomes raise the question of how students at Roxbury Prep are challenged and supported to achieve these results. Although the answers are numerous, staff members identify the teaching and learning that occurs in classrooms as their most critical priority, and teachers work to engage students by planning and executing lessons with a meticulous sense of urgency. This chapter documents some elements of planning and execution that are essential to teaching and learning at Roxbury Prep, beginning with the long-term planning that occurs during the summer. It highlights examples of team-oriented creativity that help teachers personalize their curricula, lesson plans, and teaching styles while employing schoolwide systems that maintain important consistencies. It will also discuss several ancillary supports for students that supplement classroom instruction.

ELEMENTS OF SUCCESS

Planning

Preparing for the Long Haul: August Planning Time

> The whole idea behind the curriculum is that you plan it early, before the school year starts, and that you plan it all the way through so that when you come to planning a particular lesson for a particular day, you already have a sense as to what you are going to do.
> —*Math Procedures Teacher*

The planning efforts begin in August, when staff members work full-time for three weeks to prepare for the academic year. This preparation is comprehensive: it includes a discussion of long-term goals for the year; the orientation of new staff members to schoolwide systems and routines; role-playing that depicts common classroom management challenges; and conversations about race, diversity, and the importance of communicating with families. Although teachers believe that all of these activities are important, they devote the greatest amount of time to the development or refinement of long-term curricular plans. All teachers begin the year with plans that document the content they intend to teach and the major learning activities they will use. These plans are documented on curriculum-alignment templates, or CAT, that break the Massachusetts Learning Standards, which correspond with teachers' grade levels and subjects, into clear, measurable learning objectives that staff members refer to as internal standards. For example, a science teacher's CAT breaks the Massachusetts Learning Standard on natural, Earth-shaping processes into internal standards that cover mechanical and chemical weathering and the rock cycle, respectively. Accompanying each internal standard are basic descriptions of the learning activities that teachers plan to use and the assessments they plan to administer. These descriptions may be as simple as "continental drift notes and quiz," but they nonetheless help teachers begin the school year with a general understanding of what they plan to teach at all times.

This understanding is further informed by teachers' administration of their final exams during the first week of classes, which provides information on students' strengths and weaknesses at the beginning of the year. Long-term plans may be adjusted in response to this information, and teachers may also adjust plans during the middle of the year if they think it is necessary. However, staff members agree that long-term plans are worth having, even when they must be adjusted, because they inform decisions about pacing and scope as adjustments are made. The school's codirector of curriculum and instruction explained that because teachers have a year-long plan, they get to make the conscious decision to spend more time on one standard, even if it means taking time away from other standards. In other words, the planning process ensures that teachers think strategically about how to handle learning standards X and Y if they decide to reteach standard Z. Some teachers use their Do-Now activities (which will receive more attention later in this chapter) to reteach learning standards that require additional instruction. This strategy can be particularly helpful because it enables teachers to review challenging concepts without sacrificing substantial amounts of the instructional time that they had allocated for other parts of their curricula.

Although the curricula at Roxbury Prep are standards-based, they include additional content that teachers believe is essential to their subject areas, is helpful in preparing students for high school or college admissions exams, or is simply inspirational to students. For example, a science teacher supplements a lesson on erosion with a lab that helps students understand why topsoil is important to the environment. A math teacher devotes several lessons to solving and graphing quadratic equations and deriving the quadratic formula in order to prepare students for high school. A reading teacher has discovered that her students enjoy relating themes of fairness and equity to their own lives, so she incorporates novels like *Fences* and *A Gathering of Old Men* into the syllabus and introduces *Julius Caesar* to students by asking, "How many of you have ever felt betrayed by someone you trusted?" A writing teacher designed his curriculum to introduce students to great scholars of color and to inspire community involvement. His students practice writing expository essays while considering the political and economic philosophies of Booker T. Washington and W. E. B. Dubois or examining actual data that show how young people can impact their communities by voting. Like many teachers, the writing teacher expressed a willingness to emphasize his broader curricular themes within a standards-based model:

> I think [the balance between my broader goals and the Massachusetts Learning Standards] strikes out well. I actually don't think the two are mutually exclusive. Coming into the year, I tended to be a big-picture person. The structures of the school [CATs] force you to be very focused in the way in which you approach your educational philosophy. On a day-to-day basis, can students write? What does that look like?
>
> Can I assess student skills according to what the state is saying students need to have? I can, I do it, and students can hold me accountable and parents hold me accountable, and I hold myself accountable. You can do big picture but also be very focused on a day-to-day basis.

Teachers' efforts to address "big-picture" ideas within a standards-based curricular model exemplify one of the many ways in which they work creatively while utilizing schoolwide systems to benefit students. Because students must pass the MCAS and staff members value MCAS scores as an important indicator of achievement, teachers use CATs to ensure that the Massachusetts Learning Standards are thoroughly addressed; however, because there is more to life than the MCAS, and because students will have to meet higher standards in order to succeed in high school and college, teachers' curricula also include educational themes beyond the minimal testing requirements.

In sum, teachers' August planning efforts help them create long-term curricular plans that are tightly aligned to the Massachusetts Learning Standards yet challenge and inspire students in ways that transcend what the standards explicitly prescribe. These plans help teachers make strategic adjustments during the course of the year as they strive to meet students' instructional needs.

The Weekly Grind: Details, Details

> Teachers here really think of their lessons as an event—what is going to happen in my class? And I think that drives a lot of the activities and it drives a lot of the questioning and it drives a lot of the structures in the class. . . . How that happens depends on the teacher's style, the material, . . . but conceptually I think teachers think of their lessons as events, as opportunities, and I think that makes them prepare down to the smallest detail.
>
> *—Problem-Solving Math Teacher*

Because teachers complete their long-term plans in August, they are able to allocate more time during the school year to planning their lessons. Thus, lesson plans are comprehensive and often include details on what teachers and students will do during each minute of class. For instance, in a lesson plan designed to help students investigate their learning styles, a teacher budgets two minutes toward the end of class for the following:

> Tell students they are going to work in partners with someone who is the same kind of learner as they are (kinesthetic, visual, or auditory). This can be pairs or threes. Once students are in these groups, tell them to decide which upcoming quiz/comp to study for, and then to choose one study strategy that is recommended for their type of learner. . . . On the board, brainstorm times . . . when people can study together.

Although teachers don't read their lesson plans like scripts during class, details like these give them a clear sense of how to spend each moment, which helps them make optimal use of their instructional time.

Certain elements of lesson plans are common schoolwide. For example, all teachers articulate specific objectives, which are called Aims, for each class, and each class begins with a silent Do-Now activity that lasts five to ten minutes. The Aims link directly to teachers' internal standards, although some standards may require multiple class periods to teach. The Do-Now generally reviews concepts that have recently been taught, which helps prepare students to learn new material. Teachers also prepare a 20- to 30-minute homework assignment for each lesson, and they write their assignments, Do-Nows, Aims, and agendas for each lesson on dry erasable boards in the blackboard configuration (BBC) developed by Lorraine Monroe at the Frederick Douglass Academy in New York City. This information is also compiled into weekly syllabi that teachers distribute to students at the beginning of each week. Thus, although teachers differ in their instructional styles, some parts of their lessons are consistent across the school. The codirector of curriculum and instruction noted that such consistency helps students make the transition from self-contained elementary school environments to middle school, where they have six different teachers and move from class to class. She believes that these transitions would be even more difficult if students had to learn six different sets of classroom procedures and that the consistency helps students adjust to their new environments quickly, which "allow[s] teachers and students to focus on teaching and learning."

Another common element of most lessons is independent practice time for teachers to assess individual students' learning. The logic is simple and is shared by teachers and codirectors alike—students take tests and quizzes independently, so teachers must make time to assess individual students' learning during class. Thus, although a typical class period may not entail a silent, sustained period of unassisted "testing conditions," teachers do generally budget ten to fifteen minutes of class time to circulate throughout the room and provide individual assistance to students working independently.

At their own discretion, teachers may complement independent work with opportunities for students to work in pairs or groups. For example, English and writing teachers incorporate peer editing sessions into their lessons, during which time pairs of students read each other's written work and provide both written and verbal feedback. Students in math classes often work together on problem sets after they finish their Do-Nows and Mad Minutes, and they may also help each other work on projects, such as pamphlets that show different ways to graph linear equations or find the slope of a line. A social studies teacher uses group projects to engage students in perspective-taking exercises that help them understand why different community members have different values, and how their actions may affect others. Although the implementation of effective group work can be difficult, as the social studies teacher explained, it is a goal that can be worth pursuing:

> I've been able to be more successful with project-based, student-centered, hands-on work and group work with my students this year, and as a result I feel so much more happy with what the students have accomplished. . . . And I'm still working on it. . . . The way I run my class is discussion based, so there's a fine line between when students should be talking and when students should be working [silently]. I need to be clearer about that line, and also I need to be clearer about the freedom that I'm giving . . . [by] saying

that you have the freedom to talk with your partners and groups about spe-cifically [social studies], and with that freedom comes a lot of responsibility and I expect you to step up and do your work.

Teachers' use of group work constitutes another example of their ability to accommodate their personal teaching preferences while maintaining im-portant schoolwide consistencies. Teachers are committed to the BBC, weekly syllabi, and independent work time because they believe that the structure and individual attention will help students learn. Group work is incorporated in the hope of enriching students' learning experiences all the more. As one teacher acknowledged, although the common lesson structure at Roxbury Prep means that the average lesson won't be as spontaneous as a lesson that Robin Williams might have taught in *Dead Poets Society,* teachers' thought-ful, thorough lesson planning ensures that they are able to integrate structure and creativity.

Although teachers are always well prepared, they are willing to adjust their plans during the middle of class if they discover that students are not being challenged appropriately. Sometimes the adjustments involve taking addi-tional time to provide instruction for a skill that is necessary for achieving the larger Aim; sometimes they involve challenging students with activities that require them to apply their newly acquired knowledge in a novel context. For example, during a lesson on probability statements and combinations, a math teacher discovered that one of his classes needed extra time to practice drawing probability tree diagrams. The teacher allocated the time necessary to practice this skill, and then gave students more of the originally planned in-struction during individual and small-group tutoring (which will receive more attention later in the chapter). Conversely, the teacher's next class progressed through the same lesson more quickly, which led the teacher to provide an ad-ditional activity and discussion based on why it is difficult to win the lottery. However, even when adjustments like these must be made, teachers' initial lesson plans ensure that the adjustments are strategic and informed. As the math teacher explained, "Without complete, personal understanding of [the original plan], such improvisation would not be possible." Thus, like compre-hensive long-term plans, detailed lesson plans are helpful even when the plans must be altered.

Reflecting with Colleagues

Comments shared by the social studies and math teachers exemplify how teachers reflect on their practice in order to improve it. Although much of this reflection occurs individually, teachers also have opportunities to reflect collaboratively during hour-long inquiry group sessions, which are held most Friday afternoons after student dismissal. Inquiry group sessions are teacher led, although the codirector of curriculum and instruction meets with leaders of both the literacy group (reading, writing, and social studies teachers) and the numeracy group (math and science teachers) to help set the agendas.

Currently, inquiry group leaders use a "results-meeting" format to facilitate the sessions. During each meeting, the presenting teacher shares the results of a prior assessment with the group and identifies a skill that she would like to help students improve. Teachers follow a protocol (see appendix 2.A) that allows them to brainstorm ideas, discuss them, and develop an action plan for the presenting teacher to implement during class. For example, a numeracy group session involved brainstorming activities that would improve students' ability to scale length, area, and volume for objects when the linear dimensions increased by various factors. Some of the group's ideas included using:

1. Pipe cleaners and grid paper to show the differences between scaled perimeter and scaled area
2. Scale models of rectangular prisms to show volume
3. The electronic SMART board to show algebraic manipulations while calculating scaled volume

After implementing an action plan, teachers may debrief via email, during the planning periods they share, or at the beginning of the next inquiry group session. Perhaps the most telling testament to the staff's reflective nature is that the format of inquiry group sessions—like the lessons they aim to improve—have undergone a process of revision over time. The results-meeting format was adopted with the hope of generating more ideas for teachers to consider at the beginning of each session. Thus, it seems that even the forum in which teachers reflect is thoughtfully considered in the quest to improve instruction.

Regardless of how inquiry group sessions are structured, they highlight another example of teachers' ability to work creatively within schoolwide systems. However, this example is unique, and it perhaps exemplifies the compatibility between structure and creativity at its greatest. Whereas teachers *do* work creatively within various schoolwide systems (e.g., CATs, the BBC) as they design curricula and lesson plans, these systems do not necessarily enhance creativity as they serve other important purposes. Inquiry groups are a unique system because teachers' creativity is an outcome that the system has been designed to enhance. Thus, as teachers work creatively within various schoolwide systems, at least one system—the inquiry groups—seems to help them work more creatively along the way.

Execution

Using Time Efficiently

> Every day here we try to make a perfect school day. The idea is that every day, each class is fifty minutes long and fifty minutes of class should be solely fifty minutes of teaching and learning.
> —*Codirector of Operations and Finance*

Teachers' thorough lesson planning puts them in a position to execute lessons that use every minute of class time. Students begin working on their Do-Nows during the first minute of class and continue working until the fiftieth minute expires. Teachers teach from bell to bell, circulating throughout the classroom as soon as the Do-Now begins and working with students in one way or another during each minute of class. The exact nature of this work varies from day to day and from one classroom to the next. However, a classroom observer would be unlikely to see teachers and students begin classes a few minutes late, finish a few minutes early, or take any breaks in between.

During class, several procedures help lessons run smoothly and efficiently. For example, as students work on the Do-Now at the beginning of each class, teachers circulate between rows and collect students' homework and distribute handouts for the day. This system is simple, but it prevents students from sitting idly as they wait to submit or receive their work, which gives them fewer opportunities to drift off task and ultimately preserves more time for teaching and learning. Some teachers may allow one or two students who finish their Do-Nows early to help distribute papers, but the end result is the same—everyone continues to do *something* as the papers are distributed. Timesaving strategies like these are hardly full of "pizzazz," as the codirector of curriculum and instruction admitted, but these "little things" are considered a "big deal" because doing them helps teachers and students stay on track.

When classes end, teachers dismiss students in silent lines and assume various posts in the hallway to ensure that students make a silent transition to their next classes. Staff members acknowledge that the policy of silent hallway transitions is strict, but they believe that such measures are necessary so that students move quickly from class to class, thus ensuring that teachers can begin class on time and use all fifty minutes. As a math teacher explained, "I always find that I'm trying to get as much as I can into those fifty minutes . . .

and if [students aren't] silent coming in and you have to quiet them down, that automatically [takes] time [at] the beginning of classes, which is detrimental to your Aim of having as much time as possible." The teacher also noted that he tries to give students different ways to express themselves both verbally and in writing during class, and that students also have opportunities to communicate during breakfast, and lunch and at other times during the day. Thus, he doesn't think that the silent transitions "deny students something that they really need."

Behavior Management

Teachers agree that the schoolwide behavior management system also helps them keep lessons running smoothly. This system is also simple—teachers may assign demerits to students who violate school or classroom rules, and students must attend an afterschool detention for every three demerits they receive in one week. Some common reasons that students receive demerits include talking during silent work time or coming to class without pencils and paper. Teachers may also send a student to the office if they believe that the student's behavior interferes with the learning of his or her classmates. For example, the expression "shut-up!" is regarded as very disrespectful, and a student who uses this expression must leave the classroom immediately. The teachers then converse with the students about their problematic behavior after class has ended, but they do not sacrifice class time to engage in "back and forths" with students who disrupt the pedagogic flow. This system is also strict, but the theme of making a big deal of little things emerges again, as staff members believe that it is the only way to ensure that every minute of class is devoted to teaching and learning.

Although students may be sent to the office, this course of action is the last resort and teachers agree that the demerit system usually helps them redirect students quickly and without disruption. The system seems to be particularly effective because it is used schoolwide, yet is flexible enough to be used differently within each classroom. The schoolwide nature of the system helps teachers communicate to students that the same "dignified and scholarly" behavior is expected in every classroom; however, the codirector of curriculum and instruction realizes that it would be difficult for everyone to use the system identically and thus encourages teachers to supplement demerits with their own tricks for managing student behavior.

Teachers agree that they personalize their use of the demerit system over time, and that this personalization helps them use the system more effectively. A veteran teacher, for example, has learned that she can work within the demerit system without losing her sense of humor:

> One of my strengths is my connection with kids. I can get them out of a bad mood by making them laugh, and I can move on. . . . The demerit system is there for a reason, but . . . I tend to go to demerits much later now, which is not to say that my class is unruly or out of control—quite the opposite. I also like [the fact] that if someone earns a demerit in my class, it's a pretty big deal because I don't usually do that.

Staff members also believe that their formal recognition of positive student behavior is an important complement to demerits. This recognition comes in the form of Creed Deeds and the Spirit Stick, which are awarded on a daily and weekly basis, respectively. Creed Deeds are awarded to students who demonstrate specific values in the school creed, such as dignity, community, and investment. For example, students may receive Creed Deeds for going out of their way to help others, participating in a neighborhood cleanup, or doing a particularly excellent job on their assignments. Creed Deeds are redeemable for gift certificates and prizes at bimonthly Creed Deed auctions. The Spirit Stick is awarded at the Friday Community Meeting to the one student that staff members decide has best exemplified the school creed during the course of the week.

Other Supports

Teachers' efforts to plan and execute rigorous and engaging lessons are undoubtedly essential to teaching and learning at Roxbury Prep. However, numerous additional supports are employed to promote student learning. The length of the academic day is a manner of support in itself, as core academic classes run from 8:15 AM to 3:10 PM. Students participate daily in two different math classes (e.g., problem-solving and procedures), separate writing and reading classes, as well as social studies and science. They also begin each day with a silent "Drop Everything and Read" period that runs from 7:45 to 8:15, which means that, Monday through Thursday, students engage in purely academic activities for about seven and a half hours per day. On Fridays, students are dismissed at 1:20 PM so that staff members can participate in grade-level, department-level, and whole-faculty meetings that run from 1:30 to 4:30.

Every teacher is also contracted to provide at least four periods of individual and small- group tutoring per week, which occurs before, during, or after school, to help students keep up with the rigorous instructional pace in the classrooms. Although it is true that the tutoring frequently occurs during students' enrichment periods, which include various art, music, and physical education classes that run from 3:10 to 4:15, the school communicates clearly to families that it prioritizes core academic skills over other activities. Staff members agree that tutoring sessions are a particularly important source of student remediation. There is also a Homework Center from 4:15 to 6:00 daily, which students are required to attend if they struggle regularly to complete their work. Teachers may also hold mandatory Saturday school sessions for struggling students if it seems that the extra instructional time will be helpful.

Not surprisingly, these efforts require a great deal of time and energy from all staff members. Sixty- to seventy-hour work weeks are the norm, and everyone agrees that their workdays are long and rigorous. The codirectors make this reality clear to teaching candidates early in the hiring process, and, ultimately, staff members decide for themselves whether their efforts are sustainable over time. Although all staff members agree that a substantially less rigorous work week would make it challenging to serve students in the way they do, they also agree that the results of their efforts are very rewarding. As a reading teacher explained:

> I think there are all these times where the kids and the teachers and the parents [are saying,] . . . "Oh my gosh, this is so hard!" . . . You know, MCAS scores aren't everything, but it's so exciting for us to get our scores and kids are freaking out and parents are freaking out . . . and teachers are screaming, and I think that for all the hard times, there are enough celebratory times where we all look at each other and think, we are really doing this, we have proof that we are doing this. We tell the kids all the time, "You are changing history. You are making history, you are doing things that people have never done before. You are proving people wrong." I just think that is amazing. That is [how we run this school]. It is a cliché, but there are definitely days in the winter where everybody would like to stay in bed, but when you are at a school like this you know why you are getting out of bed, and you do get yourself there and you do it because you know it is really valuable.

Preparing Students for High School

Despite the success that Roxbury Prep enjoys, staff members realize that improvements can always be made. The school's mission focuses on college graduation, and thus the mission is not fully realized when students finish eighth grade. For this reason, the school has developed a Graduate Services Program to support Roxbury Prep alumni as they progress through high school and college. Program coordinators work full-time to keep in touch with alumni and offer support that includes tutoring for academic coursework and the SAT, assistance during the college application process, and social or emotional support that may be helpful along the way. The program coordinators recently started visiting the high schools that alumni attend so that the high school officials have an opportunity to speak with the coordinators about strategies for supporting these students. Program coordinators emphasize that they do not wish to "tell high schools how to do their jobs," but instead consider themselves to be educational allies who can help alumni navigate their high school experiences.

Teachers make efforts to prepare students for high school by teaching them independent study skills, like making flash cards that review readings or notes and encouraging eighth graders to self-advocate when they need extra help. Teachers' encouragement of self-advocacy generally gives greater autonomy to those eighth graders who seem ready to handle it. For example, whereas teachers mandate tutoring for struggling sixth and seventh graders, they are more likely to inform eighth graders and their families that the tutoring is available, rather than to decide precisely which of them must attend.

* * * * *

If you visit Roxbury Preparatory Charter School on any given day, you will see staff members doing their jobs in a variety of ways. You will see smiles, stares, hands in the air, Creed Deeds, demerits, Mad Minutes, and peer edits. In some classrooms, you may encounter some banter or the occasional Viking helmet, and on Friday afternoons you will see students and staff members come together for Community Meetings that truly inspire. Undoubtedly, you will also see teachers creatively utilizing schoolwide systems to engage students in lessons that are rigorous, well planned, far reaching, and standards based. If you ask staff members about their work, you will hear focused, committed individuals speak passionately about teaching, learning, and social justice. Just remember to ask them at an appropriate moment, because there is no talking in the hallway.

CHAPTER THREE

BOSTON COLLEGIATE CHARTER SCHOOL

Bringing College to Students and Students to College

"Fifth grade, where are you going when you leave BCCS?!?"

"COLLEGE!!!"

So ends another assembly at Boston Collegiate Charter School. It is only 8:20 AM on a cold, sleepy morning, yet the energy inside is palpable as the excited shouts of eighty-five fifth graders unite to break the morning's silence. Boston Collegiate has been hailed as a success story in the charter school movement, but to these students, this is just school and today is just another day.

The morning begins with a bus ride through the winding roads and unforgiving rush-hour traffic of Dorchester, Boston's most populous neighborhood. With its gritty blend of multifamily homes and light industry, Dorchester has been plagued by years of violence and poverty. Today, as the bus reaches the corner of Boston and Mayhew streets, a silhouette of the city's skyline appears through the clouds. Here stands the newly renovated, three-story redbrick Boston Collegiate Charter School, which feels a bit removed from its less-than-pristine surroundings. Students step off the bus and head toward the front doors, where they are greeted by a school administrator.

"Good morning," "Hello," "How are you?" she says, careful to greet each passing student. The children look sharp. Boys wear navy blue, logo-emblazoned

The primary author for this chapter is Jon Valant.

polo shirts tucked into their khaki dress pants, with dark-colored shoes and belts. Girls wear the same, sometimes substituting skirts for pants. Every student carries a backpack, and every backpack appears to be full.

The bright, airy front lobby connects what was once two separate buildings—a Catholic high school and a convent—creating a facility that feels fresh and classical, and also maintains the convent's old charm. At the top of the stairs in the lobby, past a towering banner reading "College Acceptances, 2004–2007," the high school's entrance is on the left and the middle school's on the right. A group of middle school students turns right and encounters another round of friendly greetings, this time from the middle school principal and a teacher. Above them hang banners, one for each grade, reading "Boston Collegiate Class of 2013, College Graduate Class of 2017." A "NO EXCUSES" poster hangs high at one end of the hallway, a "NO SHORTCUTS" poster hangs at the other.

It is 7:52 AM, and the day's first advisory period will begin in eight minutes. A group of fifth graders hustles up a flight of the stairs to the fifth-grade hall. Here, blue doors open to classrooms on one side of the hall and tall windows open to a cloudy sky on the other. A few students notice a visitor, and they smile to say hello. One offers help in finding a classroom, another volunteers a handshake, and one even offers a hug. By 7:57 AM, almost every student has made it to a classroom and the fifth-grade hall is quiet. In the classrooms, students talk to one another as teachers greet them and get organized for the morning.

"10, 9, 8, 7 . . ." counts the teacher, as her twenty fifth graders quietly scramble to their desks. By the end of the countdown, everyone is seated and attentive, with only one student fumbling with his backpack. As the teacher collects homework, she jokes with students, setting a casual tone that triggers light conversation between students. While this draws an occasional, "Let's keep our voices down, please," the soft buzz of conversations is tolerated and the atmosphere remains upbeat. Then comes taking attendance, which is especially playful. Students are encouraged to respond with animal sounds upon hearing their names called. "Bahhh," says one student, to giggling in the classroom; "Mooo," says another. This is middle school advisory, where the focus is as much on building relationships as it is on building skills.

After attendance is taken, the morning meeting begins. Students stand in a circle in the front of the room, where they listen to announcements and are invited to make an announcement of their own. Announcements range from, "My mom's friend had a baby last night" to "There was a crime at the Shell in Dorchester." As the brief meeting concludes, the students line up to join their

BOSTON COLLEGIATE CHARTER SCHOOL
A Commonwealth Charter School, Founded in 1998

Number of Students and Grade Levels
412 Students in Grades 5–12

Race/Ethnicity
64% White
27% African American
6% Hispanic
2% Asian
1% Multiracial, Non-Hispanic

Subgroups
42% Low-Income
17% Special Education
4% First Language Not English

Source: Massachusetts Department of Education

classmates for assembly. First, though, another teacher enters to check that everyone has complied with the strict dress code. When one student confesses to having forgotten his belt, he receives a demerit. Two more demerits this week will land him in detention.

When the line quiets to the teacher's satisfaction, students walk to take their place in the fifth-grade assembly. Lacking a gymnasium, auditorium, or similar meeting space, Boston Collegiate is forced to creatively manage its large-group gatherings. For this gathering of eighty-five fifth graders, the second-floor hallway must do. Students sit cross-legged in pairs, in neatly aligned rows, as their young, enthusiastic teachers walk about them. Talking is no longer acceptable, and the methodical pace at which the students are seated—and the straightness of the rows in which they sit—suggests that they have done this many times before.

The assembly aims to be both informative and inspirational. Teachers make announcements, acknowledge student accomplishments, ask trivia questions, and tell a story that leaves students with a clear message: "When someone tells you that you can't achieve something, you put your iPods on and don't listen." Now the teacher calls out, "Fifth grade, where are you going when you leave BCCS?!?" Students join in screaming *"College!!!"* and the resulting energy carries the fifth grade into the beginning of its academic day.

Similar scenes are unfolding throughout Boston Collegiate during morning advisory. The day's homework is collected by advisory teachers and distributed to the other grade-level teachers, triggering a process in which the families of fifth through eighth graders who did not complete their homework are notified that their children must stay for today's afterschool Homework Club. In many of the high school classrooms, students gather in groups to review for an algebra test or collaborate on English essay responses.

Advisory activities differ across grades; for example, high school advisories have a more academic orientation, but they are more alike than different. An upbeat atmosphere and collegiate focus is common throughout. Each advisory is named after the advisor's alma mater; a sixth-grade student might belong to Wisconsin 6 and a ninth-grade student to Cornell 9. Advisory classmates are also teammates, and together they compete for acknowledgment and rewards for behavior, effort, and achievement. College posters and memorabilia cover most of the classroom walls. In the Williams College classroom, for example, posters, photographs, and a Williams basketball jersey hang in plain view. Just a few feet away, a board labeled "Where are we going after BCCS?" publicly displays where each of these fifth graders plan to attend college. As 8:25 AM approaches, it is time to make the transition from advisory to first period. It is time to get to work.

Still energized from the morning assembly, the fifth-grade advisory cohort walks together to its first-period reading class. Students talk as they form lines in front of each classroom, but their voices are soft and their teachers unbothered. After a minute passes and it becomes clear that class is about to begin, everyone falls silent. "Good morning," the teacher says to each student while motioning with her arm to accelerate the pace. Within seconds, all of the students are seated, and nothing can be heard but the rustling of paper as students collect their materials and immediately get to work. They have started the "Do-Now," a brief exercise that will greet them at the beginning of every class. Today's Do-Now instructs them to edit this sentence: *annemarie ran down the Street with Elen*. As the first students finish, they take out their silent, sustained reading books, hoping to get through a page or two before their classmates catch up.

At 8:32 AM, the teacher asks for a volunteer to correct the Do-Now sentence. Of the twenty students in the room, all but two raise their hands. When the teacher asks follow-up questions, at least two-thirds of the room volunteers. In fact, when fewer than half of the students volunteer, the teacher reacts, saying, "Come on, I should see every hand up." Once the Do-Now is complete, a volunteer reads the day's objective from the board: "You will be able to edit the work of your peers for basic grammar, sentence structure, and general context." The teacher then explains the day's agenda and the peer editing begins. The room remains silent through the transition, and the teacher hurries to get the activity started. Not a moment of class time is wasted.

Today, students work in pairs to edit the children's book that they have been creating over the last several days. The project integrates reading, writing, and art, and they must use their own words to convert Lois Lowry's *Number the Stars* into a children's book, complete with illustrations. The productivity of each group depends on the particular students involved. Many groups engage in ongoing, high-level discussions about whether certain passages are necessary, where stronger topic sentences might help to bridge paragraphs, and how to describe characters better. Others interact more sporadically, requiring more of the teacher's attention. Still, every group is engaged and remains on task as the teacher crisscrosses the room, answering questions and pushing the students forward.

At 9:15 AM, class is almost over. The teacher claps and the students clap in response. "Excellent job today, you guys. You did amazing work, and I'm really proud of you." The final order of business is assigning a "MAPP" score for the day. At the end of every class period at Boston Collegiate, the class is evaluated on a zero-to-one scale for each of four MAPP criteria: mindful, achieving, professional, and prepared. A class that is well prepared might receive a one-point score for the preparedness criterion, while an unprepared class would receive a fractional point or nothing at all. Our English teacher rewards the day's impressive effort with a 4.0, the highest possible score. This will be helpful to this advisory group as it works to collect enough points to earn a class party or other shared reward.

A short walk up the middle school stairs finds a familiar scene as seventh graders travel to their second-period classes. Student talk softly with teachers and other students, but the well-monitored halls are orderly and the class-to-class transitions are quick. As the beginning of class approaches, the hallway turns silent. "Please look me in the eye," says a seventh-grade teacher as students file into her classroom. She pauses to shake each student's hand. "Hi, thanks for coming," she tells one. "Hi, it's nice to see you," she tells another. Most students respond with a "good morning" or "thank you." All are careful to look their teacher in the eye. This, after all, is a form of professionalism, and professionalism is one of the four MAPP criteria.

Throughout the hallways at Boston Collegiate, an assortment of student work, acknowledgements, and posters remind students that the goal here is college. Student writing and artwork, much of it reflecting social justice themes, hang on the walls. The names of students are posted to recognize high scores or substantial improvement on interim assessments and other tests, and class lists display students' "merit point" totals. College memorabilia and information are plentiful, and one of the high school hallways displays the average SAT scores of Boston Collegiate students while another displays the colleges attended by alumni. At almost every turn, student accomplishments are celebrated and the college-preparatory mission is reinforced.

Back on the second floor, the fifth-grade advisory cohort has returned to its advisory classroom, where the advisory teacher will now serve as the history teacher. However, the relaxed atmosphere and animal sounds of advisory are a distant memory. "Everyone should be sitting outrageously professionally," the teacher says, as she moves through the classroom checking notes. Her tone is gentle but firm, and the class is fast-paced. Students are preparing for next week's exam, and today the preparation entails answering review questions and taking notes in a study guide. This teacher, like the English teacher before her, expresses dissatisfaction when participation dwindles, and she is quick to remind students that they "all know this stuff." After several questions are asked and answered in rapid succession, students are given time to quickly scribble notes on what has been written on the board.

Both explicitly and implicitly, a major focus of the class is study habits. Students are guided through the process of taking notes in a teacher-created study guide that highlights key information from the previous unit. The study guide fits in a particular place in students' class binders, and their homework in recent days has been to create note cards from the study guide that can be used for test review. When they are ready to move from creating note cards to studying, students are reminded of the "two-pile method": put the cards that you know in one pile and the cards that you do not know in another.

The teaching of study skills is both deliberate and strategic at Boston Collegiate. One sixth-grade teacher distributes note cards and envelopes to students at the beginning of another fast-paced review period. She instructs them to take notes on the cards and carry the cards around in the envelopes. As homework, the students are asked to develop individual study plans to show how they will study all of the material in the days before the test. As students get older, less hand-holding occurs. In a joint ninth- and tenth-grade world studies class, students maintain binders with handouts and notes. While students are expected to keep up with the binder collection—and are provided with a table of contents and instructions for where specific handouts should be placed—the teacher refrains from directly checking the binders. This, the teacher says, "is their transition from eighth grade to eleventh grade," and greater independence will be expected of students in the upper grades. Plus, an occasional open-binder quiz provides enough incentive for these ninth and tenth graders to stay organized.

Back in the fifth-grade history class, students quickly and quietly make the transition from test review to group work, where they compare notes with partners. Class is almost over, but one task remains: evaluate the class using the MAPP criteria. After some discussion, the class receives a 3.2, losing a half-point for professionalism and 0.3 points for mindfulness (i.e., being respectful and attentive and adhering to the school's Code of Conduct). In closing, the teacher tells them that "there will be a point when I don't remind you to sit up."

Indeed, the eleventh-grade students are not reminded to sit up straight. After quickly reviewing the Do-Now, a high school math teacher reads the day's objective: "You will be able to work effectively as a team to solve real-world problems using linear programs." He asks the students to break into groups and distributes a challenging set of problems that requires students to determine the ideal mix of products a company should produce in order to maximize its profits.

"I don't expect everyone to be on-task all of the time," he tells the class, "but after a minute of small talk, you need to get to work. After all," he says, "If you're working at Abercrombie & Fitch, you need to get the product out—need to get stuff done." This is quite different from the language used in the middle school, where the focus is as much on the process as the product. Here in the eleventh grade, students are given more freedom and are judged on their output, much like they will be in college. Interestingly, it hardly seems necessary. Over the next thirty-five minutes, students collaborate on the problem set, struggling through the questions and consulting their teacher only when truly perplexed. Most groups work hard throughout the period, finishing early. Their motivation is partly incentive-based: if they finish early, they can start their homework, reducing the night's workload. Moreover, the first group to finish has been offered five "MAPP miles" (analogous to the middle school's "merits"), which can be used toward the purchase of tangible rewards. Perhaps more important, most of these students are in their seventh year at Boston Collegiate and their work habits have been honed during this time by like-minded teachers. Surely some bad habits remain—daydreaming, for example, can sometimes creep in—but misbehavior is mild and the collective work ethic is impressive.

The fifth graders, meanwhile, remain in the early, formative period of their Boston Collegiate experience. For the rest of the day, their classes will be intense and the pace will be relentless. After history, they will travel together to writing, math, science, and art. This intensity is mitigated by a supportive school atmosphere and two more advisory periods: one at lunch and one at the end of the school day. At lunch, the lack of a school cafeteria sends students back to their advisory classrooms, where they talk with friends and teachers in an atmosphere that recaptures some of the morning advisory's controlled playfulness. At 2:50 PM, they return for one final 10-minute advisory to wrap up this day and prepare for the next one.

However, for many students and teachers, the school day does not end at 3:00. Several students in grades 5–8 will be required to attend Homework Club until 4:00 or 5:00. A second group of more persistently struggling students will stay late for structured tutoring in BCCS-Plus, a skill-building program for students at risk of falling behind. Others will stay late for mandatory tutoring, voluntary tutoring, or one of the school's extracurricular activities, such as basketball or museum club.

ELEMENTS OF SUCCESS

Boston Collegiate's approach seems to be working. To the extent that the Massachusetts Comprehensive Assessment System (MCAS), the state assessment system, is a reflection of academic quality, Boston Collegiate does well. Across grades 5–12, the school outperforms Boston Public Schools and is competitive with (or surpasses) state averages. It is the only public school in Massachusetts where all tenth graders passed the math and English portions of the MCAS from 2003 to 2006—a feat made easier by its small high school graduating classes. Beyond MCAS, year after year, every graduate is accepted to a four-year college, and relatively few students leave Boston Collegiate along the way. Additionally, waiting lists for entry are long, and parents report being highly satisfied with their children's experience at BCCS. This, along with a connection through the Boston Collegiate founder, has encouraged Uncommon Schools, a charter management organization, to accept Boston Collegiate as an associate member. This is both an indicator of and a contributor to the school's success.

Still, a humble honesty emerges as staff members confess to not having discovered a silver bullet for education reform. "I think it's just hard work and doing lots of the little things right," says one administrator. The school's website proclaims there to be "no one, magical 100% solution but rather one hundred, individual 1% solutions."

While no single attribute or activity can account for Boston Collegiate's success, these "one hundred" solutions seem to coalesce around three key factors:

- A clear, powerful mission embraced by all of the school's stakeholders
- The recruitment, development, and retention of high-quality, mission-aligned teachers
- Balancing high expectations with a warm, supportive school atmosphere

A Mission Everyone Accepts

In 2004, six years after the school's opening, the leadership team of South Boston Harbor Academy Charter School opted for a new name to accompany its new Dorchester location. Citing a desire to "adopt a name that best reflects and supports the school's mission," the team chose to be called Boston Collegiate Charter School.

Boston Collegiate's mission is elegant in its simplicity: "To prepare each student for college." It is written across a bulletin board in the front lobby and the front page of the website. Most important, though, it permeates almost every decision and conversation in the building and is embraced by teachers, administrators, students, parents, and supporters alike.

"This is a school," says one administrator, that "tries to be clear with all the stakeholders in terms of what we're about, what our mission is, what we're trying to do, [and] what our expectations are." A teacher agrees: "The mission? Whoever you talk to in the building, they all know what they're here for, and they're all passionate about it." Boston Collegiate's college-preparatory orientation is clear to anyone who walks its halls. In the back of one middle school classroom, a paper hangs for each student, reading, "My name is _____, Future college: _____." For most students, Harvard, Yale, or Boston College is scribbled in fifth-grade handwriting.

In many ways at Boston Collegiate, college is brought to students and students are taken to college. Boston Collegiate graduates sit on alumni panels to describe their experiences to their younger, curious peers, while the Bridge to Success program ensures that every student will visit a partner college at least twice per year. In school, a college lexicon is introduced, as high-achieving students are acknowledged as being cum laude, magna cum laude, and summa cum laude, and the MAPP scores mimic the traditional college grade point average. Meanwhile, students in the higher grades receive syllabi and more long-term, college-like assignments that have largely replaced the nightly busywork common in some American high schools.

The omnipresence of college language, materials, and conversations establishes four-year college as an expectation for all students. Most of these students would be the first in their families to attend college and consequently might not consider it an option. A teacher explains:

> They aren't only prepared academically. . . . They haven't been around a lot of people who went to college, talked about college a lot, and used words that they're going to hear in college. If you're the first person in your family to go to college, there are a lot of terms that you might not have heard growing up. You might not know a lot about how dorms work, or tuition, or homecoming. What's that like? What's a Greek system?

Preparing students for college has been challenging. Boston Collegiate's first graduating class began college in 2004, and the school is just now able to collect information about the performance of its graduates. The results are mixed. While students have consistently been accepted by a four-year college—which, in fact, is a graduation requirement—several no longer remain at college, citing a variety of financial, academic, and social concerns. As of 2007, the school reported that 78 percent of alumni have stayed in college.

Intent on addressing this issue, Boston Collegiate created a full-time college counselor position and, in the 2006-07 school year, established a College Readiness Committee. The committee, led by the high school principal, meets monthly to discuss ways students can become more college ready. For example, upon finding that relatively low SAT scores were undermining students' competitiveness for scholarships, the College Readiness Committee introduced three college-prep days per year. On these days, students in grades 9–11 take abbreviated SAT exams. The results are analyzed by Boston Collegiate teachers, who then create action plans to address skill deficits.

These are just a few illustrations of how the simplicity of the school's mission helps to keep the organization focused. In a school where one teacher describes "a culture of, 'we're all in this together,'" students, parents, and school leaders work toward the same goal. Reflecting in a focus group, one parent shared this about her son:

> He still goes to tutoring. He knows that he has to go to tutoring. I don't ever tell him. The teachers don't even have to tell him. He knows that, you know what, if I want to get those As and Bs so I can go to Gonzaga or the University of Miami, then this is what I have to do.

"Teachers, Teachers, Teachers"

Asked what drives Boston Collegiate's success, an administrator does not hesitate to respond, "Teachers, teachers, teachers." This administrator's response mirrors Boston Collegiate's three-pronged approach to placing a great teacher in every classroom. Careful attention is paid to recruiting and hiring strong, mission-aligned candidates; using constant, constructive feedback to improve teacher performance; and actively working to retain those who succeed.

Recruiting and Hiring

In recent years, Boston Collegiate has received several hundred applications for a few openings. This has provided the school with the considerable benefits of high selectivity, enabling it to identify what it wants in its teachers and pursue only those who "fit."

The screening process begins with a resume review and, for some, a telephone interview. If the candidate seems promising, a face-to-face interview is scheduled with the principal and other school leaders. A candidate then might be asked to teach a mini-lesson, submit a video of their current teaching, or allow a Boston Collegiate representative to visit their current classroom. Along the way, the candidate meets "just about everybody in the school" in order to get as much input as possible.

An administrator describes the characteristics of successful applicants:

> There are basic qualities we look for. Obviously, we look for people who are smart and well educated, organized, and who combine the mission and the core values of the school. . . . I'm looking for the evidence and basic qualities that I think make people really good teachers and staff people here–hardworking, professional demeanor, receptive to feedback, commitment to measurable achievement, and ability to show clear student progress over time.

Given these criteria, it should not be surprising that Boston Collegiate teachers tend to be well educated, young, willing to work long hours, and committed to the school's college preparatory mission. "[The mission] was told to me maybe a hundred times," notes one teacher about his interviews. While having prior urban teaching experience is advantageous for a candidate, it is less important than having strong character, being mission aligned, and exhibiting a strong work ethic. In an administrator's words, "We aren't really looking for great *teachers*, . . . we're looking for great *people*.

Development and Acculturation

Of course, great people only are helpful to Boston Collegiate insofar as they can be great teachers, so teacher development is critical. Through orientation, training, and regular feedback, Boston Collegiate leaders work with teachers in an individual, personalized way in order to maximize each teacher's potential. This requires that teachers have the desire to learn and grow, which is often cited by administrators as an essential characteristic for a teaching candidate. Says one administrator, "I think being receptive to feedback is kind of a sacred cow to me. It's something I look for in staff here. It's something I try to have in myself."

Boston Collegiate does not just work to build great teachers—it works to build great *Boston Collegiate* teachers. These are teachers who will embrace the school's mission, faithfully implement its systems, and contribute to its culture. The acculturation of new teachers begins early. "The induction process starts when you start recruiting," says an administrator. "You're intentional about what you're trying to convey about the school." Newly hired teachers are encouraged to visit the school as often as possible prior to the school year. They sit in classrooms, talk to current teachers, begin working through curricula, and get to know their mentors. They also attend a two-week summer orientation for new teachers. An administrator comments about the summer orientation:

> We do it to give pertinent training and orientation in preparation for the first year at the school. So it starts with philosophy—big picture, culture, mission issues. Then it really tries to get into components of what good instruction looks like, how to create a good lesson, and then some practical aspects of daily life here.

Orientation also provides an opportunity to create camaraderie and a shared sense of purpose among staff members. This will be critical as teachers work together to build a coherent curriculum and a culture of high expectations.

While the acculturation process prioritizes unity and consistency, the professional development of teachers prioritizes personalization and efficiency. These are not necessarily conflicting priorities. The school strives for consistency in its culture and excellence across its classrooms but understands that individual teachers have different needs. One administrator explains:

> Some [teachers] arrive here with this being their first teaching experience; others arrive with five years of experience. We recognize that they shouldn't all get exactly the same professional development. They want and need different things. We do short workshops for the entire teaching staff in the

mornings of professional development days and see great value in those sessions. However, it is equally important for teachers to have the opportunity to work on their goals and seek out their own opportunities, inside and outside of the school. It is important to us that there is that balance of opportunities and expectations.

The external provision of staff development sessions is rare, since many at Boston Collegiate regard it as inefficient and ineffective. Instead, the focus is on sharing best practices across classrooms, analyzing student achievement data, and occasionally sharing notes from visits to other high-performing schools or skill-building workshops.

The backbone of Boston Collegiate's professional development, however, is frequent and informal observations. The resulting feedback is considered more developmental than evaluative. Principals (one for the high school and one for the middle school) and the dean of curriculum visit most classrooms weekly, and the executive director, department chairs, and others also make regular visits. A teacher describes progress in this area:

> I think we've gotten much stronger at having feedback come from many different places. You know what the executive director sees, what your principal sees, and what the curriculum dean sees, and they're all looking for slightly different things.

After these short classroom visits, teachers receive immediate written feedback. The school uses a standard observation form—a one-page evaluation that addresses key aspects of teaching performance, from student engagement to classroom management to blackboard configuration. While Boston Collegiate teachers also receive a formal mid-year evaluation, they receive less emphasis than the informal observations. A staff member explains:

> This is a school that believes in lots of opportunities for informal feedback as opposed to the more structured formal observation process, where I'm going in and doing one or two full-class observations a year with a pre-meeting and so forth. ... We've also gotten a lot better at giving feedback constantly. So principals and the dean of curriculum are in classes much more frequently than they ever were in the past, and I only anticipate that continuing or growing.

Retaining the Best Teachers

The final step in building a strong teaching force at Boston Collegiate is retaining those who perform well and contribute to the school's culture—and letting go of those who do not. Given the demands on Boston Collegiate teachers, retention can be difficult. Long work days are nothing new to Boston Collegiate or to its charter compatriots, and they have contributed to relatively high teacher turnover in the past. Over time, as school leaders began to acknowledge and address the issue, turnover rates dropped sharply. An important moment in tackling the issue came in 2005-06 with the formation of the Teacher Retention Committee.

Teachers and the executive director meet periodically as the Teacher Retention Committee to discuss tangible ways to improve work-life balance at Boston Collegiate. As a result, teacher workloads have been made more manageable (e.g., by shifting some extracurricular responsibilities to nonteachers). The committee also has discussed on-site day care and teacher sabbaticals. An administrator explains the rationale for prioritizing teacher retention:

> We don't want to be cycling through teachers every few years. There is something lost in the school culture, in the quality of the curriculum, in the quality of the teaching if we are constantly bringing in new teachers and losing our older teachers.

Many teachers have noticed and appreciated the administrators' efforts. Says one:

> They really care about work-life balance. It is really hard in a school like this with limited funds but really high expectations. Teachers do a lot more than they are expected to and have a lot more responsibility than they might at points in their career in a traditional school. But they . . . really help us balance work and life.

The school has used other strategies to increase retention. Teachers now have monetary incentives to stay, as they are offered a $1,000 bonus for reaching their third year, a $2,000 bonus for reaching their fifth year, and a $3,000 bonus every two years after that.[1] In addition, several teacher-leadership roles now exist, providing teachers with additional experiences, exposure, and, in some cases, money. With positions like department chair, grade-level leader, advisory coordinator, culture coordinator, and mentor, after four or five years "basically everyone either has a leadership role or doesn't want one," according to an administrator.

Perhaps more than any formal systems or policies, however, Boston Collegiate's success with teacher retention derives from a deep respect that many teachers feel from their administrators, along with a sense that they are "treated as professionals." One teacher states:

I felt like they gave me all kinds of great structure. I have an office, a desk, and a desktop that works. I have a tech guy that would do everything possible to make my life extremely smooth. My principal observes, my department chair observes, and my fellow teachers observe. If I want to go do professional development, I can go do it. If I want to start this thing or think we should do this [differently], it's all encouraged.

Finally, if teachers are not performing well and do not show signs of improvement, they are fired or not invited back for the following year. "We'd sacrifice a teacher long before a student, if the students aren't learning," says an administrator. This administrator reports that Boston Collegiate has grown much more willing to part ways with low-performing teachers over the years and cites this as an important step in the school's development.

In summary, then, placing an outstanding teacher in every classroom is a key to Boston Collegiate's success. The Boston Collegiate approach is three-pronged: recruit and hire smart, hardworking, philosophically aligned teachers; provide constant, informal, constructive feedback that helps teachers grow; and actively retain successful teachers and remove unsuccessful ones.

Firm but Friendly

Weaving through the sunny, colorful classrooms and hallways of Boston Collegiate Charter School, one first notices what is here: countless college banners, motivational posters, sharply dressed students, and fast-moving teachers. Soon thereafter, one notices what is missing. There are no fights in the halls, metal detectors at the doors, or students yelling at each other from one side of the room to the other. Disagreements in class are rare, and the halls are empty while classes are in session. From day to day and classroom to classroom, Boston Collegiate is orderly, calm, and controlled. This orderliness is a product of high expectations for students and teachers, a small-school feel, and firm, consistent school structures.

The process of setting high expectations begins anew each year with a boot camp–like acculturation for students and teachers alike. Teachers meet in the summer to build grade-level cohesion as the school year starts. They strategize about how to create consistent learning environments for their students and commit to uphold the school's strict disciplinary system. This can be especially tough—and important—with Boston Collegiate fifth graders, as a middle school teacher explains:

We are strict in that they have to have their shirts tucked in or they get a demerit . . . plus, [they have to watch] their posture and sitting up straight, and they can't have their heads on their desk. So there are certain things that I think other schools would say, "Well, that's pretty picky." . . . It really does help in the long run, though. . . . Being a fifth-grade teacher in some ways can be the hardest, because it's like boot camp. Here you have these kids who are really trying to do the right thing but getting so excited. Then they end up getting a demerit. It can be very hard. There is an acculturation process that happens, and it really does help the consistency.

The merit-demerit system is central to maintaining order. Demerits are handed out liberally, especially in the middle school grades. One middle school student receives a demerit for not having a pencil ready when the Do-Now begins, while another gets one for sipping from a flavored water bottle that his teacher asked him to put away. The consequences for a single demerit are not severe: middle school students serve afterschool detention after their third demerit in a week; high school students, for their third demerit in a month. However, this lightly triggered demerit system has a powerful effect, creating disincentives for even very mild misbehavior. Severe misbehavior—like disrespect toward a teacher or classmate—is immediately punished with detention or a suspension. Demerits, though, serve as a second tier to the disciplinary system, giving students additional reason to stay on their toes, ready to learn. The school's Code of Conduct reminds students that "for every infraction there will be a consequence," and even the slightest infractions are addressed.

The Code of Conduct goes on to explain that Boston Collegiate is "unequivocally committed to providing a safe and orderly environment in which students can improve their academic achievement." Thus, the school's logic emerges: by "sweating the small stuff" related to student behavior, Boston Collegiate removes distractions that could limit student learning.

High expectations reach beyond student behavior, since much is expected of both teachers and students in the classroom. Many teachers speak of a shared sense of urgency at Boston Collegiate, and an administrator names cultivating this sense of urgency as one his most important responsibilities. Additionally, for teachers to succeed at Boston Collegiate, they must faithfully uphold the school's systems, which creates consistency and coherence. This begins in advisory, where teachers take attendance and collect all of the day's homework. In academic classes, use of the blackboard configuration that lists the day's objective, Do-Now, agenda, and homework assignment is expected of every teacher, regardless of grade level or subject area. A teacher explains:

There are a hundred things that you have to do. And it's just so hard to do them all. But if you do, . . . something really great happens. So having teachers who are willing to do a lot of little things to keep this school running smoothly, to ensure that kids are achieving, I think is one of the biggest keys to our success.

Of course, academic expectations are high for students as well. In most middle school classes, the pace is remarkably fast and unrelenting. The Do-Now begins the moment that class starts, transitions from one activity to the next are sharp (or else demerits are given), and there is virtually no downtime as teachers hustle through the day's agenda. Students are pressured to volunteer for questions and often cold-called when they do not, and reminders to "track the speaker" require students to watch the teacher's every move.

In the upper grades, meanwhile, the expectations are different but equally high. Schoolwork has become increasingly abstract and more demanding. By now, students have a strong academic foundation, making sophisticated, college-level conversations both possible and commonplace.

Virtually every day in every class, students in each grade receive homework. For those who struggle to keep up, there are both consequences and supports. Failure to satisfactorily complete a day's homework will land students in grades 5–9 in that day's Homework Club or mandatory tutoring until at least 4 PM. Here, students complete past homework and begin the next night's work. More consistent academic difficulties might lead a student to BCCS-Plus, a structured, teacher-run, afterschool tutoring program, or, for older students, to mandatory tutoring. If students regularly attend BCCS-Plus or tutoring and continue to struggle, they are eligible for teacher-staffed Saturday School, which serves grades 5–9 with tutoring and support, or the less structured Saturday Study, which serves grades 10–12. All of this amounts to a challenging school experience for students. They must arrive early, keep pace, participate consistently, stay late, and go home to a full night's homework. Any missteps along the way will likely draw a teacher's attention and earn a student a demerit or detention.

Critically, though, the rigid structures and considerable demands placed on Boston Collegiate students are balanced by a warm, supportive school atmosphere. While discipline is strict and expectations high, the school has a decidedly warm feel. An administrator explains:

We're not a super-strict model where there is no talking in the hallways and all movements are managed. We're not that. But we're also not comfortable with looseness, lots of noise, and the absence of certain basic structures. We are constantly trying to strike a balance.

Class time is sacred at Boston Collegiate, and no disruptions of any kind are tolerated. When class is over, however, the teacher-student dynamics can change. A high school teacher offers his view:

> In my old school I was very formal and more legalistic and harsh . . . , whereas here, because there is a general structure, there's not violence in the school, there's not thuggery and cursing . . . and your job is more to teach. My relationship with [students] is more like, when I'm teaching, I'm teaching. But when I'm not, I'm a person you can interact with almost like you interact with a peer. . . . I don't feel like I need to maintain a distance all the time.

These differences between work time and play time are especially visible during advisories, in hallways, and after school. Advisories range from businesslike to playful, where teachers are charged with simultaneously executing school structures and building relationships with their students. "Advisors generally know their students very well," says one teacher, "and our job is to advocate for those students." This teacher contrasts Boston Collegiate with her prior teaching experience: "Kids here love their teachers. . . . It's bizarre." This affection can be seen in the hallways, where students and teachers joke and make small talk, and after school, when nonacademic afterschool activities can offer a break from the day's academic rigor and strictness. In Role-Playing Club, for example, a small group of students huddles with a teacher in the basement science room. These students, who might not be interested in more conventional extracurricular offerings, engage their imaginations in *Dungeons and Dragons*. They are led by their "Dungeon Master" teacher, whose easygoing temperament invites these students to develop a deeper relationship with him than is possible in the confines of a class period.

This warmth in nonacademic moments helps balance the methodical, unrelenting demands of the day's academics. A similar balance exists in the school's policies and systems. Whereas the demerit system ensures that there is a consequence for every code infraction, the merit system ensures that there is an acknowledgement of every accomplishment. As demerits are to bad behavior, MAPP "merits" (grades 5–7) and "miles" (grades 8–12) are to good behavior. They may receive points for volunteering to clean up a classroom or showing considerable improvement on a test. As with demerits, merits also are lightly triggered, providing incentives for even subtle accomplishments. Thus, in both school policy and staff behavior, demanding academic and behavioral expectations are balanced with a nurturing atmosphere as students set out to reach their goals. While the balance between high expectations and warmth may subtly shift from one grade to the next, it remains intact from grades 5 to 12, leaving students feeling both pushed and supported throughout their Boston Collegiate careers.

* * * * *

These three factors—a powerful mission, outstanding teachers, and balance between high expectations and a supportive school climate—help to explain much of Boston Collegiate's success; however, they do not tell the whole story. The importance of instructional leadership as well as a commitment to self-improvement are other important factors that will be treated in subsequent chapters. At Boston Collegiate Charter School, expectations are high, excuses are unacceptable, and the work is never finished. Perhaps that is why, when you hear eighty-five fifth graders declare that they are bound for college, you just might have to believe them.

CHAPTER FOUR

THE ACADEMY OF THE PACIFIC RIM CHARTER SCHOOL

Paving the Way to Adulthood

They're wearing lab goggles like it's old hat, their adolescent bodies moving restlessly from stool to stool as they circle their beakers impatiently. Conversation bounces from football to the presidential primaries to the mass of calcium carbonate in eggshells—the subject of today's experiment. Very few of the fifteen students in this eleventh-grade chemistry class are able to sit still while they wait for the chemical reaction to take place. They mill around the large rectangular tables, checking on their classmates' beakers and "massing the funnel paper" for the next step in the process they've designed. The teacher, a slight Asian woman with a wise smile, alternates sitting at a table engaging in casual chit-chat with her primarily African American students and wandering about the room doing small tasks to occupy herself. As she casually lays paper towels on a back table, anticipating the clean-up process coming later, she entertains a student's complaint that "This is gonna take ages." She responds slowly, "Patience. It's a virtue."

It isn't particularly odd that the teacher doesn't have a lot to do during this class period. After all, the students designed the experiment and they're in charge of carrying it out. Yesterday she asked them to figure out a way to determine the percentage of calcium carbonate in eggshells, and today they are on their own, working in small clusters to actualize their plan. Her role today

The primary author for this chapter is Kristy Cooper.

is to offer encouragement in moments of frustration: "You've done this before. You can figure it out." She's also there to remind them that the lab is set up to assist them. When a couple of students have trouble remembering how to prepare their filter paper, she prompts them to "look over there," pointing to a display on the wall: "How to Prepare Filter Paper." They mutter, "Oh, yeah," and within seconds they've got their filter paper ready and they're off to tackle the next steps on their own.

It was different when this teacher had the same group of students as eighth graders in physical science three years earlier. Back then she had provided extensive directions when conducting experiments, but she believes that by eleventh grade the scaffolding is in place, and she needs to encourage her students to think for themselves. She takes a certain pride in knowing they can cope without her, and she credits this pedagogical decision to feedback from alumni who have returned to complain that instruction in the eleventh and twelfth grades was too easy, here at the Academy of the Pacific Rim. This teacher now makes a greater effort to anticipate the rigor of college in designing her high school curriculum—such as explicitly requiring that students learn from reading their chemistry textbook—rather than waiting for her to have all the answers. She knows her students will be expected to learn from college texts, and so she takes responsibility for incorporating this requirement into her practice.

In this way, this teacher is like many of her colleagues at the Academy of the Pacific Rim, who are intent on developing independence in their students as they grow and mature across the school's grade span, grades five through twelve. The dean of students, a nine-year veteran at the school, explains the school's philosophy and strategy for developing student independence over time:

> The middle school is more top down, more structured. The teachers do more of the job in terms of direct instruction, and the students access the content that the teachers provide. But, we've pulled back in the high school, which is more geared towards student participation—trying to get students to try out courses and take leadership roles and really participate much more in the planning, delivery, and even sometimes the evaluation of lessons, so that they are that much more prepared to navigate the world on their own.

Indeed, instruction is often more structured in the middle school grades, and efforts to develop and massage academic skills are evident. While their older counterparts design and carry out original experiments and meander collegially about the chemistry lab, twenty-three seventh graders down the

THE ACADEMY OF THE PACIFIC RIM CHARTER SCHOOL
A Commonwealth Charter School, Founded in 1997

Number of Students and Grade Levels
472 Students in Grades 5–12

Race/Ethnicity
57% African American
23% White
16% Hispanic,
3% Asian
1% Multiracial, Non-Hispanic

Subgroups
13% Special Education
51% Low Income

Source: Massachusetts Department of Education

hall shimmy their desks into a loose circle—bunching up in odd places as students squish in around the support columns marking the building's origins as a warehouse. They pass around a handout titled "Purposeful Talk," as the teacher, sinking into a desk to join the circle, poses the question for today's "purposeful" discussion: "Think of a reason why name-calling is wrong, and give an example from the book to support your point." A few students leaf through their copies of *The Misfits* as others eagerly raise their hands to condemn the evil act of name-calling. An orderly discussion ensues, as students share their opinions and everyone tracks one another's contributions on their Purposeful Talk papers, which include a chart on which students can award their classmates points for good contributions and respectful listening. In fact, it is this peer-evaluation system that swings the classroom to order once the discussion begins. As students call on one another to participate, each respondent demonstrates a familiarity with academic discussions by structuring their comments with phrases like, "I agree with Darryl because in the book Bobby says . . ." As the end of the class period nears, the teacher draws the discussion to a close by explaining the homework: students are to respond to the question from the discussion, drawing on both their own ideas and those presented by their classmates.

Another flight up, on the more colorfully decorated fifth- and sixth-grade floor, younger students experience the same level of purposeful structure in their math program, which is divided into two math classes each day. On a cool fall morning, fifth-grade students in the Math Foundations class sit huddled in pairs as they work through long-division problems on a two-page worksheet. The teacher calmly circles her way around the doubled-up desks, commenting over students' shoulders, "So far so good. What's your next step?" Many of the partners work together every step of the way, agreeing together on a move before writing it on their papers. In some partnerships, one person rushes ahead and then stops to wait for their partner. Others coax their classmates along with carefully worded "helping" questions. One small girl hovers over her partner, offering assistance as she helps him divide with remainders: "What times 8 equals 33?" "4?" "So, what's 4 times 8?" When her partner isn't sure, she helps him strategize from what he does know: "So subtract. What's 8 times 5?"

In Math Applications class a week later, these same students work under the guidance of a different teacher. Again they are huddled in pairs, but this time they are teamed up for group problem-solving. Their stapled packets present seven word problems, each with designated space for writing the question, the strategy or plan, showing work, and reporting the final result in a sentence. Focusing in this class on applying the algorithmic math skills they have developed in Math Foundations, students test their knowledge on problems such as, "The sixth and seventh graders at the Academy of the Pacific Rim are going on a field trip to Boston College. Four buses will carry 56 students each, and a fifth bus will carry 68 students. How many students are going on the field trip?" As the students hunker down with pencils and discuss strategy with their partners, the teacher circles through the room asking probing questions and monitoring progress.

Across the hall, a cohort of sixth graders works through the pages of a textbook, *Ancient Civilizations,* taking turns reading aloud about the geography of India. The teacher, who alternates sitting at his desk and standing up front, is creating a portrait of India's landscape on the board, and he punctuates the conclusion of each paragraph with questions like, "What two mountain passes can you take through the Himalayas?" After reading the first three paragraphs on page 95 in the text, the students pause to answer the first two questions on their worksheet: "What are three characteristics of India's geography? What are two ways geography influenced the Indian people?" The students fill in their worksheets and wait for instruction to resume.

A journey through the three floors of the Academy of the Pacific Rim's renovated brick building in Hyde Park, Massachusetts, reveals that teachers have great freedom to use pedagogical strategies of their own choosing, and their instructional styles run the gamut. The executive director explains the policy on instructional methodology:

We don't mandate direct instruction or [the] Socratic method or "discovery" or "expeditionary learning." What we do is give different tools. We expect weekly lesson plans, and we say that every week should include a range of plans that will address different modalities of learning. There is a list of them . . . ten, fifteen practices. What we don't want to see is direct instruction all week long . . . [or] independent seatwork all week long or group work all week long. So, it's not one method, but ideally it is the use of specific tools that will deliver good instruction.

The Academy of the Pacific Rim's Instruction Guidebook, given to all new teachers upon arrival, provides detailed explanations of both classroom management techniques—such as the blackboard configuration that outlines learning objectives, the day's agenda, and a "Do-Now" activity to start each period—and the pedagogical components of strategies such as direct instruction, guided practice, teacher-guided reading, independent practice, cooperative learning, and discussions. Expectations are clear that teachers will incorporate a variety of approaches in designing their courses, and the guidebook states directly that

the instructional activities that teachers plan in their lessons should always be aligned with the objective and should incorporate one or more of these strategies. A general guideline is that each hour-long lesson should include at least two of the components.

This pedagogical freedom ensures that teachers can design their own instruction to serve students' interests, learning styles, academic performance, and developmental needs as they change over time.

Adding a Little Asian Flavor

Academy of the Pacific Rim teachers receive a Culture Guidebook along with the Instruction Guidebook. The Culture Guidebook outlines another strategy that school leaders believe helps the school fulfill its mission:

To empower urban students of all racial and ethnic backgrounds to achieve their full intellectual and social potential by combining the best of the East—high standards, discipline and character education—with the best of the West—a commitment to individualism, creativity, and diversity.

The Culture Guidebook also describes the school's character-development program: KG-PRIDE. Highlighting the school's "East meets West" theme, the K and G in KG-PRIDE respectively represent the Japanese notions of *Kaizen*—continual improvement—and *Gambatte*—perseverance, while the letters in PRIDE stand for purpose, respect, integrity, daring, and excellence. These seven constructs permeate formal planning of the skills and qualities students should develop over time through the school's homegrown, grade-specific standards in character development. For example, tenth-grade character development focuses on respect and integrity, with standards noting that these students will be able to

> take a leadership role in organizing event days celebrating the school's values and diversity, take an active role in directing their own learning, monitor and encourage their peers to use respectful language at all times, and submit assignments displaying academic integrity at all times.

KG-PRIDE posters cover the walls of the building as constant reminders of the school's central focus on these elements of character.

As part of the KG-PRIDE program, middle school classes close each day with teachers' evaluation of the attributes of Kaizen and Gambatte, according to a five-point rubric. On a Wednesday morning in sixth-grade reading, an assertive young teacher circles the room as students huddle in pairs making inferences about characters' feelings and traits in passages from a story about a boy living downstairs from Beethoven. As time begins to run short, the teacher directs the students to return their coupled-up desks to their rows and stand behind their seats. Once the room has returned to its original formation, the students come to attention behind their chairs in a call to order modeled on the Asian schooling custom. Their maroon Academy of the Pacific Rim polo shirts and white button-downs are tucked neatly into their khaki pants, belts fastened tightly around their waists. A few of the students are dressed professionally today, as it is the first Wednesday of the month—"Dress for Success" day—when middle school students may opt for professional attire and attend a lunchtime seminar with a guest speaker who is representing a particular career. The teacher remarks, "I heard one disrespectful comment today and the room is not clean. So, that's a 4 for Kaizen. Most people participated in having interesting discussions, and only one person was missing part of their homework, so you also get a 4 for Gambatte." She records these scores on a chart just to the right of the front whiteboard, and the students slide back into their seats, somewhat aware that they may not beat out the other middle school homerooms for that weeks' "Class Coin," a token that can be put toward purchasing a field trip or class party at the end of the year.

In addition to underscoring the character-development program at the Academy of the Pacific Rim, the geographic East figures prominently throughout the school curriculum: students navigate the foreign syllables of Mandarin in mandatory language courses in grades seven through twelve, pictures of grinning students with their arms hooked around one another on trips to Beijing adorn the halls, and visiting teachers from the Academy of the Pacific Rim's sister school in China coteach with their American colleagues. Mirroring the Asian flavor of their schooling experience, seniors celebrate graduation at the annual senior dinner, held in Boston's Chinatown. Besides capturing the explicitly Asian nature of the school's culture, the senior dinner is also a forum for the other central aspect of the Academy of the Pacific Rim's culture: interpersonal bonds. The parent of a recent graduate recollects:

> Just before they graduated, all the parents and the faculty and the students got together in Chinatown and they had a big dinner for us. It was neat. Some of the parents were in tears. It was so emotional. It's hard seeing them move on from here because it's like a family type of atmosphere. A lot of the parents got up and said how much they appreciate what the school has done for their kids—turned their son into a man. And one kid was a special needs kid, he got up and he spoke, said how much help he got here, how the teachers were great. One kid got up and said the executive director was like a father to him.

As this parent explains, connections at the Academy of the Pacific Rim are strong, both among the students themselves and between students and staff. This supportive, bonded community is certainly due in part to the eight-years students spend at the Academy of the Pacific Rim, but personal ties also result from the school's deliberate nesting of students within cohesive structures that support cultural goals.

Sending Kids in the Right Direction

In the eleven years since the school opened, teachers and administrators have used a trial-and-error approach to developing ways to support the school's mission, and the programs at the Academy of the Pacific Rim clearly have been woven together with great care and deliberation. The third guidebook given to new faculty, the Operations Guidebook, details the current iteration of these mission-driven programs. As noted in this guidebook, a cornerstone of the Academy of the Pacific Rim's current structure is advisory—a biweekly meeting of ten to fourteen students and a school-based adult, the advisor. The guidebook explains the advisor's function:

> The advisor's role is multifaceted and includes both academic support and character education. It includes advocating for the student in the school, acting as the school's liaison to the student's family, supporting the student in his or her academics and providing the opportunity for the student to forge a healthy professional relationship with an adult.

In the middle school, students are grouped for advisory by homeroom and activities focus on character development. In the high school, advisories are cross-grade with the intention of building a small, permanent community for each student. One of the primary purposes of the advisory is tracking students' academic performance, during which the advisor explicitly teaches students to monitor their work habits and grades. An administrator who serves as an advisor explains:

> Every other Monday, we go over each student's grades. I hand them their family journal and their progress report. So they're given, literally, an up-to-date grade and information like, "This homework's missing, that one isn't." And I'll work with them. I'll ask, "Johann, why do you have three zeros on homework? Get your homework in!"—that kind of thing. So, not only are their teachers on them, but I'm another adult saying, "This is unnecessary, and we can work on this."

Another purpose of the high school advisory is to help students acquire knowledge about college—the application process, options for financial aid, and the realities of college life—to promote the school's goal of increasing college access and success for their students. On a Monday morning in October, two high school advisories gather in one classroom for the week's 30-minute activity, which has been planned by student representatives from the after-school Advisory Leadership module. Today's task places two advisory groups in opposition as they compete to determine which advisory is more knowledgeable about college. Two teachers call students up in small teams, *Family Feud*-style, to face off as one teacher reads the questions: "How many years of college earn you an associate's degree? How many teacher recommendations are usually required in a college application? What is one college that has five or more Academy of the Pacific Rim alumni?" The students, both those poised eagerly at the front of the room and those leaning back in their chairs watching, respond with great enthusiasm, mirroring that of the teachers, who encourage the competitive mentality. Loud voices reverberate off the concrete walls of the newly refurbished high school facilities on the building's ground floor, as students chatter over one another. Every question is answered correctly by the ninth- through eleventh-grade competitors. Even without their senior advisory mates, who are upstairs in the computer lab working on college applications, these students demonstrate a solid command of information on the college-going process.

This focus on college is also promoted in another structure devoted to building students' voices within the school: the community meeting. Held twice a week in the middle school and once a week in the high school, community meetings are a way for the school to develop ties, share information, and promote goals. On a Friday morning in November, students in the high school's brick-walled multipurpose room come to order as the ninth through twelfth graders congregate at blue lunch tables under high ceilings. The two twelfth-grade students leading the meeting stand at the far end of the room and call on students and faculty members to take turns standing to make announcements. Today's topics include next week's food drive, Teen Night at the art museum, the deadline for applications for the upcoming China trip, a financial aid workshop at Hyde Park Library, and Sunday's gathering to clean up trash in the local brook. This list of opportunities is followed by grade-level reports on college-week activities. Standing in front of a bright window, an eleventh-grade student pushes back her long hair as she describes how much easier it was to take the PSAT for the second time as an eleventh grader because she felt more confident and was less worried about the pressure of time. A twelfth grader gives a thumbs-up as she reports that, on her campus visit, Boston College "looked fabulous." She describes meeting up with an Academy of the Pacific Rim alumna and shadowing her to biology class to look at "stuff under the microscope." All eyes in the multipurpose room are glued to the front throughout the announcements, a short speech made by a representative from Providence College, and the presentation of a Gambatte award to a student who has persevered in her work. Throughout its 30-minute duration, the student-led community meeting is a testament to the ownership and empowerment given to students at the Academy of the Pacific Rim.

In addition to promoting student participation within the walls of the building, the school extends students' experiences into the wider world through its Pacific Rim Enrichment Program (PREP), which requires high school students to spend at least at least 225 hours over three summers participating in college or career-oriented internship programs. PREP activities range from internships in local law offices and hospitals to organized summer programs at Harvard College and Boston University to international travel in Hungary and Panama. Each September, returning high school students submit journals, write reports, and give oral presentations on their summer PREP activities. On a warm September morning, the school's administrators nestle into the back of a high school advisory meeting, abandoning their keys and clipboards on the desktops and turning their proud attention to the student presenters. As a young African American student struggles to describe his summer interactions with the white, middle-class students he encountered in a leadership program, the faces of the adults in the room beam with broad smiles. Clearly unnerved by the faculty's joyous response to his summer of hardship, the student finally turns his slight shoulders toward a white male teacher and challenges him with an emphatic gesture, asking, "Why are you smiling?!" Maintaining his composure and gleaming smile, the teacher warmly replies:

> We just love you to death. You're really getting yourself ready for college. You're going to encounter these things in college. It is tough. But we think you're a 17-year-old black man, and you're learning how to have a racial conversation with other white kids. We know you're frustrated. We know you're angry. But gosh, you are learning a skill that is going to come in really handy.

ELEMENTS OF SUCCESS

Through eleven years of innovation and hard work by school leaders and faculty, not only have the students at the Academy of the Pacific Rim out-performed nearby traditional public schools on state standardized tests, but the staff members also have reached their own internal goals of developing students' independence and helping students gain access to college. Certainly, with 100 percent of the previous year's tenth graders passing the standardized state test—the Massachusetts Comprehensive Assessment System, or MCAS—on their first try and with 92 percent of alumni enrolled in college, the Academy of the Pacific Rim can take pride in its achievements. While the factors that contribute to this success are numerous and complex, the school's goals are met, in part, through high levels of professional responsibility for student outcomes, internal accountability mechanisms to ensure that school staff members meet expectations, and clear structures for fostering student development and independence over time.

Who's In Charge?

Individuals who choose to work at the Academy of the Pacific Rim make an informed commitment to the school's high level of professional responsibility to their 472 students. This expectation is made explicit during the hiring process, and staff members accept this commitment as a condition of working at the school. The emphasis on adult responsibility for student outcomes and the pervasive belief that teachers and school leaders have the ability to promote student success are critical to the school's effectiveness in meeting internal and external goals. Adult-centered responsibility within the school is created both by structural features of the organization—such as the allocation of human resources through advisories, special education services, and the daily schedule—and by the personal characteristics of individuals who are attracted to working at the school.

Ensuring that adults are able to assume and meet the professional responsibility of serving students effectively requires the devotion of numerous human resources within the organization. Thus, a central focus of the work at the Academy of the Pacific Rim is utilizing systems to identify students' individual needs and designing strategies for how the adults will work to meet those needs. An administrator explains:

> I think we've done a good job, when a student is not performing, of looking at all angles of the problem—trying to have meetings, trying to give that student extra support, potentially referring them for testing. . . . We're never quite satisfied because we get to know the students so well and we care so much about them. There are students who do well on the tests, but we know it wasn't their best, so we continue to push them. We continue to push.

The school's attention to individual students' needs is implemented first and foremost through the advisories, in which the responsibility for ensuring the success and well-being of individual students is assigned to the advisor. The advisors get to know their advisees well, monitor their academic performance, advocate for their needs within the school community, and stay in constant communication with their families. Through this assignment of students to advisors, the school ensures that the needs of individual students do not go unidentified or unmet. Someone is explicitly responsible for each student, thus sealing the proverbial cracks in the system so that no one falls through.

The school's special education program also demonstrates a deep commitment of human resources to meet student needs. By providing a sufficient number of learning specialists, each specialist serves just fifteen to twenty special education students. Learning specialists work individually or in small groups with the students on their case load, either having them for an entire academic period during the day or working with them during the afternoon tutoring block. In addition, learning specialists hold weekly 30-minute, one-on-one meetings with each general education teacher who serves the special needs students to ensure that the students' individualized instruction is integrated directly into the work they do in their mainstream classes. Specialists also participate as members of grade-level teams to stay fully informed of instructional concerns within the grade level and to discuss individual students' tutoring needs, which are assessed monthly by each grade-level team. A shared computer network also supports cooperation between general education teachers and learning specialists by giving specialists access to classroom teachers' lesson plans. This integration of instruction enables specialists to assist students more effectively during tutoring and to plan ahead for academic supports and modifications.

Academy of the Pacific Rim's daily schedule also illustrates teachers' level of commitment to their students. The teachers' school day starts at 7:30 AM for those with morning duty, manning hallways or breakfast spaces. By 7:40, teachers are expected to have their classrooms open and to be welcoming students as they arrive. Once the school day begins, the schedule contains six hour-long class periods in the middle school and five in the high school, along with designated time blocks for advisories and community meetings at different points during the week. Teachers in the middle school typically focus on one subject for one grade level—for example, eighth-grade science. With three classes of students in the middle school grades, most of their teachers teach three periods a day and tutor for an additional period. This leaves them with two periods for academic planning, fulfilling advisor duties, meeting with learning specialists, and grading and tracking student work. In the high school, where there are currently only two classes of students per grade level, teachers teach two grades in one subject area—for example, tenth- and twelfth-grade history. Thus, at the high school, teachers typically have only one planning period per day.

Beginning at 2:30 in the high school and 3:20 in the middle school, most students' afternoons are filled with a mix of tutoring from a teacher or learning specialist, teacher-led extracurricular activities, teachers' office hours, and college counseling or test prep. All of this varies by day of the week, and the activities finish daily by 5 PM. Each Wednesday afternoon, faculty and staff members devote two full hours, 3:30 to 5:30, to collaboration. They met either as grade-level teams, department teams, middle and high school communities, or as a whole-school community. In addition to these responsibilities, teachers design their own curriculum—which they work on during the summer and through-out the school year—and many serve as department or grade-level chairs. All of this means that many teachers work late into the night and on weekends to fulfill all of their professional responsibilities. Clearly, the amount of time the faculty commits to serving students reveals the school's priorities and the be-lief that students benefit from having teachers and specialists devoted to their progress and achievement for many hours of the day.

In addition to the sheer number of hours they put in, the staff's actual work is demanding. A quick walk through the building makes this evident. Teach-ers exude enthusiasm and energy as they attempt to maintain high levels of animation during class, deans sweep trash in the hallways while ushering stu-dents into classrooms at the beginning of class periods, and instructors con-clude a day of teaching by running tutoring sessions in the afternoon. This intense commitment remains a core element of work at the Academy of the Pacific Rim. As the executive director describes:

> We expect that teachers will be extremely dedicated to the work they do, hardworking and team-oriented. . . . There's a beauty and a challenge [in] working here: the beauty is you work with dedicated, smart, team-oriented, driven individuals. The downside is that many of us are sort of overachiev-ing or Type A personalities.

Because of the clear expectation that adults who work at the school will be extensively devoted to their work and will shoulder the responsibility for stu-dent performance, the school attracts staff members who share this orienta-tion of personal responsibility. Thus, professional responsibility is not only im-plemented through structures in the school but is reinforced and strengthened by the personal mindset and selection of the staff members.

Seeing Is Believing

Although organizational structures and hiring strategies support the school's orientation toward professional responsibility, simply setting up a structure that enables faculty members to meet the needs of students does not ensure that they will actually do so. Thus, to closely monitor the teachers' work, the school leaders have implemented a system of internal accountability. This sys-tem is enforced through structures and systems that ensure that faculty mem-bers make their teaching practice transparent both to the school leadership and to fellow teachers. School leaders maintain awareness of and control over what teachers do through the review of weekly lesson plans, formal and informal classroom observations, and a biannual evaluation process. In addition, teachers are aware of and learn from the work of their colleagues through peer observations, regular grade-level and department meetings, and office space in communal faculty workrooms. This extensive system of internal accountability leads to heightened teacher performance, both because individuals feel accountable for the quality of their work and because school leaders are continually aware of those teachers who need extra support and guidance in order to improve their instruction. Similarly, by openly sharing their instruction, teachers hold each other accountable for working at high levels and holding high expectations for themselves.

As noted earlier, the school's *Instruction Guidebook* clearly articulates the fact that teachers are expected to use a variety of instructional methods across the course of a given week, focus their curriculum on the state's grade-level standards, plan units to address "big goals and essential questions," and use differentiated instruction, along with a number of other explicit expectations about how time and space are used in the classrooms. The principals at the middle and high school can easily monitor the extent to which teachers abide by these expectations through analysis of teachers' weekly lesson plans and frequent classroom observations. Teachers whose performance is considered lacking in some regard are given extra one-on-one support in the form of coaching from a department chair, collaborative lesson planning with the principal, or guidance on classroom management from the dean of students. Principals and department chairs also monitor teachers' work and target instructional support based on student academic performance, as revealed through regular six-week interim assessments and annual results on the MCAS.

In addition to all these forms of monitoring, there is a formal biannual evaluation that is directly tied to an annual salary bonus, which awards teachers between two and four thousand dollars based on the merit of their professional work. Annual evaluations, completed collaboratively by each teacher and the principal, are structured around six rubrics that evaluate professionalism, teaching, individual goal-setting, adherence to school culture, advising, and collaboration with colleagues. Although teachers say that the evaluation does not motivate them to work harder in anticipation of receiving the bonus, it does give the leadership an explicit way to signal teachers about which values they consider central to the school's effectiveness.

In addition to having structured accountability to the leadership, teachers at the Academy of the Pacific Rim are keenly aware of one another's instructional practice, and this peer awareness keeps teachers motivated and working to high standards. One way teachers share their work is by observing one another's teaching. Such peer observations have taken different forms over the school's history, from teachers selecting colleagues for reciprocal observation partnerships to administrators assigning teachers to partners. The results of these peer observations have varied over time, from casual conversations about practice to salary bonuses for teachers who are rated well by their peers. Through these structures, teachers learn from one another and push each other to higher levels of instructional practice. One teacher observes, "This culture really [encourages] self-reflection. Three or four times a year, we do peer observations where we go watch each other, and we reflect on each other's teaching. It gives us a kind of a mirror to see what we're doing."

Another expectation is that teachers will share their work with their colleagues in formal settings. For example, the math department chair makes instructional practice transparent within her department by having teachers share best practices at department meetings. As she describes, "I asked a member of the team to share this really great lesson she had on multiplication problem-solving, and it was differentiated. It's often a struggle in a math department to try and help people think through how they can differentiate when they should be hitting the standard." In this instance, not only is the department chair facilitating the math teachers' learning by connecting them with information that is hard to find in their field, she is also confirming that the teachers are expected to use one another as resources and be aware of one another's instructional practices.

Sharing also occurs in more casual settings, facilitated in part by communal faculty workrooms. These office spaces, which include a desk, a computer, and a phone for each teacher, are organized by grade level within the middle school and by department in the high school. The frequent use of these rooms is apparent in the mountains of books and papers covering the teachers' desks. This is clearly the space where instructors store their personal effects, delve into the business of designing the curriculum and tracking student progress during planning periods, and interact socially. In fact, the Culture Guidebook specifically notes that the purpose of the faculty workroom is to "promote collaboration and professionalism." One teacher explains

> I'm constantly collaborating with other teachers simply because everyone is working in the faculty room together. In the mornings, in the afternoons, you see materials that other people are working on and you're able to share materials with other teachers. So, I think there's constantly informal collaboration going on.

Beyond sharing ideas in these collaborative activities and settings, the teachers also reinforce the common expectations of the school's work ethic for teachers. In the shared time and spaces, teachers become the audience for each other's work, pushing one another to maintain high levels of commitment and providing the accountability necessary for going the extra mile toward creating innovative and challenging lessons. As the staff is comprised of devoted and driven individuals, it makes sense that transparent working conditions fuel the expectations for high levels of performance. One teacher notes, "I'm working with teachers that are extremely inspiring in terms of how well prepared they are, how well they know their curriculum, how much they expect of the students. I would say that our instruction is incredible." It is only because of this internal accountability regarding instruction and practice across the school— both between leaders and teachers and among teachers—that individuals are able to make such informed comments about their colleagues' practice and hold the school to high levels of instruction and student achievement.

Making Long-Term Investments

When the Academy of the Pacific Rim opened in 1997, it began with just one hundred sixth- and seventh-grade students. In subsequent years, the school opted to expand vertically—adding additional grades—rather than to expand horizontally—adding more students in the existing grades. As a result, the school now serves nearly five hundred students from fifth through twelfth grade, and teachers and administrators make great use of this eight-year span to design and implement both academic and character-development programs. Having the same students from ages eleven to eighteen enables faculty and staff members to purposefully scaffold students' development so that their students make great strides in developing the habits and qualities envisioned in the mission statement. As students migrate from the colorful, artful learning spaces upstairs in the middle school to the more austere, Spartan classrooms downstairs in the high school, the disciplinary structures make an opposite transition—shifting from the highly rigid behavioral expectations enforced in the middle school to the more collaborative, open disciplinary policies in the high school. An administrator explains this purposeful structure:

> In the sixth grade, seventh, and eighth grades, we're much more focused on uniform violations and respect and pushing the KG-PRIDE—making sure that students are obedient, disciplined, that sort of thing. It's as if there were no choices to be made: "You will be here at this time," and "You will take

these classes," and I think as they move on to the high school, we try to build in much more independence. So in terms of discipline, it's much more of a discussion: "Okay, you're in the tenth grade . . . why do you have that belt on?" As opposed to in the sixth grade: "You need to call your mother and you need to go home and change that belt." So there's no discussion. In the high school, we're trying to give students more independence, more choice.

Although the staff intentionally plans much of the scaffolding over time, certainly some of the variation in student behavior between the grades is simply due to students' increasing maturity and natural development. A teacher who has taught in both the middle school and high school at the school recognizes difference in students at different ages: I've taught up here in seventh grade and eighth grade for a year, and adolescents are crazy at that age and so it requires teachers to be much more proactive in the classroom. With high school, you can have more space, give more freedom." Because of the legitimacy of this observation, the school pays close attention to variations in behavioral structures across the middle and high schools. For these reasons, the implementation of the KG-PRIDE program is stricter in the middle school, including the classroom evaluations of Kaizen and Gambatte. The longitudinal structure of the character development traits, such as the emphasis on purpose and respect in the ninth grade and then respect and integrity in tenth grade, also reflects the developmental nature of the program. Other schoolwide structures, such as advisories, student-run community meetings, and PREP, punctuate the school's work in fostering and building student development, self-direction, and empowerment.

Staff members at the Academy of the Pacific Rim also put great thought into the intentional and purposeful vertical alignment of the curriculum over the years. As demonstrated by the contrast between the eleventh-grade chemistry and sixth-grade history lessons described at the opening of this chapter, staff members expect students to take on more responsibility as they mature, and structures are specifically set in place to build academic skills and independence over time. For example, one administrator describes the vertical alignment of the number of paper assignments: "We've tried to sequence our paper [requirements] in history so that sixth grade is three papers, five pages each, and then seventh grade is four papers [of] eight pages." Additionally, dividing math instruction in fifth and sixth grades into two periods that separately emphasize the foundational and application elements of middle school math is intended to support instruction at later grades so that older students are capable of effectively attacking problem-solving challenges. Teacher collaboration in planning assignments across grade levels also ensures that student expectations grow. For example, when teachers and administrators realized that the same students who struggled with their long-term research papers in eleventh grade went on to fail their research projects in twelfth grade, they implemented greater supports around the eleventh-grade paper to help students experience greater success in both years. An administrator explains, "I think we've been much more intentional about scaffolding and getting the intensive work out of the way earlier on, so that when they get to twelfth grade, they really are prepared."

Individual teachers also work on their own to scaffold the various classes they teach over time in order to help students develop different academic skills as they near their college years. A high school history teacher explains:

> My goal for the seniors is that they will be ready for the types of work that they're going to do in college, and that is discussion-based independent work, independent projects, independent thinking, longer-term assignments, assignments that generally require more analysis and critical thinking. So, really, in the twelfth grade, I'm far less concerned with any content than I am with preparing those twelfth graders for college-level work. Whereas in the tenth grade, just given the fact that U.S. history is a nationwide requirement, and it's something that I do believe . . . that all people should have a strong foundation in, I do hope that some of the content sort of sticks.

All of this intentional effort directed toward developing students' character, independence, and academic skills over time ensures that students at the Academy of the Pacific Rim develop in alignment with the school mission and receive a purposeful education that builds sequentially as they grow and mature.

* * * * *

Although there are many reasons that the Academy of the Pacific Rim has experienced success over their eleven-year history, the evidence clearly demonstrates that a sense of professional responsibility held by school staff, internal accountability for high-level work among teachers, and intentional structures for developing student independence and skills over time explain a great deal of this success. With staff members devoting significant energy and commitment to the school and students literally growing up within the school's walls, these phenomena blend together to create an interdependence that allows teachers to find meaning in their work and students to develop in accordance with the goals set for them by the school.

CHAPTER FIVE

THE MATCH CHARTER PUBLIC HIGH SCHOOL

Culture, Consistency, and Coherence

In 2001, the Ellis the Rim Man auto-parts store on Commonwealth Avenue in Boston closed. A year later, the MATCH Charter Public High School opened its doors in the same building. The iconic billboard that was perched atop the three-story building came down and solar panels went up in its place.[1] Located near the brand new athletic and entertainment venue at Boston University and across the street from aging auto-parts stores, the MATCH school retains artifacts of the past while representing what some consider the future of how schools make innovative use of people, space, and time.

8:15 AM

On this October morning, a line of students snakes around the outside of the school building and into a small entryway. Seven bleary hours ago, the Red Sox clinched Game 2 of the World Series, Boston's second appearance there in recent history. Many of these same students were just leaving the school during those early innings the night before. There is a small sliding window in the entryway where visitors must check in, similar to a bank teller's window. The young woman behind the glass types on the computer, clearly accustomed to the students waiting on the other side. For the moment, the inside door is locked, and the students chatter as they stand around waiting

The primary author for this chapter is John Roberts.

for the door to open. The students know what to expect, as some play absentmindedly with the nylon cords of their small MATCH backpacks. Under their coats, most wear white cotton shirts, and on their feet they sport black or white sneakers.

Several minutes later, the school's executive director steps to the head of the line. There is no security guard, no metal detector, and he smiles as he says, "Good morning." The students snap awake and start a slow amble through the door, their thumbs under the nylon cords of the backpack straps over each shoulder until they need to extend a right hand to the well-dressed man between them and the door. He wears a dark suit and tie, and the small room forces the students to stand close to one another and to him as they move past him into the school. Some offer a hand sheepishly, others with a joke or knowing smile. But, all must answer the executive director's question, "Why are you here?"

Inside, the school is freshly painted—white with blue and yellow accents. This accentuates the neo-Egyptian columns, iron support beams, and large windows of the main room and entryway. There is barely a trace of the auto-parts store that inhabited this space most recently.

A row of signs hangs near the main staircase. One reads, WE WON'T GIVE UP ON YOU, and another, WHAT WE DO HERE IS IMPORTANT. A smaller note at eye level reads, THIS WEEK'S DEMERITS. The students are unfazed by these familiar sights as they walk to their lockers. A small group of students is spilling out of the great room just inside the main hall, closing notebooks and finishing conversations with teachers or tutors. Although it is only 8:25 AM, some already have been working with a tutor or teacher for an hour this morning; they now exit the room quickly and with purpose. The young people shoot each other comments and jokes, even as they hurry off in opposite directions.

The main staircase splits at a landing halfway to the second floor. All the students headed to the second floor are rushing to the right, while the few coming down from the second floor use the branch on the left. The young teacher posted at the landing pulls a student out of the pack, speaks to him briefly, and gently releases him back into the upstream flow. Her comments to the young man carry kindness and concern, warmth and a warning—an important element of the MATCH culture. A few minutes later, a visitor new to the school climbs the left side of the staircase on his way to the second floor. When he reaches the second floor, the teacher on the landing calls up to him: "Can you go back down to the first floor and then use the right hand side on your way up." It's not a question. He returns to the first floor and climbs the stairs again, falling in line with the students climbing up the right side.

MATCH CHARTER PUBLIC HIGH SCHOOL
A Commonwealth Charter School, Founded in 2000

Number of Students and Grade Levels
  222 Students in Grades 9–12
  Middle School Opened September 2008

Race/Ethnicity
  62% African American
  2% Asian
  0% Hispanic
  4% White
  2% Multiracial, Non-Hispanic

Subgroups
  11% Special Education
  71% Low Income
  14% First Language Not English
  0% Limited English Proficient

Source: Massachusetts Department of Education

By 8:29, the hallways are empty. A lone student scrambles into a classroom, sliding into class on dusty sneakers. The classrooms are mostly silent. The voice of a teacher carries into the hall as she begins class: "Several students have already earned a demerit." As she circulates around the room, she adjusts the small MATCH backpacks on the back of each chair so that they all hang the same way, and her hand gently touches the shoulders of students who are now writing.

1:00 PM

Although the classes that immediately follow lunch do not formally begin until 1:05, all the students in a tenth-grade English class are already writing responses to the silent "Do-Now" exercise that begins every class at MATCH. The students write on a brightly colored piece of paper that they were required to pick up just inside the door as they entered the classroom. Teachers generally do not take time to hand out paper or assignments at the beginning of class. The packet has two double-spaced pages, previously three-hole punched to fit in students' notebooks, that are divided into four main sections—Aims, Homework, Do-Now, and Class Activity.

The worksheet gives students a place to answer the Do-Now and take class notes on Charles Dickens's Industrial Era novel, *Hard Times*. Two questions make up the Do-Now activity, which will last no more than ten minutes:

1. What does the conversation that Tom and Louisa share while looking at the fire reveal about them as individuals and as brother and sister?
2. In last night's reading, we also learned of Sissy's progress in Gradgrind's school. How is she progressing and what seems to be her major obstacle?

Some students consult a copy of the novel as they write, the pages dog-eared and littered with yellow sticky notes written with highlighters and pens. The nineteen students are seated mostly two to a table, facing the whiteboard and away from the door. In another corner of the room, a male student writes infrequently, his sprawling legs reaching all the way under the table and into the aisle between the desks.

At 1:06, the teacher announces, "You have one minute." She turns to locate the dry-erase marker as she moves from the Do-Now to the next section of her lesson. She writes "TOM" and "LOUISA" at the top of her hand-drawn chart on the whiteboard and asks the class a variation on the first Do-Now question. The conversation is brisk and lively as the teacher asks for student comments and redirects them to the day's "Aims" or to specific sections in the text. At the peak of activity, eight or nine student hands are in the air waiting for attention. Most of the students begin to write whenever the teacher does.

A few minutes later, the teacher asks, "How does Dickens's commentary reach beyond a criticism of industrialization and utilitarianism?" The class response to this question, which also appears in the student packet, is more subdued. One student makes a comment that the teacher calls "insightful" while she pushes another student to clarify his answer. After her further explanation of industrialization and utilitarianism, fewer hands reach for attention. But the conversation turns lively again as she begins to probe the students about what the typical gender roles might be for Tom and Louisa in this period of history.

Down the hallway, a math teacher's Do-Now on the whiteboard asks:

1. How do you think you did on yesterday's exam?
2. Is your effort in class and on homework assignments preparing you to do well?

He gives his eighteen students about six minutes to write and then speaks to the whole group: "I am not holding you behaviorally [*sic*] in a way that would correlate with [higher test scores]. And you're not doing what you're supposed to be doing." He's concerned about their recent grades on in-class exams and their progress toward the AP exam in the spring. He goes on to explain that he holds himself personally responsible for part of this, but emphasizes that "there are no make-up exams. These are high-stakes exams."

His tone softens as he moves to the lesson for the day: "I only want you to master two things today. I would love it if you got 100 percent on the quiz tomorrow because you took notes. [There's] no reason anyone should be doing poorly in this course." Indeed, the students seem to believe him when he says, "It brings me down."

The desks in the AP U.S. history class down the hall are arranged in a semi-circle around the teacher's overhead projector. Once again, the Do-Now that begins each class at MATCH is in progress. The students write on clean sheets of notebook paper attached to brown clipboards as the Do-Now is projected on a white screen: "In your opinion, what does a child need from the age of 1 Day until the age of 18 in order to succeed?" The AIM for the day appears just under the Do-Now: "[Students will] evaluate how egalitarian the U.S. is today and how egalitarian colonial society was in the 1700s."

After five minutes, the teacher stops the students and begins the conversation: "OK. Good morning. Good to see you all." He sits in a chair next to the projector and rests his left hand on the lighted surface so that it projects his hand onto the white screen behind him. Over his left shoulder, attached to a bulletin board, is the teacher's campaign sign for the school committee election in his suburban home. He will be up for election in just a few months. Without prompting, a student begins the conversation by asking, "How many opponents do you have?" The teacher mentions his opponent, and this elicits other more general questions from students about elections and the electoral process. Although the discussion begins slowly, the teacher's personal involvement in an election has perked the interest of several students and the engagement level of the class builds quickly. Just as some of the students' questions begin to drift toward other topics, the teacher reels the conversation back in, closer to the day's Aim. He asks, "This raises a question of who runs? Who votes?" The same student who opened the conversation suggests, "I heard more people vote on *American Idol* than in presidential elections." "That's true," the teacher says. "Actually, let's look at the statistics I brought in."

2:00 PM

Every day, all students are required to attend two hours of tutoring at MATCH. These sessions are scheduled during the regular school day, separate from core courses, with the same tutor for the entire school year. This day's AP U.S. history tutorial has five adult tutors, each seated at a table with two students. There is no regular classroom teacher in the room. The tutors are dressed in what schools often call business-casual clothing, and all of them are recent college graduates. At least one U.S. history textbook lies on each table, and each group of three works from identical tutoring packets prepared by the teacher in consultation with the tutors. One tutor reads along with two students as they struggle to understand the word "dogma" and variations like "dogmatic." She suggests definitions while they huddle around a dictionary, the page open to the *Ds*.

Tutors talk easily with students, and there is little conversation about student behavior. Nevertheless, the students look up when a tutor leaves the room to track down a student who has been in the restroom for quite some time. As they enter the tutoring room together a few minutes later, the tutor audibly remarks, "You were gone for over five minutes."

There is a professional, friendly rapport between tutors and students, perhaps the result of the time they have already spent together this school year. Tutors work with the same four or five students each day and work 12-hour days in service of MATCH's college mission. Tutors know their students' home phone numbers by heart, with whom they live, and they memorize the school schedules so they can track down the student or appropriate teacher at any time. Near the end of the tutoring session, a teacher on her prep period pokes her head in the door. "Just checking on you guys," she says with a smile as she turns to leave. A few students smile and then turn back to work.

3:30 PM

Near the halfway mark of an English class the teacher asks, "Why can't blood be a theme?" She pauses for a moment, then answers her own question. "Themes have to be full sentences. A theme is a longer, complex thought," she offers.

A lone hand goes up and a student suggests, "So would the motif be the racism?"

"I wouldn't say the motif is the racism," the teacher replies rather matter-of-factly.

In the next minute, the teacher asks the following questions in rapid succession:

"What was his name?"
"What was he doing?"

"When was he giving this away?"
"Who remembers how he won?"
"Who really did the reading?"
"Anyone know another item?"

Few students offer responses to these questions, and both the teacher and students look exhausted.

5:00 PM

Sometime just after five each school day, the doors of the MATCH school open and students spill out on to Commonwealth Avenue. They walk to the subway stop across the street, where they will board the train along with undergraduates from Boston University and professionals headed for home in the city. Many of these young people are still an hour from their homes in other Boston neighborhoods; students from the nearest Boston district high school were dismissed more than two hours ago. Some students remain inside the school as the academic day at MATCH rolls on toward the dinner hour; the windows that face Commonwealth Avenue are dark, except for the headlights of rush-hour traffic.

More often than not, students who are required to stay into the evening are having difficulty completing homework or meeting grade requirements on tests and assignments. There are forty-five tutors who make sure the homework gets done. When these sessions finish, around 7 PM, the students will board the subway for home and the tutors will climb the stairs to the school's third floor, where they live.

The walls of the stairwell between the second and third floors bear signs that read, MATCH CORPS ONLY. STUDENTS FOUND ON THE THIRD FLOOR WILL BE EXPELLED. Remodeled specifically to house the MATCH Corps Tutors, the third floor is reminiscent of the hall of a college dormitory, but it is functional and perfectly arranged for its purpose. An open room running the length of the building serves as the living room and working area for the tutors. At regular intervals along one wall are the doors for the dorm-like triples that hold the beds and personal items for each corps member. The main room is clean, organized, and full of artifacts of the tutors' ongoing hard work: manila folders labeled with the names of courses at MATCH; laptop computers displaying Excel spreadsheets; student work waiting to be reviewed and graded. At the midpoint of the hall, a large sectional couch sits in front of a big-screen television. The kitchen at one side of the room consists of a sink, two refrigerators, a stove, oven, and other appliances. At the near end of the hall, by the stairway and elevator, are several simple brown tables. A large cabinet nearby contains hundreds of hanging file folders and other crates of documents.

On this particular afternoon, several tutors are typing on laptop computers, grading student work, or preparing activities for upcoming tutoring sessions. Sometimes the tutors are responsible for creating the Do-Nows for their tutoring sessions and they need to review the material given to them by the teachers of several subjects. At other times they implement specific tutoring plans created by classroom teachers. Their work varies from subject to subject and from hour to hour, and they have to make phone calls to their students' homes each week. At the moment, most of the tutors are working alone, although they sit close to one another and occasionally ask questions or drop a folder or piece of paper on another's table. No one is watching the television.

ELEMENTS OF SUCCESS

The MATCH School's mission is to prepare its students to "achieve success in college and beyond." In order to graduate, students are required to take an AP history class in their junior year and pass two courses at Boston University. Formerly the Media and Technology Charter High School, the school is now known simply as MATCH. Most of the curriculum and activities associated with the earlier version of the school have been replaced with specific preparation for college. The grade 9–12 school with just over two hundred students has been the focus of numerous articles, reports, and awards as it has continued to post impressive Massachusetts Comprehensive Assessment System (MCAS) test scores. In May 2007, the Center for Education Reform, a charter school advocacy organization in Washington, D.C., identified the MATCH Charter Public High School as one of the National Charter Schools of the Year. Ninety-nine percent of MATCH graduates have been accepted to a four-year college since the first class graduated in 2004.

Teachers, tutors, administrators, and parents, along with multiple classroom observations, suggest that three main elements help MATCH achieve its mission: the purposeful building of relationships between adults and students; the careful and deliberate application of a code of conduct that allows teachers more time to focus on teaching; and an attitude of high expectations and urgency. These themes support the mission in a coordinated fashion and result in high levels of organizational coherence.

Citing similar themes, MATCH founder Michael Goldstein, who designed the school as his final project while a master's candidate at Harvard's Kennedy School of Government, describes his view of the these elements:

> I think visitors to our school come away with one of two "take-aways." I think only the second is largely applicable, but more people have the first. So, the first take-away when people visit is they say, "This is great. You've got a very long day. You tutor kids a lot. You have a curriculum that aligns with college. You require kids to do these unusually challenging AP and Boston University courses . . ." All of which is true.
>
> But, I think the second take-away [that many observers miss] is [that] it's possible for schools to construct the right culture, which is focused on achievement and learning. [This culture is] built through this one-two punch of a ton of adult-to-kid relationship-building . . . plus really caring about enforcing the same rules [with] everybody. . . . If you combine the relationship and the consistent enforcement of reasonable rules, you reduce the disorder enough to put teachers in a position to succeed.

Adult to Kid Relationships: Tutors, Teachers, and the "Tripod"

Teachers, MATCH Corp Tutors, and administrators cite strong personal relationships with students, families, and one another as a factor that facilitates success in many areas of school life. As one administrator suggests, "I think if you look at things here, you should look at relationships. That's the reason we're successful—[it's] not curriculum, it's not standards, it's relationships. . . . I really want to recommend that piece, that segment of the 'relationship tripod.'"

Adults who have regular contact with students use words like "triangle" or "tripod" to identify the network of people who put the student at the center of their work, and this language is consistent across school administrators, teachers, and tutors. In this construction of a relationship, a teacher, the parent, and a tutor represent three sides of the triangle or legs of the tripod, as depicted below.

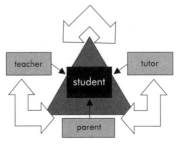

A teacher describes the importance of these relationships:

We've convinced them to stay here at school when they could go to another school and graduate with much less difficulty and with much less work. The way to do that is to create an environment where they're showing up almost like to be with their family. We've become like family members to them.

Michael Goldstein explains that the "word [tripod] describes how the parent, teachers, and tutors are trying to get the kid to reach his potential . . . and it's just easier if the same message is coming from the teachers and the parent." The principal and other administrators say that relationships with students and their families are critical, but they also use these relationships strategically, in the sense that they ensure that most parents and students understand MATCH's expectations.

MATCH Corps Tutors

One essential element for building relationships with students is the MATCH Corps Tutors. In 2005, the school introduced the MATCH Corps, a cohort of recent college graduates who live on the school's third floor and make a year-long commitment to tutor MATCH students sixty hours a week. Supported in part by a grant from AmeriCorps, MATCH Corp Tutors review daily classroom lessons and notes, provide a large amount of instruction outside of the classroom, and give attention to students who are struggling. There are forty-five corps members, and each works with the same four or five students for the entire school year. Most of the tutoring done during the school day involves a tutor working with two or three students at a time, while the afterschool sessions tend to include more one-on-one tutoring. Clearly, these "megadoses" of small-group and one-on-one tutoring have an important academic effect; however, the year-long relationship with a single tutor may also provide an important adult relationship for many students at MATCH. Several administrators and teachers suggest the same, as one comments:

Basically, [the MATCH Corps Tutors] make our kids' ties to the school stronger by building a relationship with them and pushing them. And also, they're the bridge to our parents. . . . They need to call [the parents] once a week, minimum. And they're the ones who have the relationships with the parents and the kids. . . . They're like little bridge-makers, really. The ways in which their work connects each student in the school to a caring adult are as critical as the academic content support [they provide].

Indeed, there is an easy professional rapport between most tutors and their charges. Tutors know all the students in the school by name within the first week of September, and they are carefully selected for both academic and social aptitude through a highly competitive and protracted hiring process. Recruited from some of the most prestigious colleges and universities in the United States, the academic and social training of MATCH Corps Tutors is evident in the professional and confident manner with which they approach their work at MATCH.

Importantly, administrators, teachers, and tutors describe the role of a tutor in somewhat different terms. For example, administrators generally emphasize how the tutors help to communicate the school's culture in addition to their academic work. The same administrator quoted above went on to describe the tutor role: "First they're academic coaches. That's what they're here for. A lot of it is content, but a lot of it is just making sure that our kids don't give up. And it's all the intangible stuff, right?"

Some teachers see tutors and tutoring sessions as means to review or re-teach content in a uniform way, while others see the sessions as individualized instruction that meets the academic needs of each student. Generally, teachers are most likely to describe the impact tutors have on the amount of content that can be covered with their help. One teacher even identifies the tutors as an important factor in MATCH's success on standardized tests: "I think you could have had this interview four years ago [before MATCH Corps was started] and I would have said, 'We're not there,' and it was very difficult. [Today] I would say the tutoring has really enabled [high test scores] to happen."

A MATCH Corp member offers a third view of the tutors' role that seems to combine both the academic and social elements of the job, noting the importance of relationships for academic success:

> Match Corps allows me to work with students one-on-one. I actually do have some curriculum component of my job . . . but I'm not totally responsible for an entire classroom of thirty kids. So, I'm able to make a bigger impact, I think, by working one-on-one with each kid and making that bond, . . . that connection with parents. As a tutor . . . I'm responsible for calling parents at least once a week to give them an update on behavior issues with their students, academic issues with their students, goals that we have for each student . . . just basically keeping them in the loop for what goes on here. . . . I have the ability to make a nice, tight little triangle, I guess, around each student.

Teacher-Student Relationships

Teachers, too, are expected to build personal relationships with students. While classroom observations typically show more formal interactions focused on the academic work, other opportunities are available outside of classes and after school for teachers to connect with students. Building these relationships, according to school founder Goldstein, is a value shared among the teachers:

> All the teachers think they have a role of building some level of relationships with kids. If you asked a teacher here, "Can I call you a failed teacher if any of your kids would describe you as not having a close personal relationship with them?" . . . I think our teachers would be willing to say, "Yes."

Phoning Home

MATCH believes that phone calls made to students, parents, and guardians each week help facilitate the creation of these relationships. At MATCH, like other charter schools, the phone call is a required element of each teacher's and tutor's daily professional life. The purpose, as a teacher observes, is "just [to have] a chance to check in with students about a day if somebody noticed something was wrong. . . . I think for a lot of them it means an awful lot. . . . [to have] someone calling that day and [asking,] 'Is everything okay?'" One parent expresses a deep appreciation for this level of attention and communication:

> What I like most about MATCH is, if you do have a concern, . . . it's a family. [My son's teacher] would call me to tell me, "Your son needs to do such and such." "He got a 70 on a test, . . . I think he can do better." . . . I wasn't special. He called everyone. And I think that was real important, and I think that's what's unique about MATCH. Yes, my son has a father, and yes, he has a role model, but to actually have people that are not in your family to care, and I mean really care, and to push and to have high expectations.

The adults at MATCH place hundreds of phone calls each month, representing a strategic effort to build trust, offer support, and engage with students and families to meet the school's high expectations.

Student of the Month

Monthly assemblies note the achievements of some students. For example, the tutors and faculty grant four Student of the Month awards, one in each grade, and invite parents to attend the awards assembly. During an assembly this spring, several immediate and extended family members stood at the back of the great hall during the ceremony, watching the student body erupt in cheers when each young woman's name was announced (four girls received the awards at this particular assembly). There were tearful hugs exchanged between the students and family members after each speech.

At this assembly, a male student who had been observed as being engaged in his classes and a member of the MATCH Hip-Hop Club, opened the event with a rap performance. The boy had written the rap piece several weeks before, and this was his first public performance of it outside the club. The performance was an elaborate analogy of the ways the MATCH school might share characteristics with a prison: the student used the words "slavery" and "emancipation" as he referenced the very long school day and the demerits and detention system. His classmates shouted cheers of encouragement at each pause in the performance as several tutors and teachers looked on. While some might view this as a negative event, this seemed to be an appropriate time and space for the student's performance, given the student-centered nature of the assembly on this day.

It is clear that the number of adults working in the MATCH school—particularly since the creation of the MATCH Corps in 2005—increases the likelihood that on any given day, a student will experience an interaction with an adult who knows her well or feels responsible for him. Some students demonstrate their appreciation for this. As one teacher observes:

> You know, they stay because of the relationship piece. Watch . . . what happens during summer and during vacations . . . some kids just hang around after school. They want to stay and do their homework here, or even stay and not do their homework . . . just talk to adults here.

MATCH administrators, teachers, and tutors all seek to create a school environment that produces frequent student-adult interactions because they believe that creating powerful relationships is a key component in meeting their mission.

Focusing Behavior with the Code of Conduct

A second important element of the school's success is a consistent enforcement of the clear rules that govern student behavior, which is based on the theory that this will provide the orderly environment students need in order for learning to occur. The rules of conduct, which normalize student behavior and achievement, are the backbone of the belief system among both adults and students at MATCH.

Central to this belief is the Code of Conduct, which outlines the school's attendance policies, dress code, and actions for which a student may receive various levels of demerit.[2] The Code of Conduct clearly outlines definitions for academic, cheating, and safety violations, student contracts (used in cases of readmission or numerous violations), and step-by-step procedures for suspension and expulsion. According to the Code of Conduct, first-degree demerits are "given for misbehaviors that may seem relatively minor but their combined effect diminishes the culture and community of MATCH." These include actions such as poor posture or leaving a book bag on the floor of a classroom—a fire-code violation. Second-degree demerits are more serious and are what some school personnel might describe as disciplinary issues, such as disrespect, roughhousing, inattention or wasting time, unprofessional behavior, and disrespecting property. An academic violation can also trigger dismissal from the school. As stated in the Code of Conduct handbook:

> Learning is our most important activity at MATCH. Students who accrue 8 academic violations [and] have repeatedly chosen to behave in an inappropriate manner that interferes with learning will be asked to leave MATCH. Academic Violations are given for:
>
> 1. Disrespectful or insubordinate actions in class, tutorial, or other school functions (including passing in the hallway)—this includes ignoring or walking away from staff or faculty members when they are speaking to a student
> 2. Any behavior that leads to a student being asked to leave class and report to the office
> 3. Lying; intentionally deceiving a staff or faculty member; not reporting to office
> 4. Receiving 10 second degree demerits in one week

Though the code might seem strict and prescribed to some, the adults who work at MATCH see it as one of the ways to "foster learning"—they consider it an essential element of the school's drive for academic success. The school justifies the code, stating, "We do not believe that anything should get in the way of giving our students access to the education that they deserve, and our rules and consequence exist in order to create an environment where our mission can be fulfilled." The school's founder explains that a consistently enforced Code of Conduct reduces the chaos, the disruptions, and the interruptions he believes are present in urban schools. He describes these conditions as a tax on learning and elaborates the "tax" to mean

> a lot of interruptions and a kind of low-level distraction, and . . . just extremely chaotic classrooms where almost no productive exchanges happen.

I describe that as the tax on learning. . . . [For schools] that get these good results, I think that more than anything, they make the hours that they have with kids much more productive.

The Code of Conduct, then, is an explicit strategy to maintain order in the school in order to maximize opportunities for learning and increase time spent on academic tasks.

Consistent Enforcement

Having a Code of Conduct in a handbook is one thing; ensuring its consistent application is quite another. Consistency is important, school personnel believe, because discrepancies are obvious to students. An administrator, using a military analogy, asks, "What do you think it takes to keep that kind of culture running? A lot of times, it means sixty adults being on the same page. . . . If there's any soft part in that sixty-person front, you better believe that two hundred kids are going to try to go through that one hole."

MATCH is careful to employ multiple strategies to actively manage the application of the Code of Conduct. Absent this awareness, school policies and the culture defined by these policies could drift and become meaningless. Goldstein stresses the need for constant vigilance: "Every day you have to re-win the relationships with the kids and parents. Every day you will have pressure on the rules. It will never end." MATCH explicitly guards against this gravitational pull, expecting teachers and tutors to take actions that are in compliance with the code, which specifically states: "At the MATCH School, faculty and staff actions determine the climate of the classroom and hence of the school. As good educators have different management styles, the exact nature of an educator's consequence may vary, but will always be in compliance with the Code of Conduct." While the exact consequences may vary, there is a clear expectation that everyone will comply with the code.

Another way the school works for consistency is through administrative supervision. For example, administrators are particularly interested in whether and how tutors enforce the Code of Conduct. The corps is seen as a central actor in the progress students make, but they are also the primary correspondents of the messages that the school values. Indeed, because MATCH tutors spend a great deal more time with individual students than do classroom teachers or administrators, the leadership maintains a vigilant attitude toward the tutors' work. The leadership values their work as much as they do the work of any classroom teacher; this is not surprising, given that the forty-five tutors hired each fall comprise the largest group of employees in the charter school.

The school supervises the tutors with a highly integrated data-management system, through which tutors report their progress with each of their students on a daily basis. Teachers and administrators say that they use this information in order to "red-flag" students who are struggling to complete homework, whose grades are below passing, or who are not following the school's Code of Conduct. This gives them a clear picture of the tutors' efforts as well.

Screening for Fit

In addition to direct supervision, the school manages enforcement of the code through its process of selecting tutors and teachers. These processes put a heavy emphasis on hiring tutors and teachers who share the school's values because there is a sense among the staff that even very talented people cannot be successful at MATCH if their values are different from those perpetuated by the school's culture. What this looks like during the hiring process is that the school tries to find ways to reveal how a candidate will interact with students and apply the Code of Conduct in the classroom. In the interview process, tutors and interns are asked what response they might make to hypothetical situations potentially involving code enforcement. The MATCH Corps director explains how "negative" the experience at MATCH might be for tutors who could not comfortably and consistently apply the Code of Conduct: "It's going to negatively stress you out if your values are far off of how we run things here. So, in an interview, we're trying to get a sense of, 'How close are you to how we run things?' . . . I want to get somebody whose [way is] close [to ours]." The persistent question of whom to hire grows out of a hiring practice that makes lesson demonstrations important but also seeks to determine whether the teacher can efficiently communicate the culture of the school through the delivery of that lesson. The teachers and the principal believe that they can recognize these candidates during a protracted hiring process. The principal explains that these qualities are somewhat more difficult to identify than what he calls the "mechanical" parts of teaching, but that "there's sort of the intangible one, which I think is always the hardest: 'Would they fit into the culture of the school?'" His concern with the difficulties of answering the "intangible" question is a profound challenge, given that teacher turnover has historically been a problem in charter schools—one that MATCH has not entirely avoided over its eight-year history.[3] One also sees this in the comments of teachers who have been at MATCH for at least two years and serve on hiring committees. One teacher recalls that "we have gone through so many teachers over the years that we're at the point where we want to make absolutely sure that the person coming in here, that this is the best place for them, and that the fit is right."

Summer Academy

MATCH admits approximately sixty ninth graders from a lottery each spring. Newly admitted students attend a summer academy each day for five hours, Monday through Thursday, for five consecutive weeks at the Massachusetts Institute of Technology (MIT), for a total of one hundred hours. The summer academy gives students a head start on intensive academic learning and gives the school a forum to introduce the Code of Conduct. Each day, MIT students tutor the ninth graders for two hours in math and two hours in English. The fifth hour of the day is devoted to a "culture class," taught by the school's principal, which introduces students to the MATCH Code of Conduct. Students who miss more than four days of summer academy are not permitted to attend MATCH in September; they are replaced by the next student on the waiting list.

The culture class communicates to students and families whether they fit into the MATCH culture as defined by the Code of Conduct. To those students who do not "fit," the Code is unapologetic:

> We realize that MATCH may not be the right fit for every student. No school is perfect for each individual. We are a "choice" school: parents and students choose to enter our lottery, and for that we are humbled and grateful. To honor our commitment to provide an environment where all students can and will learn, continued or serious misbehavior by a student means that MATCH is not the right fit for that particular student.

Parents also must buy in to the culture, which is not for everyone. During a parent focus group, a parent relates the following story:

> There are also a couple of kids who uh, fell through. There's too much work. My niece got into MATCH—she had special needs. She was really struggling, and my sister, you know, I kept trying to talk to her. I was like, "You know, she's gonna struggle, but it'll get better." My niece was also under a lot of peer pressure and influences. She liked the thought that she was getting challenged and she was doing okay; even though she was failing, she was doing stuff she never thought she would be able to do. . . . I used to come and pick her and my daughter up at eight o'clock practically every night, and her sisters were already at home, hanging out, on the phone, so there was that, you know . . . she missed being able to just hang out, and my sister got

sucked in. She didn't stand her ground. I was like, "Don't give up! Let her do it for a year and see if it improves." But she took her out after a few months.

In a document posted on the school's website, "Common Criticisms of High-Performing High-Poverty Public Schools and MATCH School Responses," the school addresses student attrition:

> We work relentlessly to keep kids and parents at MATCH who want to leave. Why do they leave? The number-one reason is, "It's too hard. . . . From a kid's perspective, we're offering the educational equivalent of spinach and the other school is offering Twinkies. . . . The number-two reason kids choose to leave our school is [they] don't like the rules.

Demerits and Detentions Made Public

The school maintains consistent awareness of student behavior by posting lists of those with demerits and detentions. Each Friday, the names of students who have earned demerits and detentions for the week appear in the main entryway of the school. While the code discusses demerits in detail, positive merits, called MATCH dollars, are less prominent. The names of those who earn MATCH dollars are not frequently displayed and are instead maintained on a teacher's computer. Public assemblies afford opportunities for students who have made the honor roll to receive recognition.

While the public display of demerits might seem harsh, it is important to understand the spirit of the Code of Conduct. MATCH staff members enforce the code because they believe this provides every student an opportunity to learn in a disciplined, safe, structured environment. Therefore, adults at MATCH talk about detentions, a love for students, and student learning in the same breath:

> Despite our rules, I think [MATCH] comes off as a very warm place and a very loving place where we are willing to tell the kids we care about them, that we love them, and to hug them. It's being there during tough times, and it's also saying, "I'm going to require you to come for detention because I care about you and I think . . . you shouldn't be doing things like that."

The explanation for this attitude is that when the Code of Conduct is consistently enforced, teachers can spend more time teaching, and more time teaching is a form of caring for the academic life of a student. The consistent application of the code embodies the belief that the careful application of equal parts structure, discipline, and cultivating relationships with students creates the conditions and school culture that enable students to meet the school's high standards. Clearly, this requires a delicate balance, but the rewards, according to MATCH policy, are worth it. According to one teacher, "We try to balance strict, consistent enforcement of the rules with individual attention to each student—helping him or her to maximize academic potential and ultimately graduate from a four-year university."

Urgency and Expectations

A third element of success, one intricately related to both personal relationships and consistent discipline, is a sense of urgency around the amount of work that needs to be accomplished each day. There is both pride and anxiety in how teachers describe their work here, and the expectations for teachers are as real for them as they are for students.

Doing More

MATCH teachers, tutors, and administrators frequently express having a feeling of professional responsibility to their students and, to a lesser extent, to families. These adults share a common feeling that they need to do more for students, make more phone calls, or cover more content in class. A teacher describes the feelings she tends to internalize:

> My expectations for myself frequently become unreasonable and I need someone to kind of ratchet me back down and say, "Okay, I understand that you'd like to be perfect and magical. Guess what? You can't do it every day, but here are the tangible things you can do." That was a big challenge—trying to keep [my] expectations realistic at a high-performance school.

Her teaching colleague describes his transition from a traditional school to teaching at MATCH:

> The culture hurdle coming from another school to this one is that I got used to my old school and the fact that a lot of kids failed. . . . [At MATCH] there's so much pressure because there are times when you do have a kid who legitimately is not doing much [work] for you . . . [but] you have such a complex system here [that] we say, "There has to be a way."

Tutors express a similar feeling of urgency and responsibility:

> Those hours in tutorial, those hours in class, they have to be extremely productive, even when they're not in class and they have their silent sustained reading or they have their study hall. They are supposed to be working

during that entire time. They are not allowed to communicate with other students. It's not going to be running in and out of the bathroom. They need to be getting work done.

"56 minutes is . . . 56 minutes"

MATCH communicates these expectations and sense of urgency to students via a common lesson format. All MATCH teachers and the large majority of tutors use the same lesson structure, the blackboard configuration (BBC), which includes four elements: (1) Do-Now, (2) Aims, (3) Class Activity, and (4) Homework. At MATCH, the BBC appears on the whiteboard at the front of the room or in a handout to students. This required lesson structure supports the sense of urgency that drives teachers' work in classrooms. There is little variation from this lesson structure across classrooms at MATCH; most lessons include handouts generated by the teacher or by tutors to direct students in note-taking and practice. Tutors and teaching assistants help with grading in some classrooms, but they otherwise do not usually assist during regular class time. This lesson structure encourages teachers to deliver content to the whole class at the same time while students take notes and answer teacher-generated questions.

This sense of urgency translates directly into what is emphasized in classroom instruction. While the principal believes there is flexibility in how teachers teach, *no* teacher may waste instructional time:

> We have a greater school culture that allows each teacher the maximum opportunities . . . to use [class] time well. Our culture allows fifty-six minutes of learning to really be fifty-six minutes. . . . It's not like we have unique, amazing ideas of how to teach math. . . . We don't have an overarching philosophy of "How to actually teach," "How to actually instruct." It's more making sure that there is no time wasted; how to use that time is up to you.

This view of teachers' instructional practice sees good teaching, in part, as the degree to which MATCH students are on task. Founder Michael Goldstein explains:

> I think that more than anything, [the teachers and tutors] make the hours that they have with kids much more productive. Not through magical instruction or highly innovative ways of teaching literature or math, but [where] the average classroom is one where the kids' eyes are on the teacher, they've got a notebook out, they're actually trying practice problems the teacher just put on the board. These are very fundamental things.

Teachers at MATCH work extremely hard every period of every single day. The staff members' high expectations and shared sense of urgency means that teachers need to be "on" for entire class periods because they drive the instructional content. In fact, visitors to the school have commented on the incredible energy this requires. In a letter to the staff, a group of visiting teachers quoted the educator Rafe Esquith to describe how MATCH teachers are "teaching like their hair is on fire."

* * * * *

Each morning, MATCH students must answer the question, "Why are you here?" As they enter the school, they look an adult in the eye, shake hands, and state that they are there to learn, to be courageous, and to persevere through difficult coursework and exams. Just as important as why they are there is where they are going—and it's likely they're going to college. Personal relationships, a consistently enforced Code of Conduct, and a sense of urgency support the culture of the MATCH Charter Public High School in coordinated ways, creating what those involved with the school see as the right conditions for student achievement.

CHAPTER SIX

BUILDING A FOUNDATION FOR CROSS-SCHOOL THEMES

What Effective Schools and High-Performing Nonprofits Have to Say

It's a tall order to digest all of the information and details presented in the previous chapters about these five Massachusetts charter schools. Each school has a specific feel, culture, and mode of operation; staffs differ, systems vary, and buildings are distinct. All five schools are certainly energizing, engaging, and decidedly effective, but each in a way that reflects its "unique climate or personality" (Purkey & Smith, 1985, p. 357). Because of their uniqueness, these schools might be dismissed as special, nonscalable cases of high performance.

Yet some important commonalities exist across these schools—commonalities of approach and best practice. What exactly do these schools do that enables them to outperform other schools in their districts on statewide assessments, while also addressing the particular needs of a high-poverty student population? How do they reach compliance in certain subgroups with regard to No Child Left Behind (NCLB)? It is by examining these schools, exploring and exposing commonalities—and some important differences—that important lessons emerge, lessons for practitioners and school leaders in all types and levels of schools and for policymakers who seek to improve the education of all children.

The primary author for this chapter is Katherine K. Merseth.

This chapter sets the stage for the major findings about what makes these schools successful. To place these findings in a research context, the chapter briefly examines theories about what goes into creating effective schools for urban youth, followed by a consideration of the elements of successful non-profit organizations, with a brief reference to for-profit models and strategies. Bringing these two literatures—effective schools and high-performing non-profits—together, the chapter then offers a conceptual framework to represent the way these schools work. This model offers a helpful diagnostic tool to assess the performance of any K–12 school that seeks to serve urban children. The chapter begins with a review of the literature on effective schools.

Effective Schools for Urban Youth

In a seminal work published more than twenty years ago, Purkey and Smith (1985) undertook an ambitious challenge to review the literature of the day about "effective schools." Before that time, several projects were working to identify characteristics of "city schools" that were "instructionally effective for poor children" (c.f. Edmonds & Frederikson, 1979; Jencks, 1972; Mosteller & Moynihan, 1972). Much of the heat generated by these earlier studies came from methodological debates over the research design and the use of "correct" schools and "appropriate" measures. This work also addressed a suggestion advanced earlier that schooling did not strongly influence student performance (Coleman et al., 1966; Jencks et al., 1973). Purkey and Smith's (1985) review was comprehensive and included fields besides education, such as innovation and management (e.g., Cohen, 1988; Kanter, 1983; Meyer & Rowan, 1978; Rutter, Maughan, Mortimore, & Ouston, 1979; Sarason, 1971).

Their efforts resulted in a list of eleven elements, regrouped here in the following general categories: values and culture within the organization; the individuals in the enterprise; and the operational aspects of the school (Purkey & Smith, 1985, pp. 358–359)

And, finally, Purkey and Smith commented on the limitations of theory alone and the power of common sense in the world of research. They declared that findings of the effective schools literature "square with common sense and with the experience of practitioners. While neither common sense nor experience guarantees correctness, they do strengthen the case beyond the realm that can be reached by theory alone" (pp. 355–356).

Moving forward, the school reform literature of the early 1990s was replete with multiple reports, diverse opinions, and clarion calls for the improvement

Values and Culture
{
Sense of community
High expectations
Public recognition of academic achievement

Individuals
{
Strong leadership
Staff retention
Staff development
Parental support

Operational Aspects
{
Maximize academic learning time
Support from central office (or charter authorizing board)
Collaborative planning and collegial relationships
Local school-site management

of American schools (c.f. Barth, 1990; Fullan & Stiegelbauer, 1991; Sizer, 1992). The Coalition of Essential Schools presented its Common Principles to serve as a guide for the creation of effective schools, while Seymour Sarason (1971) continued to remind readers about the power of school culture to resist change, and historians David Tyack and Larry Cuban (1995) explained the historical reasons for the slow pace of reform. Much of this work focused on individual schools and how they could transform themselves internally with strong professional development (Lieberman, 1995; Little, 1993).

During this period, parents were expressing dissatisfaction with schooling writ large (c.f. Rose & Gallup, 2007); they did not want fancy reforms or coalitions, networks or movements. They wanted safety, order, and basics for their children and they wanted to know that their tax dollars were being spent to achieve these outcomes (Public Agenda Foundation, 1996). In 1994, young Teach For America alumni Dave Levin and Mike Feinberg began dreaming up a network of schools to serve inner-city youth. Some time later, in 2000, their dream became a reality when they received private foundation support to establish the Knowledge Is Power Program (KIPP), in which they offered what they believed to be the five essential principles for effective inner-city middle schools: high expectations, choice and commitment, more time on task, principals with the freedom and discretion to make decisions, and a focus on results.

As the end of the twentieth century approached, states jumped more actively into the school reform game, fueled by legislators who felt the heat of taxpayer concerns about fiscal accountability. States defined curriculum standards and established tests to determine what students were to know and be able to do. A new notion emerged about how to reform schools: with standards and accountability. States now were determining what children should know and what teachers should teach. As Patricia Albjerg Graham (2005) observed in her historical review of public schooling in America:

> By the late 1990's school reform advocates had dismissed "restructuring," "systemic reform," and even "goals" as these battle cries were replaced with "standards." This last term . . . translates somewhat better into practice than its predecessors since it, in fact, defines what a teacher should instruct the students and what they should learn. (p. 185)

Ultimately, achieving specific curricular outcomes became the driving force in school reform. Schools and society now had clear (though sometimes contested) targets. Researchers and practitioners rushed to offer still more advice to those operating urban schools in this new context of standards, accountability, and testing. Carter (2000), for example, studied twenty-one high-performing, high-poverty schools (including Levin and Feinberg's KIPP academies in Houston and New York) and identified characteristics that he felt led to stellar performance on standardized tests. Bearing a striking similarity to the KIPP five pillars, his list included having a principal with control over budget, staffing, and curricula; high nonnegotiable expectations for students, faculty, and administrators; extended learning time; parental involvement; and a heavy emphasis on having the "right teachers" in the building.

At about the same time, Reeves (2000) was writing about "90/90/90 schools," which were schools that had 90 percent or more students eligible for free and reduced-price lunch, 90 percent or more students of color, and 90 percent or more of their students meeting the district or state academic performance standards in reading. Building on lists generated by others, Reeves responded to the now data-rich environment and added several new elements he considered important for success, including data-driven instruction and teachers working collaboratively to assess student work. Lists of "best practices" proliferated, often without empirical proof, and networks like No Excuses Schools and Turn-Around Schools with their "turn-around formulas" appeared.

Student accountability, as measured by standardized tests, and schools measured by aggregated test scores received an enormous boost of legitimacy and importance with the passage in 2001 of the federal legislation known as the No Child Left Behind Act. This reauthorization of the Elementary and Secondary Education Act required states to set performance standards, to design their own way of determining what their children should know and be able to do, and to offer a plan to the U.S. Department of Education for how 100 percent of the students in the state would be deemed proficient in language arts and mathematics by 2014. NCLB represented an extraordinary change in how schools, states, and the federal government would do business. Because different states had different exams and cutoff scores for proficiency, wide disparities in student "proficiency" emerged across the country. Nearly half of the states moved to institute high-stakes tests and awarded diplomas only to students who were deemed "proficient" on statewide tests. For schools, performance became the watchword. There was no guesswork or hearsay; a child was either proficient, or not. This was accountability with teeth.

One group, the Education Trust, which had a particular interest in closing the achievement gap between low-income and minority youth and other students, began highlighting schools across the country that were rapidly reducing the gap. Their website, "Dispelling the Myth," was an enormous interactive database that anyone with computer access could search to find descriptions of schools with particular achievement levels, mix of students population, or geographic location (Education Trust, 2007). Their work helped identify schools that were successfully helping children achieve basic proficiency. Again, the common characteristics emerging from their database were similar to those mentioned previously. However, they added that successful schools would explicitly embrace external standards and assessments along with a culture of high expectations and frequent use of assessment data for the design of instructional tasks. The successful schools listed in their database exhibited a culture of high standards combined with extended learning time and structured academic support for students (pp. 14–27).

Running parallel with the standards movement, the charter school movement had also been receiving increasing attention since the opening of the first charter school in St. Paul, Minnesota, in 1992. As the standards movement came into full bloom in the early twenty-first century, reports began to surface about the characteristics of both successful and unsuccessful charter schools. The metrics for successful charter schools differed from state to state, but they often included above-average academic performance for students on state high-stakes assessments, organizational viability, appropriate financial management, and evidence of community interest and support. Many reports provided specific descriptions about the structures and operations of charters at the state level and more general information about the movement at the national level (c.f. Carnoy, Jacobsen, Mishel, & Rothstein, 2005; Ericson &

Silverman, 2001; Hill et al., 2001; Lake & Hill, 2005, 2006; Lake, 2007; Rothstein, 2004; RPP International, 2000; U.S. Department of Education, 2004; Buddin & Zimmer, 2005; Zimmer & Buddin, 2007.

As the number of charter schools grew from one school in 1991 to nearly four thousand schools in forty states some fifteen years later, several charter management organizations (CMOs)—nonprofit networks of charter schools—were founded, including Victory Schools, DC Prep, Mastery Charter Schools, Light House Academies, Uncommon Schools, and others. As these CMOs sought to "scale up" the number of charter schools in their networks, they found it helpful to articulate their specific design principles so that schools within a particular CMO would have common characteristics. These organizations built their lists of characteristics more from practical experience than from empirical research. For example, Achievement First, a nonprofit CMO with strong academic performance results in Connecticut and New York, offered several core elements that the organization felt were essential to operating effective schools: an unwavering focus on student achievement combined with a disciplined, achievement-oriented culture; the use of consistent standards-based curricula and interim assessments with frequent use of data; increased time on task; principals with the discretion to lead and closely supervise instruction; and the aggressive recruitment of staff coupled with high-quality professional development (Achievement First, 2008).

Finally, to round out the review of "successful" charter schools across the country, Nicola Filby and her colleagues at West Ed briefly visited eight charter schools to determine their common characteristics. After two days of observation at each school, they declared that these schools (one of which was MATCH) had strong, mission-driven cultures that focused on college preparation and offered students a rigorous, relevant, and engaging curriculum, with "wrap-around support" (Filby, 2006, p. 6). Importantly, they noted, these schools had cultures that demanded high accountability from teachers, administrators, and students.

Taken together, the multiple reports, pronouncements, and somewhat limited empirical research easily coalesced around several individual elements or characteristics that authors and advocates identified as being necessary to achieve strong student outcomes. This twenty-year span of literature suggests that effective schools—both charter and traditional—for urban youth will exhibit:

- A clear mission
- Strong leaders with the discretion to make local decisions

- A dedicated staff of teachers who have ample opportunities for collaboration and professional development
- Data-driven instruction and planning
- Opportunities and structures designed to extend academic learning time
- A culture of high expectations for student performance
- Parent and community involvement
- Supportive environments that foster and produce high achievement for students on statewide accountability measures

These statements suggest that many, if not all, of the above elements must be present in order to create an effective school experience for urban students. However, is this all it takes to create successful learning opportunities for children? Do school leaders and charter school founders only need to implement the items on these lists to guarantee successful schools for urban youth?

The answer to these questions is decidedly no.

Many school leaders who try to implement these elements one-by-one get less than satisfying results. Sometimes the reform effort gets stuck on a certain item, such as lack of staff commitment, wavering expectations that lead to a "dumbing down" of the curriculum for lower achieving youth, or money and/or patience that runs out and the champion leading the reform moves on. Moreover, partially implemented reforms or reforms implemented in a disconnected, disassociated fashion are usually more harmful than no reform at all. For example, consider implementing data-driven teaching in a culture of low expectations; this could result in a particularly deadly combination of drill-and-kill instruction for students. Well-intentioned school reformers sometimes suffer from a notion commonly called the "Christmas tree ornament" approach to reform: add one ornament here, another there, until the tree is full of disconnected decorations. Teachers jokingly refer to this approach as the "reform du jour" and have well-developed techniques to "duck and cover" until the next new idea comes along.

What is wrong with this element-by-element approach for charter schools, as well as for traditional schools, is that a list of characteristics frequently fails to acknowledge that there is more to successful school reform for urban youth than a series of one-step efforts individually implemented. Lists have a tendency to obscure the important connective tissue that brings coherence to the overall effort; in other words, lists ignore how the organization operates as a whole. What is missing from these lists is the importance of coherence across the organization. To explore this critical element, this chapter now turns to the literature on high-performing organizations, both for-profit and nonprofit, which sheds light on how actions and processes in organizations like schools must cohere or be congruent. Building an understanding of this organizational literature begins with the views of one of management's greatest gurus, Peter Drucker.

Management of Nonprofit Organizations

Peter Drucker (1990) playfully (and characteristically) offers some straight talk about what defines a nonprofit. He attacks the vagueness of the term "nonprofit" and reminds the reader that the term only really describes what the organization is *not*—it is not a business and it is not a government agency. Nonprofits do not deliver goods and they do not create regulations. Instead, he claims, the product of a nonprofit is "*a changed human being* . . . non-profit institutions are human-change agents" (p. xiv). Using Drucker's definition, then, schools are nonprofit organizations: they seek to change human beings by imparting knowledge to students and therefore operate as "human-change agents."

Like the effective schools literature, the nonprofit literature covers an extensive range. While the language these authors use may not be immediately familiar to educators or policymakers, the lessons and characteristics of successful nonprofits do apply to schools. This literature concerns itself with the internal workings of organizations that help them deliver their product. Letts, Grossman, and Ryan (1999), for example, devote a significant portion of their work on high-performing nonprofits to the organizational processes. These internal workings—the actions, processes, interactions, and decisions that help define and mold the organization—help it perform its function. In business terms, these actions are the organization's strategy, which is

> the whole set of decisions that are made about how the organization will configure its resources against the demands, constraints, and opportunities of the environment within the context of its history. . . . On one hand, strategic decisions implicitly determine the nature of the work the organization should be doing or the tasks it should perform [to achieve the desired outcome]. On the other hand, strategic decisions, and particularly decisions about objectives, determine the system's outputs. (Nadler & Tushman, 1980, pp. 39–40)

Applying the business notion of strategy to education in her *Note on Strategy in Public Education*, Harvard Business School lecturer Stacey Childress

(2004) offers a further interpretation: "Strategy is a set of actions an organization chooses . . . that fit together to create a clear picture of how the people, activities, and resources of an organization can work effectively to accomplish a collective purpose" (p. 1).

In the for-profit world, the overarching purpose of strategy is to create a product that customers value over another product (Nadler & Tushman, 1977; Porter, 1980, 1996). Clearly, this strategy is essential in a highly competitive environment, but it is also important for nonprofits and for public schools. Some may argue that competition is inappropriate in the education sector, and yet, charter schools are attractive (to many) precisely *because* they introduce competition into a market that operates as a monopoly, giving families that do not have financial resources a chance to send their children to private schools. Since charters are publicly funded in a method similar to traditional schools (i.e., the consumer does not necessarily know the specific cost of the service), cost is not a factor in the choice consumers make between traditional public and charter schools. Therefore, charters must differentiate their product from traditional schools in ways other than price in order to be attractive to customers and stay in business.

Like businesses, charter schools need a distinctive product in order to survive. Whereas some parents might value a neighborhood school for its convenience, others may, if given the choice, choose not to send their children to their low-performing neighborhood school and instead travel across town for a product they value more than convenience. The five charters in this study differentiate themselves from other traditional schools by advertising that they offer students a chance to achieve high scores on state tests, have more options for the high school they attend, and a better chance of being successful in college. These are outcomes to which the five schools dedicate their actions, decisions, and energy.

Organizational Models

Instead of offering lists of important elements, as found in the effective schools literature, the nonprofit and for-profit literature often use models or conceptual diagrams to depict how the myriad elements of organizations fit together. Organizational models project relational images, helping individuals see how changes in one element may impact another element of an organization. As noted by two long-time organizational management scholars, David Nadler and Michael Tushman (1980), a model shows how . . . factors are related—that is, which factors or combination of factors cause other factors to change. In a sense, then, a model is a road-map that can be used to make sense of the terrain of organizational behavior. (p. 36)

Called a congruence model in later publications (Tushman & O'Reilly, 2002), this model stresses the "fit" among component parts:

Our *congruence model of organizational behavior* is based on how well components fit together—that is, the congruence among the components; the effectiveness of this model is based on the quality of these "fits" or congruence. (p. 39)

Bradach (1996) offers another organizational model called the 7-S, which takes elements from Nadler, Tushman, and O'Reilly (Nadler & Tushman, 1977, 1980; Tushman & O'Reilly, 2002), as well as Waterman, Peters, and Phillips (1980) and others, adding several helpful details. His model includes the elements of strategy, structure, systems, staffing, skills, style, and shared values, and it offers a means to connect to findings from the effective schools literature discussed previously with regard to values and culture, individuals, and operational aspects.

Faculty members at Harvard Business School and the Harvard Graduate School of Education also worked with the models of Tushman, O'Reilly, Nadler, and Bradach to develop the PELP Coherence Framework (Childress, Elmore, Grossman, & King, 2007), which articulates how elements within a school district can lead to a focus on student learning. They add an additional element, the "instructional core"—that is, the relationship between student, teacher, and content (see figure 1)—to their model. The advantage of this model is that it combines elements from business strategy and education and stresses the internal operations of a school district. However, the PELP model gives somewhat less attention to the external environment in which a school district exists than would be the case in business models (Leschly, 2007). With charters operating in an arguably more competitive and regulatory environment than traditional urban schools, a slightly different model is required.

While the "instructional core" is in the center of the PELP Framework, the framework does not intend to suggest that instruction is the central outcome of schools and districts. The outcome by which all schools and districts are typically measured is student achievement, just as the outcome of a for-profit business might be profits or market share. The centrality of the instructional core in the diagram illustrates that these authors see it as "the most highly

FIGURE 6.1   The PELP Coherence Framework

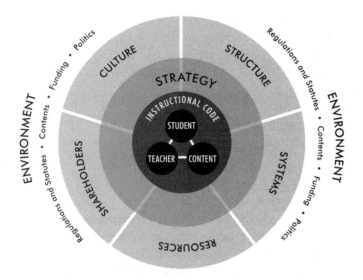

Source: Childress, Stacey, Richard F. Elmore, Allen S. Grossman, and Susan Moore Johnson, eds. *Managing School Districts for High Performance* (Cambridge, Massachusetts: Harvard Education Press, 2007), 3.

Copyright © Public Education Leadership Project at Harvard University. Reprinted with permission.

leveraged *means* to generate student achievement at scale. . . . All of the elements of the framework (including the instructional core) are organizational constraints or enablers of the ultimate outcome (student learning)" (S. Childress, personal communication, September 9, 2008). To achieve the outcome of "student achievement" at scale is to manage *all* of the elements of the framework in a coherent, coordinated fashion. Like its business predecessors (Tushman & O'Reilly, 2002; Nadler & Tushman, 1980), the PELP model stresses balance, consistency, and "fit"—coherence—among and between its elements.

Childress and her colleagues (2007) state:

> In today's accountability environment, public school districts face an imperative to achieve concrete performance goals related to student achievement. In order to accomplish these goals in all schools, not just some schools, the organizational elements of a district—its culture, structure and systems, resources, stakeholders, and environment—must be managed in a way that is coherent with *an explicit strategy to improve teaching and learning in every classroom, in every school.* (italics added, p. 1)

When we applied the PELP Framework to the operation of these five charter schools, we found less emphasis on the instructional core than on the other elements of the framework. Across these schools, our interviews and observations documented that a focus on an "explicit strategy to improve teaching and learning in every classroom" varied widely, and in several instances it received less emphasis than the elements of structures, systems, people, culture, and mission.

The central goal for these schools is high test scores, which are a necessary precondition for students to have increased options at the high school and college level. To achieve this goal, the schools employ impressive and exemplary strategies in terms of the culture they create, whom they hire, how they structure the school day, and the systems they employ. One administrator in the study explains:

> [Schools] that get these good results, I think that more than anything [they] make the hours that they have with kids much more productive—not through magical instruction or highly innovative ways of teaching literature or math, but through turning somersaults in very sort of interlocked ways. . . . [They] make the average classroom one where the kids' eyes are on the teacher, they've got a notebook out, they're actually trying to practice problems the teacher just put on the boar . . . very fundamental things.

While we did observe a number of exceptional teachers, this level of practice was not consistent nor its execution uniform. The consistency and coherence found in so many aspects of these charter schools did not necessarily extend to the teaching and learning in their classrooms. The success of these schools appears to be due instead to tightly linked structures, systems, people, culture, mission, and purposes. This finding led us to create a variation of the PELP model called the Charter School Coherence Model (CSCM). It is described in the following section.

Elements of the Charter School Coherence Model

The model presented here, the Charter School Coherence Model, describes the practices these charters employ that lead to their success (see figure 2). The CSCM emerged from the key elements articulated by interview subjects, and from a thorough analysis of information and documents written about these schools. It reflects many of the theories articulated previously about high-functioning organizations and schools.

The CSCM offers a helpful heuristic to frame the remaining chapters in this book. As noted previously, any given element, such as the people in an

FIGURE 6.2   Charter School Coherence Model

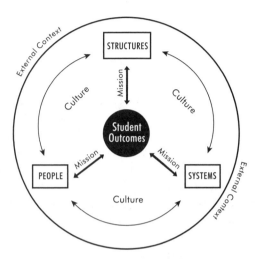

organization or its structures and systems, relates inextricably to the others. In other words, the functions of these key elements work interactively and synergistically, all playing an essential role in achieving successful student outcomes. The "external context" surrounding the model represents the context in which these schools operate, including the fact that they are charter schools operating independently from other schools and are competing with other charters and traditional public schools for their students and community niche. A brief discussion of the major factors in the model follow here.

Culture

Each school in this study has a distinctive culture, where "culture" refers to the beliefs, assumptions, and habits of those who inhabit the organization (Schein, 1985). Culture influences everything in an organization, whether it is a nonprofit or a charter school. While distinctive, these five schools do share several common characteristics, which are presented in chapter 7. For example, whether a K–8, 6–8, 5–12 or 9–12 school, all share a clear mission and purpose, and dedication and attention to culture-building. These schools also ask a great deal of everyone involved with the organization–parents, teachers, administrators, and students. School cultures of high expectations are ubiquitous and contribute to the high value placed on continuous improvement. These five schools continually ask, "How can we do this better?" They are never satisfied and are constantly assessing their effectiveness, planning new programs, and rethinking their work to make changes that will help achieve high student outcomes as measured by MCAS scores.

People

Both the effective schools and nonprofit literature discuss the importance of the "right people." However, it is not sufficient to simply have these people in the organization; they must be motivated and engaged in the organization's activities. Thus, a key component in the success of these charter schools is getting the right people motivated to implement the school's mission. The leaders of these schools play an important role in communicating the culture and mission to parents, teachers, administrators, and students. They do so by employing processes for publicity, recruiting, hiring, and enculturation. These processes help reinforce a deep engagement with the schools, and, indeed, every adult associated with these schools expresses having a strong buy-in to the core mission and strategy of the organization. Chapter 8 offers further details about the individuals who play important roles in the success of these schools.

Structures and Systems

Structures and systems illustrate the purposefulness with which these schools make decisions about how to design and implement their daily operations. In essence, they define the work of the organization. The approach offered here builds on the work of Bradach (1996), who defined structures as "the way in which tasks and people are specialized and divided" (p. 3) and systems as "the formal processes and procedures used to manage the organization" (p. 4). A specific focus on structures to guide the schools' use of their personnel and time resources are as fundamental to ensuring coherence as the systems of student behavior management, data use, and internal and external accountability. This aspect of our five schools appears more fully in chapter 9.

Student Outcomes and Instruction

The nonprofit and for-profit literatures are unrelenting in their emphasis on the importance of outcomes. Now, because of the age of accountability, the same can be said of K–12 schools. Outcomes determine whether the organization achieves its purpose, and having the freedom to determine that purpose is a fundamental concept of charter schools. Purpose varies widely in the American education system, from organizations designed to deliver "wit" to those focusing on the "character" of the young (Graham, 1984). The primary outcomes desired by the schools in this study are high MCAS scores, increased options for secondary school, entering and completing college, and individual personal growth. Everything these schools do is in service of achieving these outcomes. Although the schools' mission statements often include college entrance and success, the first step on the way to college is passing the MCAS, which then permits students to receive high school diplomas.

The close examination of operational practices within these five successful charter schools unearthed relatively few comments from teachers or administrators about instructional practice or the instructional core. Precisely because this instructional "dog did not bark" and was therefore not part of the CSCM, the researchers collected additional data within classrooms. Chapter 10 presents the findings from this aspect of the research, describing a range of structures surrounding instruction that includes common blackboard configurations, alignment of curricula with the Massachusetts Curricular Frameworks, and urgency around the use of instructional time and test-preparation activities. Beyond these commonalities, however, the data show a range of variation in instructional activities both within and across the schools. Surprisingly, the coherence that permeates the operation of these schools appears to stop at the classroom door.

Conclusion

The five schools in this study present an impressive and unique collection of practices found in effective schools and high-performing nonprofit organizations. Across the board, they have taken the essential elements of both worlds and creatively combined them to create high-functioning public organizations that serve a public need. The CSCM, which is based on these successful practices, offers a practical template for K–12 charter and public school practitioners and policymakers to use in assessing the performance of any K–12 school. The book now turns to the elements of the CSCM in the next several chapters.

CHAPTER SEVEN

CULTURE, MISSIONS, AND THEORIES OF ACTION

An administrator at the Academy of the Pacific Rim, reflecting on his feelings when he first learned about the charter school movement several years ago, still bubbles with enthusiasm:

> When I found out about charters, I had this "aha moment"!! It was like, "WOW! This is great!" A school, you know, a *public* school without any fees, tuition, enrollment, etc., but [you could] have the *culture* work like independent schools . . . [with] high expectations, [the idea that] you're going to college, and all of that!

And over at Roxbury Prep, one of the codirectors declares:

> So for us, the culture is driven by what happens inside of the classroom. A lot of schools, very high-achieving schools that I think are fabulous, spend a lot of time on culture, on building culture, and on explicitly teaching culture. We do some of that with our advisory class and with our Community Meeting. But I would say the culture of Roxbury Prep . . . is defined by what happens inside of the classroom.

These charter school leaders use the word "culture," but what exactly does it mean? It is such a frequently used yet elusive term in the world of schools and organizations (c.f. Lieberman, 1988; Meyerson, 2008; Peterson & Deal, 2002; Sarason, 1971; Tushman & O'Reilly, 2002). Certainly, every school or organization has a culture, so the important question is, what kind of culture is it? Is the

The primary author for this chapter is Katherine K. Merseth.

culture productive, coherent, and supportive? Or is it dysfunctional, divisive, and toxic? Does the culture support or subvert the organization's work and mission? Is the culture broadly understood, or are there conflicting and competing subcultures within the organization? As seen in the previous chapter, the nonprofit management and effective schools literatures work with similar definitions of culture. Edgar Schein (1985), an emeritus professor at the Sloan School of Management at the Massachusetts Institute of Technology, offers one of the most widely cited definitions of culture:

> [Culture is] a pattern of basic assumptions—invented, discovered or developed by a given group as it learns to cope with its problems of external adaptation and internal integration—that has worked well enough to be considered valid and, therefore, to be taught to new members as the correct way to perceive, think and feel in relation to those problems. (p. 9)

Schein is saying that as organizations evolve, culture helps them manage two important issues—how to interact and react to the external environment surrounding the organization, and how to inculcate individuals into the organization's set of beliefs and values.

School researchers articulate culture in similar ways. Peterson and Deal (1999), for example, note that cultures build up over time and can create powerful expectations about professional norms. Peterson (2002) describes school culture:

> Every organization has a culture, that history and underlying set of unwritten expectations that shape everything about the school. A school culture influences the ways people think, feel, and act. Being able to understand and shape the culture is key to a school's success in promoting staff and student learning. (p. 10)

Today, a preponderance of consultants and tools are available to examine and potentially transform a school's culture. Multiple resources, such as the School Culture Triage Survey (Wagner & Masden-Copas, 2002), the School Culture Survey (Richardson, 2001), and the *Shaping School Culture Field Book* (Peterson & Deal, 2002), are available to diagnose, develop, improve, or alter a school's culture. There is even a Center for Improving School Culture[1] ready to help schools bring about cultural change.

Taken together, then, these perspectives on culture establish a basic fact: culture is the marinade, the soup in which operational elements such as the people, the structures, and the systems operate and in which instruction, an important task of these schools, floats. While these elements help define the culture, it is also true that culture helps define these elements. The circularity and interactivity between a school's culture and the elements within it indicate the level of an organization's coherence and internal alignment with the mission.

This concept of strategic coherence appears throughout this book. As business strategist Michael Porter (1996) observes:

> Strategy is creating fit among a company's activities. The success of a strategy depends on doing many things well—not just a few and integrating among them. If there is no fit among activities, there is no distinctive strategy and little sustainability. (p. 75)

The aim is not simply coherence for coherence's sake, for one can have an organization that coheres around goals yet might not achieve the mission. It is, rather, a set of goals and activities that cohere strategically around the mission that helps define who these schools are, what they do, and how they do it.

The Importance of Culture

Why is culture important? In the charter school context, culture is important for several reasons. First, many argue that student performance reflects school culture and that when a school immerses students in a context where learning and achievement are valued, they are more likely to learn and achieve (e.g., Barth, 1990; Elmore, 2004; Lieberman, 1988; Peterson & Deal, 2002).

However, establishing a causal relationship between culture and student achievement is challenging at best. The empirical literature instead offers *correlations* between school culture and student achievement. For example, one study of eighty-two middle schools in Virginia found significant positive relationships between student achievement and teacher professionalism, academic pressure, and community engagement (the latter having the strongest positive correlation; Tschannen-Moran, Parish, & DiPaola, 2006).

Second, culture is important in the charter school context because the schools in this study began as start-ups. They are not conversion schools—nothing existed before these schools received their charters—and therefore, at least initially, they developed their cultures purposefully, making them their own. Creating culture or influencing an existing one is not an easy task; doing either can be an uphill battle, but they are battles that differ. With a start-up, the focus is on establishing core beliefs and values, while in an existing school the task is to change beliefs and values. Regardless of the situation, the cultures in these five schools offer insights for all school leaders. Furthermore, culture is important to these schools because they stand alone—namely, they are not part of districts or charter management organizations and thus they are solely responsible to their customers and to themselves. The only formal external influence they encounter is the Massachusetts Department of Education, which requires the schools to go through a reauthorization process every five years. Finally, culture is important because it is a powerful vehicle that fosters the realization of a school's mission. Culture both defines and unites an organization around common goals and desired outcomes.

There are several useful ways to begin to understand a school's culture. One is to consider the set of beliefs and values conveyed in the school mission statement, another is to explore the school's "theories of action" (Argyris & Schön, 1974) or "theories of change," which also express certain assumptions about activities that lead to the attainment of the school's goals. Another perspective on the culture of these schools emerges from the values expressed by organizational members. This chapter sets the stage for discussions in the following chapters about how human resources, systems, and structures enable these schools to sustain and manage their cultures. After all, every school and organization has a culture, and every school has people, structures, and systems that operate within that particular culture. However, what is striking about these five schools is the degree of coherence and strategic alignment among the various elements of the organization and the stakeholders' consistent values and assumptions.

Organizational Missions

What is a mission and what are the characteristics of a good one? Oster (1995) declares that "among nonprofits, mission statements typically identify both the audience and product or service being offered. They answer the twin questions: What are we producing and for whom?" (p. 22). Drucker (1989) poses the same questions in slightly different terms and adds a third: What business are you in? Who is your customer? What does your customer value?

Strong mission statements serve three functions: (1) they describe why the organization exists and what it does; (2) they motivate and send a signal to the individuals involved in the organization; and (3) they help frame the evaluation of the organization's products (Oster, 1995). To summarize, then, effective mission statements are memorable and easily and quickly understood by multiple constituencies. They describe, in unambiguous terms, an organization's goals and serve as a guide to establish metrics or benchmarks of the organization's output and impact. So how does this nonprofit language apply to the mission statements of this study's schools?

Missions in Schools

Like culture, having a mission statement for a school is a rather unremarkable thing. A mission statement may express what a group or an individual, at one point in time, thought their school or organization stood for. On the wall of the school office or in the handbook of nearly every K–12 school in America, one can usually find the school's mission statement. Many are vague, leaving the understanding of the school's purpose open to multiple and possibly conflicting interpretations.

For example, one middle school mission statement declares, "We will respect ourselves and one another, appreciate individual differences, and encourage one another to reach our potential." This statement does not go far in answering Oster's question of what the school is producing. The statement of a Boston public middle school that shares the same general student population as Roxbury Prep expresses the desire "to develop ethically and academically successful world citizens with input and ownership by students and parents." Many such well-intentioned mission statements fall short on providing specificity, clarity, and easily defined, measurable outcomes. Indeed, they succumb to a common tendency "to make the mission statement into a kind of hero sandwich of good intentions" (Drucker, 1990, p. 5).

Now consider the following mission statements from the schools in the study:

Academy of the Pacific Rim Mission
The Academy's mission is to empower urban students of all racial and ethnic backgrounds to achieve their full intellectual and social potential by combining the best of the East—high standards, discipline and character education—with the best of the West—a commitment to individualism, creativity and diversity.

Boston Collegiate Mission
The mission of Boston Collegiate Charter School is to prepare each student for college.

Community Day Mission
Our mission is to provide a kindergarten through grade eight school that will draw upon our considerable experience in working together as a community to develop and implement a curriculum that discovers and supports

the special characteristics and unique learning styles of each student. We will engage that student in meaningful learning experiences for the purposes of clearly stated goals in the areas of understandings, knowledge, skills, habits, and social competencies. The curriculum will be embedded in the reality of city life and will reinforce the positive aspects of our city: its culture, art and economy, its working class history and strong work ethic.

MATCH Mission
The MATCH Charter Public High School prepares Boston students to succeed in college and beyond.

Roxbury Prep Mission
Roxbury Preparatory Charter School, a public school that serves grades 6–8, prepares its students to enter, succeed in, and graduate from college.

Using the criteria established above—specificity, clarity, and measurable outcomes—three of these mission statements receive high marks: Roxbury Prep, MATCH, and Boston Collegiate. These three missions are clear, specific, and lend themselves to outcome measurement. It is possible to determine whether students are prepared for college by examining their admission rates and their desire to attend. While MATCH's "and beyond" may present some challenges in measurement, retention and completion rates would certainly lend a degree of understanding to whether the students were successful in college. Roxbury Prep's mission statement is noteworthy for its scope and clear ambition, although it is perhaps not so immediately useful because the school would need to wait ten years (in the case of sixth graders) to determine whether it was successfully meeting its mission.

On the other hand, Community Day and the Academy of the Pacific Rim offer more expansive mission statements that include information about *how* they intend to achieve "full intellectual and social potential" or engage students in "clearly stated goals in the areas of understandings, knowledge, skills, habits, and social competencies." Actually measuring these particular outcomes will be more challenging than for the other three charter schools. Perhaps sensing this, administrators from the Academy of the Pacific Rim and Community Day both offer a more action-oriented translation of their school's mission into specific and easily measurable outcomes. At the Academy of the Pacific Rim, for example, when asked about the school's mission, one administrator stated:

Everything is focused on that particular goal [of academics]. . . . We're not trying to be everything for everybody, so we don't have a vocational program and we don't have a strong sports program. We don't have all these interests that might compete when it comes down to academics. I think being clearly focused on academics first, and everything [else] coming second, makes it much easier. . . . We're very clear and everything revolves around that.

Another administrator at the same school makes the connection to college as an outcome measure even more overt:

Ultimately we want to prepare them for college and then living in a global world. I think our measures of doing that are how many of our alumni are going to graduate from college and what are they going to do [after they graduate]. . . . Those are probably the best measures that we have, since what's the most tangible for people is college prep and college success.

While Community Day does not specify the exact levels of their "clearly stated goals in the areas of understandings, knowledge, skills, habits, and social competencies" in their mission statement, in practice, achieving their mission relates closely to the Massachusetts Curricular Frameworks and to results on the Massachusetts Comprehensive Assessment System (MCAS). The executive director—who brought nonprofit management experience to the job—explains:

I always managed through specific, measurable goals and objectives . . . so it kind of amazed me that [in] schools . . . there wasn't a more specific orientation towards what are your goals or standards that you need in every grade [and] how do they link, one to the other?

Thus, in these schools, teachers and administrators articulate their mission in very similar ways. The common language, shared understanding, and core of beliefs are remarkable in these organizations; nothing is ambiguous about the work of these schools. A teacher at Roxbury Prep, for example, attributes the success of the school to the fact that the "mission of the school is very explicit," while a Community Day teacher notes that mission permeates everything: "From everything everybody does, more so than any school I've taught at before, everybody here is on the same page and everybody wants the students in the school to be successful." Finally, an administrator at the Academy of the Pacific Rim stresses the reverence for, indeed almost sanctity of, the mission while discussing various changes and midcourse corrections the school has undertaken, noting that whatever happens in the school "has always been guided by the mission."

Espoused Values: Theories of Action and Intended Impact

An approach that offers a different perspective on the culture and organizational assumptions made about these schools is to explore their "theories of action." A theory of action can serve as a roadmap to a particular destination. Childress (2004) suggests that "a theory of action represents the organization's collective beliefs about the causal relationships between certain actions and desired outcomes" (p. 1). Similar to a theory of change or intended impact as articulated in the nonprofit and for-profit worlds,[2] a theory of action describes what conditions must be present and what activities need to occur in order to achieve a desired outcome. Some organizational consultants argue that focusing on intended impact or a theory of action helps develop clarity about outcomes: "Another approach . . . is to help an organization's decisionmakers develop clarity, not about mission, but about what we call 'intended impact' and 'theory of change'" (Colby, Stone, & Carttar, 2004, p. 1).

What, then, do the decisionmakers in these five schools articulate as their theory of action regarding "improved outcomes for students"? When asked directly about their school's theory of action, leaders provided the following responses via email:

Academy of the Pacific Rim
We believe that all students can learn to the highest academic standards/ expectations. We believe that this requires hard work, and that it may take some students longer, and some students may require more support, but with effort, all students can achieve. (Codirector)

Boston Collegiate
We believe that combining high academic and behavioral expectations with tremendous support; ensuring consistency, order, and structure throughout the school; and, ensuring that all teachers are outstanding and supported will prepare students to excel in college and beyond. (Executive director)

Community Day
We believe that in order to ensure opportunity for our students, it is necessary to hold all stakeholders (students, faculty, and parents) to high standards. We do everything we can to maintain our focus on these standards while supporting the individual needs of each student. (Executive director)

MATCH
If a school creates a culture in which teachers are freed from behavior management issues and organizational operations to focus on teaching and kids are focused and trying reasonably hard to learn, then students will achieve academic success. (Founder)

Roxbury Prep
When students are provided a safe, structured environment and teachers provide rigorous, engaging classes that are aligned with standards and reflect content expertise, all children can make tremendous academic progress and be prepared to enter, succeed in, and graduate from college. (Codirector of curriculum and instruction)

Looking across these schools, the similarities in their theories of action are striking, even though they describe work in different cities, at different grade levels, and with different populations. Academy of the Pacific Rim and Community Day stress the need for student support and accommodation; one is a 5–12 school in Boston while the other serves K–8 children in Lawrence. Boston Collegiate, Roxbury Prep, and MATCH all mention the work of teachers, while Roxbury Prep and Community Day specifically stress the importance of standards alignment. Taken together, these theories of action indicate the belief that the collective action of individuals working within a school around a shared mission will lead to desired student outcomes. These statements reflect a culture of agency that assumes the mission is achievable and the belief that school personnel have the skills and ability to bring the mission to fruition. From the perspectives of school leaders, these theories of action reflect assumptions and beliefs that create conditions under which their goals will be achieved.

Assumptions and Operating Norms

Another means of exploring the culture of schools is to examine commonly held values and expectations about the ways that schools and the individuals in them conduct the business of teaching and learning. Sara Lawrence Lightfoot (1983), in *The Good High School,* eloquently makes this point about all schools:

Schools must find ways of inspiring devotion and loyalty in teachers and students, of marking the boundaries between inside and outside, of taking a psychological hold on their members. . . . I do believe that good schools balance the pulls of connection to community against the contrary forces of separation from it. . . . The protection and solace good schools offer . . . may also be partly approached through ideological clarity and a clear vision of institutional values. (pp. 322–323)

Noteworthy assumptions and values in these five schools include high expectations for students regarding their work ethic and behavior, high expectations for families and how they support the students, and high expectations for teachers and their commitment to the job. Permeating the culture of all these schools is dedication to continuous improvement and pride in being adaptable organizations. The following section examines these values, as evidenced by comments from individuals working within the schools and researcher observations.

High Expectations for Students

In all of the classrooms in all of these schools, the expectations for student engagement and behavior are palpable. Students are expected to work hard, behave, and participate at all levels. As described in the chapter on the Academy of the Pacific Rim, for example, students in their PREP program are required to do some kind of internship or other program for each of the three summers they are in high school This sends a message to the students that they must participate in the world at large and gain experience beyond the school's walls. At MATCH, the founder takes pride in the fact that his school's culture establishes high behavioral expectations:

> We think that if you show that you really care about each individual, you then are in a comfortable position to create high expectations both about classroom decorum but also actually about doing your work.

Expectations for students relate not only to behavior but also to the level and amount of work they do. At Roxbury Prep, a seventh-grade teacher describes how the school tracks classes according to ability while still holding the same high expectations for all levels:

> I really hold extremely high expectations for all of my students. We have three different sections—703, which in a tracking system could be considered the high group, 702 the middle group, and 701 the lower group. The expectations I have for 703 are the same for 701, and I just make sure that I provide all the support to make sure all students can meet these high expectations.

This same teacher goes on to say that he sometimes must defend his level of expectations to parents who suggest the program is too rigorous:

I had a parent question me and say she felt the curriculum was designed more for high school. I said no, I have high expectations. I said let's . . . look at the high schools we are trying to get our students to go to. There is a lot of catching up to do and the competition for proficiency at these high schools is going to be high. I would be remiss as a teacher for not equipping my students with the tools they need to be competitive at that level and also to get to college.

At Community Day and Roxbury Prep, the assumption is that eighth graders will gain admission to a secondary school of their choice; at the high schools, that graduates will go to college. An Academy of the Pacific Rim administrator speaks for the secondary schools:

College prep is what we do. There's a lot of language in the middle school, but . . . it intensifies in the high school. In ninth grade they go on a college field trip . . . [and] there's information nights for parents. The tenth through twelfth grades attend our college fair. In the eleventh and twelfth grades, the students have specific SAT classes that we provide and pay for. They have college counseling class once a week that runs in the eleventh- and twelfth-grade year. We have seminars, one-on-ones with the college counselors . . . From the very beginning, at sixth grade, we're unapologetically college driven.

High school choice or college attendance is a nonnegotiable expectation established at these schools early in each student's academic career. Class time is sacred, and the limited time they have to achieve these goals creates a sense of urgency and the need for students and teachers to stay focused.

The schools also deploy precious resources in the service of students' achieving their secondary school choice or college attendance, which illustrates a coherent strategy to meet their goals. Academy of the Pacific Rim, for example, deploys two full-time college counselors for a high school with fewer than two hundred students. Boston Collegiate has a full-time director of College Advising and Alumni Programs and also a College Readiness Committee that solicits feedback from graduates about the quality of their preparation for college and then reviews and adjusts the school's curriculum based on this feedback. At the eighth-grade level, Community Day makes families aware of their choices for high school. While noting that Lawrence High School is a choice, the individual responsible for secondary school placements also mentions that Community Day graduates attend other regional schools that participate in a statewide school choice program, parochial schools, and vocational schools. This individual believes that her role is "to help families by laying out those options and being able to help them craft a list that seems most appropriate for their child." The other middle school in the study, Roxbury Prep, also commits funds to support a graduate services coordinator. And at both Community Day and Roxbury Prep, the placement coordinators collect data on the performance of their graduates in high school and college.

Beyond allocating precious staff resources to fulfill their mission of high school choice or college attendance, the schools in our sample organize field trips to visit high schools or college campuses. In these ways, the schools demonstrate a coherent strategy to achieve their goals. A teacher at Roxbury Prep, for example, describes with pride and enthusiasm his recent trip to Amherst College with his middle school students, even though it could be five years before these students begin the college application process. The placement coordinator at Community Day takes students to visit secondary schools that she decides are appropriate for them. She explains how she chooses which high schools to visit:

> I work on that choice because it's not fair to send a child who has absolutely no chance, for example, [of] getting into Phillips Academy to visit there. That would be cruel. So I work with the head of school and the teachers [to] craft what seems to be possible options. . . . I say to the kids all the time, the better high school you go to, the better college you go to, the better job you have. That's just reality. But what I'm really looking for is for each child to attend the school that is right for them.

In addition to these direct actions, the schools communicate their high expectations for students in some subtle and subliminal ways. One approach is through role modeling. The forty-five college-graduate tutors who make up the MATCH Corps offer an intriguing example. Because MATCH students develop strong professional and personal relationships with the tutors, they always have access to informal information about life after high school. If a student wants to know what college is like or what to expect, a tutor can tell stories, answer questions, or give hints about how to survive. Furthermore, there is a conscious strategy to recruit MATCH Corps members from top-ranked public and private colleges, thus sending a message that such achievement is not only possible but expected. Other schools send not-so-subtle messages by naming classrooms for the teachers' alma maters, such as Cornell 8 or Dartmouth 10, and by displaying college materials throughout the halls of the schools.

High Expectations for Families

Expectations about college or choice of secondary school are made clear not only to students but also families, sometimes even before a student applies or enrolls in the charter school. One codirector of Roxbury Prep describes this deliberate process:

> When families come for information sessions, which means they're just fill-ing out applications and have a 50/50 chance of getting in through the lot-tery, we start really at that moment. . . . We explain the school—we state all the great things . . . and then we say that the way we've been successful is that the school is incredibly strict and incredibly well structured, and the school's incredibly demanding academically. We say, "I don't know how many of you have more than fifteen minutes of homework a night, but now you're going to have two-three hours of homework a night. And, I don't know what it's like in your school hallway, but in our school hallway it's silent. And, I don't know what you normally do on Saturday, but each time you need it, you will spend a Saturday in school." We're just very clear about it. . . . You may agree or disagree with the way that we do things, but we're going to be really clear about it and that just is who we are.

These schools also host activities to help parents fill out secondary school or college applications and financial aid forms. As an Academy of the Pacific Rim parent observes, with a sense of amazement in her voice, "They really try to help the parents with the process. We come in and they help you with the financial aid forms. . . . They have a night where all the parents come in and they'll . . . sit with you at the computer and help you do the form!" Going even a step farther, Community Day *requires* parents to attend a parent night at which area high schools set up tables where families can get additional infor-mation. Last spring eighteen high schools were represented at the fair.

This emphasis on secondary school or college admission and persistence is important, because the national charter movement is awaiting data about the long-term impact of these schools. As recently as 2007, Gill and his colleagues (Gill, Timpane, Ross, Brewer, & Booker, 2007) from the RAND Corporation note that there is "as of yet almost no evidence on the long-term effects of charter schools on the academic attainment of their students, including ef-fects on high school graduation and college participation" (p. 110). They com-ment further on the importance of the mission and culture of these schools: "As small schools that are intended to operate with a strong sense of academic mission, charter schools may be likely to affect students' identification with school and academic ambitions more than their scores on state achievement tests" (p. 110).

High Expectations for Staff

"Expectations," as Elmore and his colleagues (2004) note, "are collective in nature and they characterize the shared norms and values of school participants developed to get the work of the school done. They are formed out of relationships among individuals, and they operate in often powerful ways to shape individuals' behavior and values" (pp. 139–140). In keeping with that viewpoint, these five schools set extremely high expectations for staff.

While teachers are hired because they have a deep commitment to the job (described more fully in the next chapter), once they are actually on the job the schools work hard to intensify that commitment and to create cultural norms of professionalism, shared ownership of problems, and a strong work ethic. According to one Academy of the Pacific Rim teacher, these expectations account for the school's success: "I think, in general, the high academic standards and high level of professionalism among teachers and students is something that sets the school apart from many charter schools . . . it sets it apart from many . . . urban schools in general." A teacher at Community Day makes a similar comment:

> You work hard consistently, and it's not something where you can just kind of rub off your shoulder and say, "Oh, I don't care." If you do that, you don't end up being here very long. . . . The teachers' work ethic kind of leads down to the kids, kind of bleeds down to them . . . so I think part of the success is our hard work that fans out to the kids, and the kids see that and they try to produce the same thing in a lot of ways.

Several methods are employed to build high expectations for staff. One example of this is to encourage 60- to 80-hour teacher workweeks, which are common. Describing the interview process at Roxbury Prep, one codirector notes that he looks for a candidate's reaction to his description of a long workweek: "I also look at people's reaction when I say it's a 60-hour workweek. If that makes your jaw drop, then no matter how good you are, you are done. Because I feel like that's what it takes. You have to be willing to do it." A Boston Collegiate teacher has a similar perspective:

> People work long hours. . . . You know, usually I get here at 7:30 AM . . . and I'll leave between 5:00 and 7:00 PM. So 11-hour days are pretty common. . . . It takes a lot of hours to give the kind of feedback that students need, to

make that feedback immediate enough that it's relevant when they get the papers back or they get the work back.

No one, teacher or administrator alike, suggests that working at these schools is an easy job. The intense commitment to do "whatever it takes" can take a toll, as another Boston Collegiate employee admits:

> It's a challenge having all of these extra things that we do. Extra groups, tutoring, Homework Club, detention, progress reports, report cards. We wrote a paragraph for each kid for their report card. It's hard. And I spent a lot of hours here every day doing things that are not grading or planning my class. And that's really hard. I think the biggest challenge for a teacher is that time-management kind of work/life balance.

A Roxbury Prep teacher also notes the extensive time commitment and observes that it is part of the culture:

> There's no competition of who works the most, but ... this is the blessing and the curse of Roxbury Prep. It's my fifth year, I'm teaching only three classes and I'm still here on Saturday or Sunday getting prepared. I think people are here all the time—early, late—and it's become almost this self-righteous thing that we like to brag about while still knowing it is not healthy and probably not self-sustainable in the end. I also think in order to really believe in that mission, you have to understand that you're going to have to be working sixty-seventy hours a week ... it doesn't make sense that you're going to teach six hours a day and go home and that's it.

While some may argue that all schools in Massachusetts feel the pressure to increase student performance and have their children do well on the MCAS and on No Child Left Behind measures, the culture of urgency is different for these schools because they face the prospect of closure every five years as part of the charter renewal process (although charter school critics correctly point out that charter closures for poor performance are rare).

A Commitment to Continuous Improvement

Another value that helps move these schools toward high academic outcomes as measured by standardized tests is a commitment to continuous improvement. An axiom in these schools is, "Desired outcome = actual outcome + continuous improvement." These schools constantly ask, "What could we do that would better serve our students? How can we improve?"

Organizational scholars talk about the peril for nonprofits in either resting on their successes or being unwilling to subject their products constantly to concrete measurable assessment (c.f. Christensen, 2006; Drucker, 1985; Letts, Grossman, & Ryan, 1999; Oster, 1995; Porter, 1980). Those who study organizations note that the successful organizations—those that endure and continue to make strong contributions to society—are those dedicated to continuous improvement. Successful nonprofits are never static, Drucker (1980) says, since the "focus is always on improving the product, improving the process, improving the way we work, the way we train. And you need a continuing strategy for doing so" (p. 60). Porter (1996), a business theorist, comments similarly: "The operational agenda is the proper place for constant change, flexibility, and relentless efforts to achieve best practice" (p. 78).

Nonprofit and for-profit organizations, and in this case, high-performing charter schools, study their processes and work hard to make modest and sometime major adjustments to meet their desired outcomes. An administrator at the Academy of the Pacific Rim states this attitude clearly: "If something's not working, then we use the data to figure out what will work, so people, I think, ultimately remain open-minded with that goal as the prize." These schools are never satisfied; they constantly assess their effectiveness, they plan new programs, and they rethink their work to make changes that will better serve students' needs.

The creation of the Homework Club at Boston Collegiate (described in detail in chapter 3) is a perfect example of the culture of continuous improvement. Despite the fact that the Homework Club is now a common part of daily life at Boston Collegiate, at one point it did not exist. The club originated when teachers came together and noted how getting homework done was a huge battle in every class. Describing the process, one teacher recalls:

> It became this brainstorming session and . . . another teacher . . . suggested, "Why don't we just collect homework in the morning and go through it? Whoever hasn't done it stays." It was this period of [asking], "Can we do that? How would that work? It sounds great. Would that be a task that would just take up so much time that it wouldn't be worth it? . . . What's the worst that could happen? . . . They're not doing their homework, so why not try it? It would mean some phone calls . . ." And it worked. And then, obviously, it's evolved from there. Now we can't even imagine not having Homework Club.

The commitment to continuous improvement has other benefits as well. For one, it demonstrates to teachers and staff that their views, ideas, and voices matter. Continuous improvement presents an opportunity for buy-in and ownership. As one teacher notes, "There's very much the feeling within the school that if you have a good idea, you can do it, you can make it happen . . . you just need to build a consensus and as soon as you have that, it's going to take off."

Another advantage to a culture of continuous improvement is that a school can jettison something that is *not* working. For example, in MATCH's original charter they took the name Media and Arts Technology High School. Early school documents reflect the technology priority:

> Bridging the Digital Divide. Technology is not taught as a separate subject, but directly integrated into math, English, science, history. For example, students studying the presidential election have filmed public service announcements about federal policy issues, produced personal radio diaries exploring character, and conducted telephone polls about the Presidential debates—all in addition to, not instead of, traditional debates, essays, and readings. (MATCH Charter Public High School, 2001, p. 5)

However, after several years, the school dropped its emphasis on the role of technology in favor of a greater emphasis on preparation for college. By the 2006-07 school year, the school's annual report no longer referenced integrating technology into instruction. Instead of being the Media and Arts Technology High School, the school henceforth was known simply as MATCH. Drucker (2006) endorses this continual reassessment of activities in an organization:

> Every product, every operation, and every activity in the business world should be put on trial for its life every two or three years. Each should be considered the way we consider a proposal to go into a new product, a new operation or activity. . . . One question should be asked of each: "If we were not in this already, would we now go into it?" And if the answer is "No," the next question should be: "How do we get out and how fast?"(p. 4)

Nimbleness

Hand-in-hand with a commitment to continuous improvement is a sense of nimbleness—an innate agility that enables schools to move and to make changes quickly, if necessary. Nonprofit scholars describe this agility as being

> much like a navigator guiding a vessel on a long-term journey. Constantly sensing the shifting winds and currents and constantly adapting the course, the executives of successful organizations use the ideas and learning generated by their organization to fine-tune their strategies (Kaplan & Leonard, 2005, pp. 18–19)

It is one thing to espouse continuous improvement, but without action it is meaningless. Being nimble is something that not all schools, and especially those existing within a larger district bureaucracy and management system, can necessarily institute. However, the schools in this study are small and self-managed, which means they can make and implement decisions quickly. Indeed, when asked what practices they employed that were not replicable for traditional schools, a charter administrator responded:

> The nimble way that we're able to address issues. For example, our schedule, for a very long time, had been set at 8:25, one bell rings. . . . We decided in October that we needed to have the bell ring three minutes earlier because . . . we actually needed a quick passing period. *In one day* we made a decision as a leadership team, we re-did the bells, and we sent out an email saying that at 8:22 a bell would ring. It was so easy to do.

However nimble, each of these schools has a clear commitment to and a reverence for the school's mission. Stakeholders at Community Day, as well as at MATCH and the other schools, describe ways their schools have changed and while maintaining a focus on their founding missions. One administrator sums up the commitment to the mission while endorsing a nimble view of continuous improvement: "I think one of our great strengths is that we have been true to our mission and guided by our mission through all of the changes."

Coherence and Strategic Alignment in Schools

To a remarkable and impressive degree, the administrators, teachers, and parents in each of the five study schools coherently describe the mission of their particular school. How is this coherence achieved? Through clarity of purpose and through the mechanisms of choice.

These schools work hard to send clear messages about what to expect at their schools. From parents' nights to culture handbooks for teachers and summer sessions to introduce new faculty and students to the school's culture and value systems, nothing is left to chance. Critics might argue that these schools' laser-like focus on student outcomes is too narrow. Some legitimately point out that such a singular focus restricts students' free time and limits their choice of extracurricular activities. Others suggest that their theories of action are too instrumental and ignore children's social and emotional needs. As one critic declared during a case discussion of the KIPP charter schools, "They are stealing children's childhood!!" However, these schools do not entertain these concerns, as they are unequivocal in their goals for students and in their strategies for achieving them.

Achieving coherence in these schools is also possible because they are schools of choice. As discussed in the subsequent chapter, "The Right People," no student, family, or teacher is *required* to attend, support, or work in these schools. Students who attend these schools do so because they or their families want what these schools offer. Thus, as Oster (1995) observes, "A clear mission statement can limit struggle within an organization, both because it attracts people with similar ideas and because it makes clear the basis on which decisions will be made" (p. 23).

Finally, two other factors that contribute to the coherence around mission found in these schools include school size and policies around entry points for new students. These five schools are intentionally small. For example, in 2007-08, the Community Day student body totaled just over 330 in grades K–8, while MATCH had 220 students in grades 9–12, the Academy of the Pacific Rim enrolled 472 in grades 5–12, Boston Collegiate had 412 in grades 5–12, and Roxbury Prep weighed in with 187 students in grades 6–8. These populations are all below the mean size for comparable Massachusetts schools. For example, the average size of a K–8 school in Massachusetts is 429 students, while the average secondary school size is around 880 (National Center for Education Statistics, 2007). We know from extensive work by Lee and others (Lee & Ready, 2007; Lee & Smith, 1995; Lee, Smith, & Croninger, 1995) that small schools tend to be more coherent. Coherence is about creating a student community small enough so that each child is known well by the adults in the school and the children know each other.

Another factor that helps maintain cultural coherence derives from school policies that govern admissions. All of these schools prefer to admit students only at certain grade levels. For example, the Academy of the Pacific Rim will only enroll new students in their fifth and sixth grades; Roxbury Prep admits only new sixth graders (and no students in other grades) up until February 15 of each year. MATCH admits students only into the ninth grade, while Boston Collegiate admits new students throughout grades 5–8; their high school students must have attended Boston Collegiate's middle school. Community Day will admit new students in any of their K–8 grades, depending on various factors, including cohesion of the class, size of the class, and openings in other grades, but after the K–1 year, this rarely happens.

Restricting the grade level of admission is a key feature in maintaining cultural coherence. These schools admit students who are at the formative stages of learning about the school's culture. Even a ninth grader at MATCH is likely to attend more fully to cultural norms when older students are near. This practice helps both students and staff inculcate newcomers easily into the existing culture.

Lessons for Replication

Several lessons about culture and coherence presented in this chapter are important for those wishing to adopt or transfer similar elements to their charter and noncharter schools. Though it may already be evident to the reader, several practices of these charter schools will not easily transfer to traditional public schools because of the degree of school-site autonomy present in these schools. For example, depending on a district's organizational structure and size, having an intentionally small school or controlling points of entry may not be possible. Districts may not have the building capacity or enrollment patterns that allow for limited enrollment. Furthermore, the notion that a school could deny entry to a student in an upper grade would unlikely be acceptable in most district systems. On the other hand, several traditional districts, such as Boston's and New York's, are noticing the advantages of autonomy. Through their respective Pilot Schools and Empowerment Schools, these cities now recognize the advantages of giving greater autonomy to at least some of their schools.

The nimbleness to make changes quickly would be another characteristic of these schools that may not easily transfer to district schools because of the collateral impact of a change. In a larger district, for example, extending the required school day for tutoring could impact citywide bus schedules and union contracts. However, *within* the school building, acting nimbly to implement improvements fully endorsed by staff should not present problems.

Many other features about these schools related to culture, mission, and theories of action *are* within the reach of all school practitioners. Specifically, the notion that a mission is a vehicle to communicate the purpose of an organization is good management practice. Making efforts to ensure that the mission and purpose of a school are understood clearly by the entire organization is essential for any school, charter or noncharter. Unfortunately, such initiatives and discussions do not occur as frequently as they should. The creation or re-creation of mission statements can be an appropriate place to begin the process of defining a school's purpose, but the work does not stop there. Leaders, with their actions and words, communicate the mission and purpose of a school every day in every venue. Faculty meetings and community forums where all opinions about the purpose of the school are voiced and respected are also an ongoing requirement for a coherent culture. These conversations may not be easy, but they are essential to creating a shared culture. The bottom line is consistent and open communication.

Conclusion

Culture, that seemingly invisible yet enormously powerful influence on organizations, plays a large role in the success of these five schools. The energy generated by urgency, coupled with the high demands placed on stakeholders and a laser-like focus on mission, makes these schools intense yet enormously rewarding places to study and work. The importance of coherence across the schools, combined with the work ethic and a commitment to continuous improvement, produces strong student outcomes.

CHAPTER EIGHT

THE RIGHT PEOPLE

It's a winnowing process. A teaching job is posted, and hundreds of resumes and cover letters flood in. Perhaps ten candidates receive a phone interview, and maybe two make it through to the next stage. They're invited to the school for an on-site interview and possibly a tour. Then, if these candidates are teaching in the area, they are observed at their posts: maybe one makes it through this round, and then he or she comes back to teach a sample lesson. When the lesson is finished, there is feedback—feedback from teachers, feedback from administrators, feedback from students. The candidate leaves, and his or her strengths and weaknesses are debated—their teaching experience and content knowledge, their ability to relate to students, a willingness to take on long hours. And, finally, the most important question is considered: "Would they fit into the culture of the school?"

This question of "fit" is a routine question asked at the five charter schools in our study, a question not only asked of teaching candidates and potential administrators, but also considered by prospective students and their families. And it is an important one. Research supports the premise that "people decisions" are crucial to the success of an organization (Drucker, 1990). Business researcher James Collins (2005) includes these types of decisions in his "principle[s] of greatness": "Getting the Right People on the Bus within Social Sector Constraints." He explains: "*The* number-one resource for a great social sector organization is having enough of the right people willing to commit themselves to [the] mission" (pp. 16–17). Chapter 7 explains that a strong

The primary author for this chapter is Mara Casey Tieken.

guiding mission unites stakeholders (Nadler & Tushman, 1977, 1980); education researchers underscore the importance of mission-driven teachers and administrators within a school (Achievement First, 2008; Carter, 2000; Education Trust, 2005; KIPP Foundation, 2007; Purkey & Smith, 1985) and find that involved or supportive parents also promote effective schools (Bauch & Goldring, 1995; Henderson & Berla, 1994).

As shown in the Charter School Coherence Model (CSCM) in chapter 6, a clear mission helps produce the coherence among people and practices that these five charter schools exhibit. As a teacher at Community Day describes, "From everything everybody does, more so than any school I've taught at before, everybody here is on the same page." In this sense, then, it does "take a certain person," as an administrator notes, a certain person who has knowingly, willingly, and enthusiastically bought in to the school's mission. At Boston Collegiate, an administrator observes, "This is a school that . . . tries to be clear with all the stakeholders in terms of what we're about, what our mission is, what we're trying to do, what our expectations are." Through actions and decisions, words and beliefs, stakeholders implement this mission on a daily basis: a school leader may envision future professional development workshops or plan a trip to visit colleges; a teacher may give feedback on an assignment or hand out a demerit; a parent may sign a reading log or remember the stipulations of a home/school contract; and a student may finish a college essay or stay after school to attend a prep session for the Massachusetts Comprehensive Assessment System (MCAS).

Taken together, these studies and remarks suggest a key element of school effectiveness: an institution filled with people—leaders, teachers, students, and parents—who are deeply committed to their school's educational philosophy and operating procedures. These people are vital to the school's success, for they determine whether its mission will be fulfilled. While this factor—a deliberateness in making thoughtful "people decisions"—distinguishes these five schools, what is perhaps more interesting is that these schools do not always accomplish this objective in the same manner.

Leadership

Without a doubt, the leadership of an organization matters. So how do these schools choose their leaders? How are critical transitions at the top handled? These schools suggest a model that illustrates their deliberate approach to choosing their leaders, and, in turn, these leaders are deliberate in finding the "right" teachers and attracting the "right" families and students.

A Model of Leadership Succession

Research on charter school leaders is relatively scarce, with few empirical studies. Relatively recent research (Henig, Holyoke, Brown, & Lacireno-Paquet, 2005) examines the characteristics of people who found charter schools. They suggest that charters generally can be subdivided into "mission-oriented" and "market-oriented" categories, and that the leadership in each type is markedly distinct. Mission-oriented leadership resembles that of a nonprofit, while market-oriented leadership may have more common with Charter Management Organizations (CMOs) that are operated as for-profit businesses. Within the five schools in this study, the emphasis lands squarely on mission-oriented leadership.

Because a leader's primary responsibility is to support the mission of their organization (Drucker, 1990), it may seem obvious to argue that leadership stability—especially the continued presence of the founding leader(s)—is enormously important to a school. However, the literature is equivocal on the question of leadership stability. For example, one study of Pennsylvania charter schools concludes that leadership stability matters more than any other leadership characteristic and that stability is associated with higher math and reading test scores (Nelson & Miron, 2005). However, other leadership theorists, primarily those from the for-profit and nonprofit sectors, highlight the ossifying tendencies that stability can engender; for example, stability can stunt organizational growth (Churchill & Lewis, 1983; Terry, 1993). Still other studies have found that many charter schools have given little thought to leadership succession (Campbell, 2007).

The five charter schools in this study do not provide a clear answer to the question of leadership retention: turnover within leadership teams varies across these schools. At all of them, however, the founders tend to stay relatively present. The founding leaders at two of the schools still serve in key leadership positions years after the schools' inaugurations; a third school's current head joined the leadership ranks early in the school's life; and other founders currently sit on their school's governing or advisory board. At Community Day, where the founder has served as the executive director since the school's beginning, a teacher observes, "We wouldn't be where we are at all without [the executive director]. I think that we ... would have been really overwhelmed with MCAS. ... [The executive director] has been the driving force." According to this perspective, stability in the top position has allowed the school to keep pace with—and even stay ahead of—the standards and accountability movement; the director's vision, provided over thirteen years and through a number of changes in other leadership and teaching positions, has enabled the school to remain committed to success on the MCAS and to their standards-based philosophy.

Beyond the founding leaders, however, these schools vary in the stability of their leadership teams, especially in positions directly below the executive director. MATCH, for example, has had only two principals in eight years, while Community Day has employed, by one staff member's count, four different heads of the Lower School and six different Upper School heads in thirteen years. These various leaders all brought different leadership styles, different approaches to the relationship between teachers and the administration, and different personalities—differences with very real, and sometimes difficult, consequences for those employed at Community Day. Eventually "they finally hired within," as one teacher explains: "They took [as head] a fifth-grade teacher who had been around. . . . He was here for three years . . . and he gave us some stability."

While these five schools vary in the *amount* of leadership turnover, they do offer a consistent model for *how* leadership succession, if necessary, should occur. It is a model of "homegrown" leadership in which leaders emerge from the ranks of the schools' teachers. Because leaders face so many decisions and activities that call on them to enforce and shape the school's culture—hiring and firing staff members, developing new procedures, interacting with teachers and students and families, conducting school assemblies and staff meetings—it is particularly important for a leader to know intimately, and even to embody, the school's culture. This knowledge can come from having served the school in different capacities over a number of years.

Currently, all five schools employ teachers-turned-leaders, and most have several. Homegrown leaders, one MATCH administrator notes, "know the culture of the school . . . know the students," and, as an Academy of the Pacific Rim administrator explains, there is an advantage to "continuity, familiarity with culture, knowing our expectations." This knowledge allows for a smooth transition between teaching and leading, as one teacher-turned-leader observes: "[I] just changed chairs . . . and had more responsibility, obviously."

Another advantage to the process of homegrown leadership is that the possibility of moving into leadership positions attracts teachers to these schools. A Boston Collegiate administrator explains:

> Charter schools are quickly becoming known as schools where the transition between teacher and leader doesn't have to be this laborious process with a lot of red tape. So I think we are, as a charter school, attracting candidates who are interested in leadership.

The transition from teacher to leader is typically gradual and hands-on, characteristics that research finds make for a more effective changeover (Campbell, 2007). The progression from teacher to leader unfolds over years, as this Academy of the Pacific Rim leader describes:

> I've been at the school for eight years. I started off as a tutor and basically [filled] in whenever I could, then worked my way up to the sixth-grade history position, eventually became the team leader for the sixth-grade team. Then there was a position for the deanship in the high school . . . [and] I went for it, and I've been here ever since.

A Roxbury Prep administrator describes how individuals are groomed for leadership roles:

> So you know, [another current administrator] came here in the second year of the school, and I think [the school's founders] pretty quickly . . . figured out that he had the capacity for leadership and could be a good school leader, so they started giving him more responsibility. . . . Each department is facilitated by a department coach, each grade-level team is facilitated by a grade-level facilitator, and all of those people teach a full load and then take on these other duties, and we use that as training time, an indoctrinating time, so that when the time comes for new leadership, if you've worked very closely with the leadership of the school, you've shaped the leadership of the school.

It is through such purposeful mentoring that many of these schools develop specific teachers for leadership roles, thus ensuring smooth transitions when leaders leave the school and guaranteeing the continuity of the school's culture and functions.

However, internal hiring is not always a problem-free solution to finding strong leaders. Insiders can be perceived to have loyalties to particular staff members or a history of hostilities, and other internal candidates may harbor resentment, feeling overlooked or underappreciated (Hollander, 1978). Boston Collegiate is well aware of the potential tensions of hiring from within and takes steps to mitigate hurt feelings. An administrator explains:

> We've become more formal in terms of . . . advertising our positions to the staff within, so that there is not . . . the idea of there being certain people who are hand picked. . . . That feels like a very important step for the institution . . . in [making] an effort to be as transparent as possible about how these positions work. You want that person in the leadership position . . . to be seen by the staff as having achieved that position legitimately, and I think

that when there aren't many candidates from within, you need to look externally to have a healthy number of candidates.

Thus, a potential downside to homegrown administrators is that internal hiring can both limit the number of job candidates and cause resentment among others in the school. In addition, while internal hires may save precious time because there is no need for them to learn the organization's structures and systems, this approach to choosing leaders only works if the school is successful in meeting its current goals and wishes to preserve the same priorities. If the outcome measures or mission should change, leaders from the outside, with new ideas and approaches, may be preferred.

Clearly, a key factor in ensuring a mission-driven school's culture is for leaders to make careful and deliberate personnel decisions. As Collins (2005) notes, "Those who build great organizations make sure they have the right people on the bus, the wrong people off the bus, and the right people in the key seats. . . . They always think *first* about 'who' and then about 'what'" (p. 34). Given that a principal characteristic of the "right people" is their commitment to the mission (Collins, 2005), one of the most important jobs of charter school leaders is finding teachers who can do the everyday work of implementing the founding mission and then evolve into the next generation of school leadership. Accordingly, leaders approach the hiring, training, and even firing of teachers with careful attention and a deliberate strategy.

Teachers

With the school's mission stable and well defined, a leader's focus turns to those who will carry out this mission. Myriad papers, articles, and research document the importance of getting and keeping effective teachers in the education process (c.f. Darling-Hammond, Ancess, & Ort, 2002; Miles, 2001; Miles & Darling-Hammond, 1998; Murnane & Phillips, 1981; National Commission on Teaching and America's Future, 2003; Rockoff, 2004). It is not surprising, then, that many participants in this study believe that their school's accomplishments are due to their teachers. When asked about the source of their success, a principal at Boston Collegiate simply replied, "Teachers, teachers, teachers," while a Community Day administrator named "committed teachers" as a success factor. A Roxbury Prep administrator drives home the point:

> Hiring is the most important thing that [we] do. It's a huge, huge, huge luxury that cannot be overstated. . . . In my experience in a regular district

school, it's very unlikely that I would have a lot of power over who I could hire [and] certainly over whom I could let go. So that's a huge advantage . . . [that] we [can] spend a significant amount of time on the hiring process.

An administrator from MATCH similarly asserts that hiring is crucial "because a teacher who struggles here will really make or break the year. It has a huge impact on the students and on how the year goes. It's a very important decision that we make. . . . We don't want to just hire someone on the fly."

All five schools, without exception, focus on the teacher hiring process, although the nuances of the process, the details of induction procedures, the offer of retention incentives, and the frequency of firing differ among the schools. Once again, these schools have the same goal—"choosing the right people"— but they achieve this goal in different ways, which illustrate different values. Developing a complete understanding of these processes is important; as Robin Lake (2007) asserts, "To help charter schools improve and grow, we must learn more about how they can recruit and keep talented teachers" (p. 5).

Hiring: The Candidates and the Process

Across the five schools, recent hires look similar: they tend to be young, academically strong, and passionate—"a very idealistic, reform-minded, hardworking group," according to a Community Day administrator. However, within the hiring process, the different missions and priorities of the schools emerge. For example, Community Day emphasizes a candidate's commitment to standards-based accountability, asking questions like, "How do you feel about the MCAS? How do you feel about standards? Are you familiar with the Massachusetts standards?" At Roxbury Prep, administrators focus on candidates who have a "passion for their content," tying this passion to the school's mission of college preparation:

> We look for a few things. One is that teachers are experts in their content area, . . . [that] if they weren't here and they didn't want to teach, they would be working at a high level in their field. . . . Another important factor is that they've had some proven experience with an urban population. . . . So [we seek] urban experience and then someone who is passionate about the mission and completely committed to making sure kids are prepared for college.

Emphasizing a slightly different element of the effective teacher equation, the Academy of the Pacific Rim and Boston Collegiate seem to highlight a candidate's ability to form relationships with kids. Academy of the Pacific Rim looks for candidates who will "build relationships with our students." A Boston Collegiate administrator explains what they seek:

High school is a hard time and kids can get very sullen. They can get pretty apathetic, and when your mission is to get them prepared for college . . . they need to be surrounded by love at the school. . . . If they're not, then we're in big trouble, so I'm eager to meet as many candidates as I can that are going to love our students.

Ideal candidates must also dedicate their full youthful energy to the school. MATCH wants an enthusiastically devoted teacher who is

pretty much ready to sell their soul to the devil, who's not going to have any sort of private life at all—[or] a minimal one. Because when you come, you have to obviously devote yourself to at least twelve hours a day, and that doesn't include weekends. [We] want someone who is very young and has a lot of energy.

However, youthful passion by itself may not be sufficient—it must be youthful devotion *channeled toward a particular end,* devotion to the mission that inspires working long hours and giving dedicated service to the school. As a Roxbury Prep administrator states, "I'm looking for people who are willing to do whatever it takes." In sum, these schools want candidates who have a deep commitment to student success, who care about the students, and who are "passionate about the mission."

Indeed, the hiring standards are high, and some cases have increased over the years. As one administrator explains:

I think we're really harsh, and we need to be because what we demand once you're here is so challenging. It's exhausting and it's heartbreaking, and we have gone through so many teachers over the years that we're at the point where we want to make absolutely sure that the person coming in here, that this is the best place for them, and so that the fit is right.

This rigorous process, then, ensures that hires will immediately and exactly fit the school's culture. Any hesitancy about the mission can spell a short tenure at the school. As a Community Day teacher comments, "Some of the people that were kind of hesitant to buying into [the mission], those are the people that don't stay around very often."

Thus, clearly articulating the school's mission and goals is essential to the entire process. A recent Boston Collegiate hire, when asked whether the school's mission was mentioned during the hiring process, responded, "Oh yeah. I mean, it was told to me maybe a hundred times. In fact, in the interview they ask what kinds of things you could contribute to [the mission] or how you would see yourself fulfilling that, how do you feel about that. . . . So I felt that I got the mission articulated to me." A Roxbury Prep teacher noted similarly, "I definitely had a good sense of the mission [during the interview process]. The mission is very, very clear."

Induction and Mentoring

A teacher's induction begins during the hiring process, as a candidate hears the mission and expresses their commitment to it. Once a member of the faculty, a new hire attends summer meetings with administrators or returning teachers who introduce him or her to the school's particular systems and structures. For example, at Roxbury Prep, teachers participate in role-plays focused on appropriate disciplinary actions and work together to set the year's curriculum and lesson plans. Boston Collegiate's summer orientation is a two-week session of "major acculturation," during which teachers, school alumni, students, and department heads are "teaching them about the culture." New teachers at the Academy of the Pacific Rim and Boston Collegiate receive detailed notebooks—the *Red Books* at Boston Collegiate and the *Culture, Instruction, and Operations Guidebooks* at the Academy—that not only outline school policies but also offer detailed suggestions about teaching practices.

In addition to these summer sessions and guidebooks, Boston Collegiate, the Academy of the Pacific Rim, and Community Day also offer longer-term mentoring of new teachers, a process that reflects their beliefs about teacher development. An administrator at the Academy of the Pacific Rim notes why this mentoring is important: "Certainly some of the new folks are struggling here . . . [because their] experience isn't necessarily translating into success in this environment." At Community Day, the similar expectation is that

> brand new teachers aren't going to be really effective no matter where they come from. . . . It does take experience. . . . We're trying to understand about supporting teachers in their very early years and keeping them with us a bit longer, but also giving them the kind of help they need so they don't become discouraged.

The formality of the mentoring programs at these three schools varies to some degree, both within and across schools. At Boston Collegiate, for example, the mentoring relationship is typically "a pretty informal relationship," although it can be more intensive—"more like a cooperating teacher relationship," says one teacher—if the new teacher is also new to teaching. Academy of the Pacific Rim's mentoring program consists of weekly meetings between the new teacher and his or her mentor:

> Every new teacher at [the Academy of the Pacific Rim] has a mentor who they can meet with once a week. [The mentors are] either in your department or in your grade level, depending on your content experience: if you're switching from third grade to sixth grade, we'll probably put you with a sixth-grade teacher. . . . But if you're new to teaching, we tend to put you with your department chair.

Even though Community Day uses a coteaching model in all kindergarten through sixth-grade classrooms, new teachers also are paired with another mentor from a different classroom. This mentoring program also recently increased from a one-year to a two-year program—a move suggesting growing attention to teacher retention.

MATCH and Roxbury Prep do not have formal mentoring programs per se, although at Roxbury Prep, new hires can get assistance from Friday inquiry groups and through close contact with department heads and frequent observations by administrators. At MATCH, tutor support occurs as a by-product of their intense living accommodations and close supervision. Thus, the support for new teachers occurs at all of the schools, but the structure, formality, and intensity varies.

Teacher Attrition

The emphasis on teacher hiring and support highlights another issue shared by these five schools, as well as other charter and traditional public schools nationwide: the dilemma of teacher turnover. At the national level, statistics about new teachers suggest that 30 percent leave within three years and nearly 50 percent leave within five years (Darling-Hammond, 2004; Ingersoll, 2001, 2002, 2004; Smith & Ingersoll, 2004). Most charter schools, including these five, employ teachers on a yearly contract; their teachers are not granted tenure, which typically is given to traditional public school teachers after three years of successful employment. Thus, charter school leaders have the opportunity to consider every year whether to rehire a teacher. This year-to-year arrangement enables schools to reshuffle their staff without the restrictions often imposed by union contracts in traditional schools.

As figure 1 reveals, annual turnover rates at these five schools ranged between 8 percent and 30 percent from 2004 to 2007, with a high of 46 percent for MATCH's 2005-06 school year.[1]

FIGURE 8.1 Annual Teacher Attrition Rates in Years 2004-05, 2005-06, and 2006-07

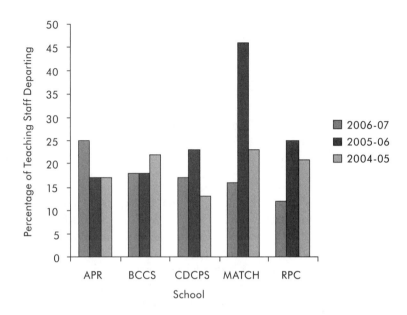

The implications of these statistics are not clear. Lake (2007), in her recent comprehensive review of charters, states, "We also do not know whether charter school turnover rates are high compared to schools serving similar populations or, for that matter, whether high turnover rates are actually a problem for charter schools" (p. 5). However, as Miron and Applegate (2007) assert:

> Such extensive attrition [of new teachers] cannot be characterized as desirable. High attrition consumes resources of schools that must regularly provide pre- and in-service training to new teachers; it impedes schools' efforts to build professional learning communities and positive and stable school cultures; and it is likely to undermine the legitimacy of the schools in the eyes of parents. (p. 2)

For a general comparison, in the Boston Public Schools, the estimated three-year teacher attrition rate is around 47 percent (Birkeland & Curtis, 2006), while the national charter school attrition rates are "between 20 and 25 percent [each year]; for new teachers, however, the attrition rate is close to 40 percent annually" (Miron & Applegate, 2007, p. 2).

Whether a teacher voluntarily decides to leave a school or an administrator deliberately chooses not to renew a teacher's contract, the literature shows that high teacher turnover can disrupt school cohesion and impair performance (Ingersoll, 2004). Clearly, attrition can cost a small, cohesive charter school dearly.

Although average turnover rates across the five study schools are relatively similar, these schools approach the issue of teacher turnover and retention differently. Administrators at Roxbury Prep and MATCH indicate that teacher turnover is not necessarily a problem they feel the need to remedy. One administrator at Roxbury Prep notes that even though they may wish that effective teachers stayed longer, there is an expectation that some teachers will leave within a couple of years:

> [Do I wish that] everyone who's good, everyone who came and it worked out and was very effective, stayed for five to seven years? Sure, the school would be stronger. But when I interview, I think about what's going to be best for kids next year. There are plenty of people that are on the hallway now that I interviewed that I didn't think, either for personal or professional reasons, would stay beyond a year or two. . . . Some of them . . . have just defied my expectation and are still here. And others were great for [the] kids for the year or two and then decided they wanted to go to grad school, and ultimately, it's a fine exchange.

Instead of worrying excessively about attrition, Roxbury Prep accommodates turnover with carefully documented and easily accessible curricula and veteran teachers placed in key positions.

MATCH also views turnover as a trade-off they are willing to make. They accept the fact that the talented, hard-working recent college graduates they hire may not be looking for a career-long job—longevity is exchanged for youthful energy. And when staff members begin getting married or having families, MATCH administrators acknowledge that balancing personal and professional demands can cause a teacher to leave: "We lose teachers every year, when teaching staff have children or they get married—especially when they have children, it seems to be really challenging trying to balance both here. But we lose a few teachers every year . . . this just isn't the environment for them."

In contrast, the Academy of the Pacific Rim and Boston Collegiate seem to prioritize retention by actively working to keep teachers. An administrator at Boston Collegiate explains:

I think the perception is that charter school work is harder and that there's more asked of teachers. And there is. But I think that one of the things that we're interested in is finding a balance for our staff so that we can be sustainable and replicable. If you can't work here and also have a family and manage your life and grow in a career, we're failing as a school. If we're just turning people over who are young and allowing them to leave as soon as they get married and have families, that's not acceptable and that's not the school we want to be.

At the Academy of the Pacific Rim, the cost of a teacher's departure is felt throughout the school: "Culturally it's devastating for students when teachers leave [because] it's such a small school, it's such a close-knit community." Even leaving after three years can be too soon in the opinion of one Boston Collegiate administrator: "We don't want to be cycling through teachers every three years. There is something lost in the school culture, in the quality of the curriculum, when you are constantly bringing in new teachers and losing old [ones]."

To address the retention issue, Boston Collegiate has established a Teacher Retention Committee that meets on a regular basis to discuss these concerns. Community Day, Boston Collegiate, and the Academy of the Pacific Rim also use incentive programs, including financial bonuses and leave for graduate study. Academy of the Pacific Rim, for example, offers a performance-based pay system that gives a bonus of $2,000 to $4,000; a portion of this bonus reflects individual incentives linked to indicators like attendance and collaborative effort, as well as a schoolwide component tied to MCAS scores. As an administrator noted, "We try to reward high-quality teachers through our performance-based salaries." Boston Collegiate ties financial incentives more explicitly to longevity. Teachers receive a $1,000 bonus as they enter their third year, $2,000 at the beginning of their fifth year, and $3,000 every two years thereafter. The Community Day administration does not use financial bonuses, but they find other ways to encourage teachers to stay, like paying for a teacher to attend graduate school at night or allowing a teacher to take a sabbatical to explore personal interests. Furthermore, this school links its two-year mentoring program to retaining teachers, noting that "it hurts when you have them for a year, you get them up to speed [and] doing well for you, and then they go someplace else. . . . One year doesn't do it. You still have to mentor and follow along and continue their growth."

All of the sample schools, however, will dismiss a teacher if their performance is subpar: no matter how rigorous the hiring (and mentoring) process, sometimes the system fails and a recent hire proves inadequate. Indeed, as important as it is to have "the right people on the bus," it is just as necessary to get "the wrong people off the bus" (Collins, 2005, p. 14). The decision to replace a teacher is not taken lightly, however, and, one Academy of the Pacific Rim administrator notes that "there's due process," even if not required by a union. Expressing a slightly different view, one of the Roxbury Prep codirectors comments:

> All of our contracts are at will, and the organization as a whole is committed to making sure it's working. And it doesn't happen often, but there are times where we've just made the wrong hire. . . . You know, we do everything we can, but we aren't shy about things if it isn't working for us.

Some administrators indicate that they have become more comfortable with letting teachers go as their schools have matured. Boston Collegiate, for example, has "gotten stronger and more confident in who we are as the years have gone by, and better able to assess whether the shortcomings are critical enough that the person shouldn't be at this school." The motivation for action as drastic as firing is clear: "We'd sacrifice a teacher before a student if the students aren't learning."

Clearly, the practices of hiring, mentoring, induction, and firing are jointly involved in the goal of getting the best possible teachers in the classrooms with the children. All of the schools want to get the right people; however, important differences exist in the approaches taken by these five schools. MATCH and Roxbury Prep seem to have adopted a philosophy of hiring that prioritizes a perfect match between a potential hire and the school, an ideal teacher who, at the moment of hiring, meets all qualifications that promise success at that school. As a MATCH tutor describes, candidates "have to have the *exact same* goal and the *exact same* drive with students"—a level of exactitude that requires an intensive hiring process that is, according to one Roxbury Prep teacher, "pretty scary and pretty intense . . . and [which] showed me they weren't just going to take anyone off the street." Therefore, these two schools have less need for a formal mentoring program, perhaps due to the candidates' immediate ability to fit. Retention issues also receive less formal attention, as teacher turnover is tolerated. The other three schools—Community Day, Academy of the Pacific Rim, and Boston Collegiate—take a different strategy. Like the administrator at Boston Collegiate who emphasizes that they look for "great people, not great teachers," these schools invest more resources into training teachers to become ideal teachers.

However, it is important to note that, regardless of which approach the schools take, their turnover rates are not that disparate, suggesting, perhaps, that differing philosophies can yield similar results. No matter how these schools approach getting the right people, the process involves a complicated mix of hiring, induction, mentoring, retention, and firing practices—practices executed deliberately for the purpose of ensuring that the school's teaching ranks are filled with people who are willing, and able, to fulfill the school's mission.

Students and Families

A good fit between the school and administrators and teachers is not all that matters at these schools; they also work hard to establish a good fit between the school, the students, and their families. These schools approach the processes of attracting and preparing students and families with the same deliberate consideration they give to teacher hiring practices and the development of teachers and leaders. This attention parallels the teacher hiring process, in that getting the right people is dependent on both the recruitment process that matches a family with a school and the development process that occurs once a family has been accepted. The application and lottery promote an initial fit between school and family, while school structures ensure a family's continued cooperation and buy-in.

Just as with administrators and teachers, the power and influence of choice are important to families. Charter schools *are* schools of choice—all require that families choose to have their children attend. Bosetti (2001), for example, stresses the influence of this choice in her study of charter schools in Alberta, Canada:

> Parents select schools which reflect their own values and meet the learning needs of their children. . . . [Charter schools'] mandates, explicitly defined in their charter, help to define the choices available to parents. . . . The ultimate goal of choice is to provide the best fit between the educational process and the needs of the learner (Boyer, 1994). With charter schools, parents . . . determine the best fit between educational programs and their children's learning needs. (p. 102)

Similarly, Lubienski and Lubienski (2006), in a study using data from the National Assessment of Education Progress to assess traditional public, charter, and private school performance, comment on the power of parental choice:

In private and charter school sectors, parents are positioned to select a school based on academic quality, and to choose another if their school fails to meet expectations. . . . Additionally, private and charter school parents, through the act of choosing, demonstrate a commitment to their children's education—a characteristic that goes beyond typical SES [socioeconomic status] measures and is associated with higher student achievement. (p. 7)

If too many students choose the same school, administrators use a random lottery to select the incoming class. While by law this lottery procedure does not permit schools to handpick their students, the process promotes buy-in from parents and students, as parents must know about a charter school, decide to enter the lottery, complete the necessary paperwork, and then participate in the lottery process.

This level of choice can have academic returns. As a Community Day teacher explains, "So you have parents that are more interested, which research tells you [means] their kids are going to do better because parents are interested." Indeed, this theory has a lot of research support. Several comprehensive studies document the positive influence of parental involvement on student achievement (Bauch & Goldring, 1995; Bryk, Lee, & Smith, 1990; Henderson & Berla, 1994). Parents who are "active choosers" deliberately select a school based on its reputation and mission and a perceived set of shared values; this choice represents a commitment to these beliefs, a commitment that engenders greater participation and, so the theory goes, heightened student achievement.

For charter schools, then, it is crucial that potential students and families are aware of the school's mission, for this knowledge begins a positive cycle of commitment, participation, and achievement. A Roxbury Prep administrator explains:

The kids who have the most success here are not the kids who had the best grades [before coming here]. The kids who are most successful are the kids for whom the families, the teachers, and the administration are all working together and doing whatever it takes. . . . If the kid doesn't buy in and the family doesn't buy in, then it usually doesn't happen.

An administrator at Community Day corroborates the importance of parental investment: "It's about parent buy-in, because if a parent is going through the time and the effort to fill out the application, to meet due dates, they know about us. . . . They have bought in."

Word of mouth and public announcements broadcast a school's mission, and all of our schools publicize in a number of venues, including newspapers, local middle schools, and well-trafficked community sites. At this initial stage, a school's reputation can also go a long way to ensure that the families applying to the school are aware and supportive of the school's mission. Boston Collegiate, for example, has a strong reputation as a college-preparatory school, so families hoping to send their children to college may be more likely to enter that lottery. In fact, Boston Collegiate even changed its name to communicate their college focus more clearly. And it has worked: a recent parent survey confirmed that the school's college-preparatory focus is one of the leading reasons why parents choose Boston Collegiate.

Achieving Family and Student Buy-In

Once the euphoria of "winning the lottery" has passed, the shared responsibilities of schools and parents begin in earnest: ongoing family support is critical to the operation of these schools. In many cases, parents and guardians will be responsible for transporting a student to and from school, often at very early or very late hours; for ensuring that lengthy homework assignments are completed and done well; for attending conferences and school events and engaging in consistent communication with teachers. Indeed, some of our schools view the relationship with parents as a crucial partnership. MATCH describes a relationship "tripod," in which teachers, parents, and tutors jointly support a student. These tutors, as an administrator notes,

> make our kids' ties to the school stronger by building a relationship with them and pushing them. And also they're the bridge to our parents. . . . They need to call [the parents] once a week, minimum. And they're the ones who have the relationships with the parents and the kids. . . . They're like little bridge-makers, really. The ways in which their work connects each student in the school to a caring adult are as critical as the academic content support.

At Community Day, the relationship between parent and teacher is strongly emphasized. A parent describes the relationship: "It's a partnership [in which] the teachers have made a commitment and the parents have made a commitment. . . . It's really a partnership [in which] they made a commitment towards the children, and the parents have made a commitment towards the teachers." This mutual and explicit commitment to other stakeholders ensures accountability, as each is willing and able to enact their responsibilities on behalf of the students' education.

Schools use a number of mechanisms to ensure parental cooperation. Starting with extensive and frequent communication between home and school in the form of routine phone calls, the reach of the school into the home is extended through regular newsletters, emails from teachers, and clearly communicated learning goals.

Some schools use even more explicit strategies to get families to participate from the moment of entry, including providing detailed family information sessions, holding interviews with prospective parents, and using contracts that outline parental responsibilities: As a Roxbury Prep administrator notes, "You may agree or disagree with the way that we do things, but we're going to be really clear about it and that just is who we are." Community Day administrators interview incoming families before accepting students in order to communicate their expectations of parents' commitment to the school. One administrator explains:

> I'll actually do an interview with the parent and the student as we're looking . . . at the top five in the lottery. And [we] talk to them about expectations, saying, "We expect [that] . . . you'll partner with us. You're here and you come in, you attend meetings. If you can, you come to one PAB [Parent Advisory Board meeting]. If you can, participate in a field trip." We want parents to be able to be involved, and we try to educate them on ways that they can be involved.

Thus, when students finally enter Community Day, their families are well versed in their responsibilities. Boston Collegiate is currently entertaining the idea of conducting small group sessions with an administrator and a few parents and students who have been accepted in order to introduce families to the school, its culture, and its basic expectations. These kinds of policies may, in fact, serve a dual purpose: they provide information for parents and students and also set a norm of involvement.

Roxbury Prep, Boston Collegiate, MATCH, and the Academy of the Pacific Rim all have family contracts that specify the particular actions a family must take to uphold its responsibilities. For example, Boston Collegiate uses a "Family Accountability Contract" that families must sign to secure enrollment. The contract reads:

> This Family Accountability Contract describes important responsibilities and school expectations that families accept once they choose to enroll at this school. . . . We know that the choice you made in coming here is a precious one and we want to make sure that you have a full and clear understanding of your responsibilities.

While Community Day does not have a formal contract describing a family's obligations to support the school's mission, each report card describes a student's personal education goals (PEGs), which are based on a student's target test score for the year. The PEG lists the steps the teacher, student, and parents will take to ensure that these goals are fulfilled, and the document is signed by the teacher, student, and parents as an indication of their commitment to these steps.

The schools also deliberately work to ensure that students fit the school, using summer orientation sessions and student handbooks to introduce students to school norms and policies. During the five-week MATCH Summer Academy, students attend a "culture class" to learn the school's Code of Conduct and the expectations of the school. The MATCH Code of Conduct is explicit:

> MATCH may not be the right fit for every student. No school is perfect for each individual. We are a "choice" school: parents and students choose to enter our lottery, and for that we are humbled and grateful. To honor our commitment to provide an environment where all students can and will learn, continued or serious misbehavior by a student means that MATCH is not the right fit for that particular student.

Should a student miss more than two days of Summer Academy or fail to meet MATCH's behavioral or academic expectations, the student will be replaced with the next student on the waiting list. MATCH, then, is very clear that fit requires work and commitment on the part of students and families, and they only want those students who are "the right fit."

Finally, it is also important to note that, just as these students and families buy-in to these schools and their missions, they also have the option of "buying-out," that is, of transferring to their regularly assigned public school. It's a take-it-or-leave-it situation: students and families are "active choosers," but buy-in is required. Whether this buy-in is developed through clear communication and family-school relationships or mandated by contracts and consequences, the buying-out option helps to ensure that only the most committed families and students remain.

Lessons for Replication

As mission-driven schools filled with students and teachers who choose to attend and work in them, these five charter schools take advantage of choice in a way that many traditional schools cannot. District personnel agreements, student assignment policies, and staff tenure practices can often limit the flexibility of regular public schools. However, there are some lessons from these five charters that even traditional schools operating under these constraints can adopt.

Take hiring, for example. Traditional schools could address an often limited hiring pool by making their application procedures more efficient and effective, thereby enabling more candidates to apply and be reviewed. Schools could also broaden their hiring criteria to focus on finding "great people," again expanding the pool. Furthermore, during the hiring process, other staff members should be involved to provide input and feedback, and making the mission of the school explicit to candidates should be a priority.

Many traditional schools already employ mentoring programs for new teachers, and these programs could be expanded to focus simultaneously on the development of homegrown leaders. By purposefully placing long-serving teachers in these mentoring relationships, new teachers would learn the school's philosophies and practices from veterans well versed in its culture, and some of these veteran teachers may eventually aspire to other leadership positions. Such purposeful placements would establish a means to develop internal leadership—a practice crucial to effective schools. Traditional schools could also work to develop other leadership skills, skills cultivated by communication with community stakeholders or by the creation and execution of professional development programs. Broadening and expanding the teachers' roles to include leadership responsibilities can be a powerful force for creating a strong, engaged faculty. Then, as leadership positions open, there may be a number of potential internal hires with extensive school knowledge.

Finally, even within traditional districts, schools could develop and manage a reputation built on their mission. This reputation could attract potential students from across the district in areas where crossing enrollment zones is permitted. Schools could promote buy-in among incoming students and families through explicit information sessions, during which schools and families would enter into voluntary partnerships to support the education of students. Consistent home-school communication should accompany such agreements so that all stakeholders can be aware of and fulfill their responsibilities.

Conclusion

It is a simple principle—the success of an organization depends on the people within that organization—and these five charter schools deliberately and carefully manage the process of getting the right people. Each school has its own

distinct approach, a unique mixture of screening, hiring, developing, and letting go, and while the processes are not all the same, they share the same goal:
ensuring that they have the most dedicated and informed leaders, teachers,
students, and families. A good match between student and school, between
family and educational program, helps make charter schools a viable educational opportunity for those who choose them. "It takes a certain person," and
these schools are deliberate in their quest to find these people.

CHAPTER NINE

STRUCTURES AND SYSTEMS

Getting Organized for Instruction

Bells ring. Lines form. Up this staircase, down that one. Homework goes here, backpacks over there. Lunch is served at 12 past 12. If you want to see your counselor, fill out a pink sheet in the guidance office and deposit it in the box on the nurse's desk; your counselor will send a referral slip when she's ready to see you. Ah, the familiar rhythm of *your school*. All around the world, at all minutes of the day, school folks chug along in accordance with the intricate series of structures and systems known only to the people inside each school. Visitors to unfamiliar schools feel as though they've stepped into the inner workings of a machine—wheels turn, levers lift, and pulleys pull. People travel in purposeful directions. Designated players fulfill discrete roles. Papers transmit critical messages: who's where, who's missing, and who's misbehaving. Despite differing locations, building configurations, and individual personalities, the structures and systems that organize the work of schools are remarkably similar.

Many of the commonly recognized structures and systems found in most U.S. schools—the parts of the building, the routines for traveling through the hallways, the tools for keeping records—are also found in the five charter schools described in this book. Yet, there is something remarkably effective about the ways these five schools organize their work that warrants the attention of those who want to understand their success. It's not just that they are organized to get things done. Many schools are. But for these schools, carefully

The primary authors for this chapter are Kristy Cooper and Chris Wynne.

constructed and minutely detailed plans for allocating people and time and for facilitating instructional accountability enable them to aggressively pursue, and ultimately reach, their internal goals (Elmore, 1995, 2004). Armed with a workforce dedicated to their mission, each of these schools works from the premise that achieving the mission requires structures that organize people and time in ways that allow teachers to focus on instruction and monitor the progress of every child. They further believe that equipping students to meet academic expectations requires systems that hold teachers accountable to school leaders and that hold students accountable to teachers. This chapter provides a detailed look at how such purposeful structures and systems enable these high-performing charters to meet student achievement objectives.

Structures

Who is responsible for what? Who reports to whom? How long does each class run? Where should everyone be on Friday at 10:30 AM? All schools rely on basic internal structures. The 7-S model of organizational alignment, introduced in chapter 6, defines structure as "the way in which tasks and people are specialized and divided and authority is distributed" (Bradach, 1996, p. 3). As organizations, schools divide and distribute tasks and people in two key ways: by organizing people—both adults and students—into a hierarchy of roles and reporting structures and by organizing time into distinct segments with functional purposes for each block. In these five schools, purposeful planning of these structural features enables leaders and teachers to focus their efforts on intended outcomes.

Putting People in Their Places

Along with ultimate missions of college success or personal development for their students, these schools also identify short-term or intermediate goals, such as raising standardized test scores or strengthening writing skills, which, in turn, serve their missions. These schools are organized to meet immediate goals by allocating people to focus on teaching each student every day. This is done first by identifying leaders to improve and maintain instructional quality throughout the school, and second, by appointing particular individuals to oversee small groups of students to prevent any student from falling through the cracks of disservice and inattention. Structuring these priorities into the fabric of the institution's organizational scheme increases the likelihood of these schools meeting short-term goals.

The allocation of particular administrators to positions of instructional leadership, as practiced within these schools, aligns with theory on effective school structuring. The PELP Coherence Framework (Childress, Elmore, Grossman, & King, 2007) notes that structure includes "how people are organized, who has responsibility and accountability for results, and who makes or influences decisions." In traditional schools, the distribution of labor typically consists of an administrative team—a principal, assistant principals, and office support staff—that handles school management, while an instructional team—teachers, learning specialists, teaching assistants—performs the organization's central task of educating students. Organizational theorists have decried this model because it fails to coordinate instruction across classrooms within a given school (Meyer & Rowan, 1978). Certainly, if a principal is preoccupied with bureaucratic organizational management, then teachers will determine individual classroom operations and practices from room-to-room will vary greatly. Theorists describe such schools as "loosely coupled" organizations in which teachers work in isolation under a "logic of confidence" that they will meet students' needs if simply left alone to work as professionals (March & Olson, 1976; Weick, 1976, cited in Meyer & Rowan, 1978). This loose coupling, theorists contend, results from a lack of inspection of both teaching and student output and ultimately creates disjointed schools in which no one has authority over instructional improvement or quality (Elmore, 2004; Meyer & Rowan, 1978; Miles & Frank, 2008). Recent standards-based reforms and standardized tests attempt to address this lack of direction and information about classroom practice.

Elmore (2004) declares, however, that little has changed since the inception of standards-based reform in the late 1990s. He blames a prevailing reverence for teacher autonomy and an educational structure that impedes instructional leadership:

> The educational change literature is full of injunctions to respect the autonomy of teaching and the mystery of its fundamental practices—hence the inviolability of individual teachers' choices about what to teach and how. This normative environment is a direct result of an institutional structure that is deliberately and calculatedly incompetent at influencing its core functions. (pp. 47–48)

As a solution, Elmore argues for instructional leadership, "the holy grail in educational administration" (p. 48). He asserts that unless administrators structure their work to have an impact on teaching, instructional practice will continue to vary widely and reforms will rely solely on teacher volunteer-ism. Not surprisingly, then, within these five high-performing schools, a core source of effectiveness is the existence of one or several roles devoted primar-ily to instructional leadership.

The organizational charts of these schools reveal the purposeful positioning of instructional leaders. For example, figure 1 shows the organization of Com-munity Day, with shaded boxes to indicate instructional leadership positions. At Community Day, each school division has its own instructional leader—the school head—and a fourth instructional leader oversees the special needs department. The actual systems by which such leaders manage instruction ap-pear later in this chapter, but the organizational charts of all five schools re-veal structures that provide for instructional leadership and also demonstrate the willingness of these organizations to explicitly devote people and money to instruction.

Of course, instructional leaders could not focus on instruction if managing basic operations bogged down their days. Thus, structures for executive-level leaders to handle overall school management—for example, the executive di-rector at Community Day—enable the instructional leaders to focus on what happens inside classrooms. Certainly, some executive administrators in these schools also play a role in deciding instructional issues, but because the execu-tives "clear the crud" of school management through structured differentiation of roles, those with instructional responsibility have considerable time and en-ergy to address issues related to instruction.

In addition to organizing leadership roles to create an instructional focus, these schools have structures that allocate particular adults to monitor indi-vidual students and help them form connections with adults. American sec-ondary schools have long been criticized for letting students "fall through the cracks" as they proceed through school anonymously, often as a result of at-tending large schools where adults cannot address students' individual needs or make meaningful connections with them (Eccles et al., 1993; Fine, 1991; Lee & Ready, 2007; Valenzuela, 1999). Furthermore, research on motivation asserts that when students feel cared about by others and experience a sense of belonging in the school community, they enjoy school more, have fewer behavior problems, participate more in school, and have higher academic achievement (Connell, 1990; Osterman, 2000). Already helped by their small size, these schools go a step further by structuring adult responsibility for in-dividual students and relationships between adults and students into the foun-dation of the organization.

FIGURE 9.1 Organizational Chart for Community Day Charter Public School

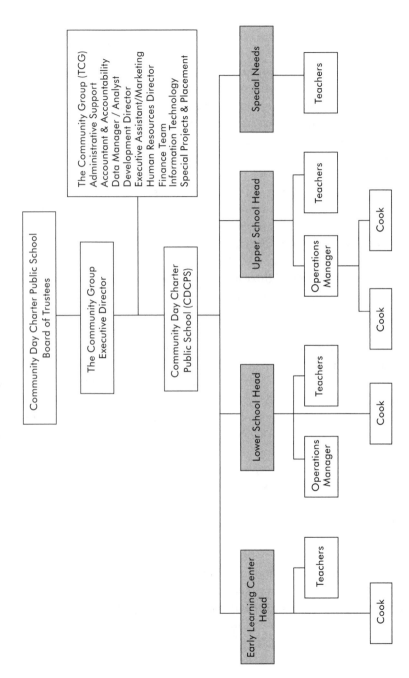

The structures that create responsibility and relationships vary across the five schools, but all include assigning small groups of students to particular adults. At Boston Collegiate, Roxbury Prep, and the Academy of the Pacific Rim, students participate in advisories, which are small groups of ten to twenty students assigned to a particular adult on campus—their advisor—with whom they meet regularly as a group. Depending on the school, advisors are either all teachers or a mix of teachers and administrators. The frequency of meetings varies, occurring once or twice a week for forty minutes at the Academy of the Pacific Rim, three times a day from between ten and thirty minutes at Boston Collegiate, and three times a day from between eight and twenty-five minutes at Roxbury Prep, which also provides a period-long advisory lesson each Friday. The exact nature of the advisory systems for monitoring academic progress, building relationships with and among students, and communicating with families varies by school (see chapters 3 and 4 for descriptions of advisory systems at Boston Collegiate and Academy of the Pacific Rim, respectively). However, all three of these schools give high priority to providing individual student attention. At MATCH, tutors serve a role similar to that of teacher-advisors at the other secondary schools, working with the same small groups of students each day throughout the school year. In addition to forming personal bonds with students, tutors take responsibility for monitoring student progress and communicating with parents. Tutors also alert school administrators to concerns about particular students, as detailed in chapter 5 on MATCH and later in this chapter.

In grades K–6 at Community Day, students spend the day in self-contained classrooms, a common practice in elementary schools. However, all teachers in grades K–6 at Community Day work in pairs as coteachers so that all students spend their entire day with two teachers, both of whom take responsibility for overseeing their students. In grades 7–8, students remain together as a cohort and travel between four teachers for various subjects. In this case, the teachers work collaboratively to ensure that they meet each student's academic needs and attend to each child's well-being.

Clearly, these high-performing charters do not operate under structures that assign leaders and students in the most common or conventional ways. In fact, these structures are expensive in terms of salaries, time, and opportunity costs. Yet, strategic decisions for organizing people focus on meeting instructional goals and serving individual students in the pursuit of ambitious student outcomes.

TABLE 9.1

Length and Number of School Days and Total Number of School Hours for Students in the Five Charter Schools and Boston Public Schools*

	Starting time of regular school day	Ending time of regular school day	Number of school days	Approximate number of hours for students during school year
APR	7:45 am	3:05 pm	190	1,393
BCCS	8:00 am	3:00 pm	190	1,330
CDCPS	8:00 am	4:00 pm	183	1,464
MATCH	8:30 am	5:00 pm	185	1,572
RPC	7:45 am	4:15 pm	181	1,432
Prototypical BPS elementary school	8:30 am	2:30 pm	180	1,080
Prototypical BPS middle school	7:20 am	1:30 pm	180	1,080
Prototypical BPS high school	7:45 am	2:30 pm	180	1,080

*In the Boston Public Schools, actual start and finish times vary across the district for elementary, middle, and high schools, but the number of in-school hours reflect the prototypical schedules noted here.

Making Every Minute Count

Allocating time in schools is more than just logistics. It is a philosophical and pedagogic decision and an investment of a critical resource. Unlike considerations for structuring people, where hiring can expand the reservoir of human resources, schools have a finite amount of time, the allocation of which involves weighing alternatives and accepting trade-offs. For all schools, decisions regarding the distribution of time to various activities impact the school's ability to create an effective, productive, and focused learning environment. When schools make these decisions strategically, as these five charter schools have, the rationing of time becomes central to meeting the mission and maximizing outcomes (Elmore, 1995). Important strategies used in structuring time include maximizing the number of instructional hours and allocating those hours among content areas to emphasize instructional priorities.

All the schools in this study have an extended school day and extended school year. As a result, their students spend many more hours at school than do their peers in traditional public schools (see table 1). For example, at Boston Collegiate, the 2007–08 school year ran from August 27 to June 27 and consisted of 190 school days that were seven hours long, giving students approximately 1,330 hours at the school. These are approximate numbers and do not take into account the school's early release days or the amount of time students may spend in tutoring or homework sessions, which run for an additional hour or two at the end of the seven-hour school day and on some Saturdays. In comparison, in the Boston Public Schools, the school day is approximately six hours long and the 2007–08 school year consisted of 180 school days, giving students approximately 1,080 hours at school. Thus, counting only regular school-day hours, the school year for students at Boston Collegiate is approximately 250 hours, or 23.1 percent, longer than the school year for students in the Boston Public Schools. Clearly, attending one of these charter schools requires an extraordinary time commitment from students and families.

Within the actual hours at the school site, the Commonwealth of Massachusetts requires 990 hours of structured learning time for all secondary students and 900 hours for elementary students. "Structured learning time" means time when the students are actually in class and does not include passing time or lunch or other nonacademic activities (Massachusetts Department of Education, 1997). While measures of structured learning times at these charter schools and across the Boston Public Schools are difficult to obtain, it seems clear that charter school students also have access to more structured learning time than their counterparts in traditional Boston public schools.

Some observers might question the long days, worrying about the trade-offs to arriving early in the morning and staying late into the evening. Personnel at these schools are conscious that students make extensive time commitments, and despite the intense focus on academic work, some of the schools offer extracurricular activities late in the day. At Roxbury Prep, for example, enrichment programs include percussion, guitar, musical theater, fitness, hip-hop, and politics, while at Boston Collegiate students can participate in clubs and activities organized around skiing, role-playing, drama, student government, basketball, and baseball, among others. Despite these few extracurricular offerings, there is no question that time—a most precious resource—is primarily allocated to academic goals.

Having maximized the amount of time students spend in school, these charters then purposefully allocate that time to various classes and activities throughout the day and week, often tweaking schedules and calendars each year to reflect updated priorities and initiatives. Figure 9.2 shows the 2006–07 middle school schedule at the Academy of the Pacific Rim (before adding the fifth grade and dividing sixth-grade math into Math Foundations and Math Applications). The schedule is an intricate, detailed matrix of time, differing by day of the week and grade level. Note first the various purposes of homeroom, which serves alternately as an actual homeroom, an advisory, and Providing Opportunities with Everyday Reading, or POWER, a silent reading period. Moreover, in the sixth grade, all class periods do not start and end at the same time. For example, in homerooms 1 and 2, first period ends at 9:30, while in homeroom 3, first period ends at 9:15. Language arts and math receive more instructional time (an hour and 15 minutes each) than reading, history, and science (45 minutes each). Also note that in the seventh grade, Chinese instruction occurs three times a week, making way for an extra hour of math or English twice a week. Finally, physical education and performing or visual arts share a time slot, with students receiving instruction in these subjects on alternate days. Clearly, this schedule reveals the school's instructional priorities and beliefs about what matters most.

MATCH similarly demonstrates instructional priorities through academic scheduling. The Monday–Thursday schedule for a typical eleventh grader at MATCH consists of eight 56-minute periods, extending from 8:30 AM to 5:00 PM. Also, as discussed in chapter 5, all eleventh graders at MATCH take Advanced Placement U.S. history, which is divided into two class meetings a day *plus* a small-group tutorial. In addition, students have a study hall, which interview and observation data suggest is also often devoted to AP U.S. history. Indeed, with the exception of a 29-minute break for lunch, students at MATCH are engaged in academic work throughout the school day, Monday through Thursday. On Fridays, the school adds in other activities that do not fit into these eight academic class periods. For example, a given Friday might start with a whole-school assembly, after which ninth graders might have physical education, while tenth graders take MCAS practice exams, eleventh graders complete a chemistry lab, and twelfth graders attend a class at Boston University. In addition, most students are dismissed at 1:00 on Fridays to make time for staff meetings in the afternoon. This academically intense schedule clearly illustrates the purposeful allocation of a valuable resource—time—to academic tasks.

The purposefulness with which these schools structure time illustrates their priority for academics and facilitates the pursuit of their missions. By extending

FIGURE 9.2 Academy of the Pacific Rim Middle School Weekly Schedule

Trimester 3

	Homerooms	HR 1 Grade 6	HR 2 Grade 6	HR 3 Grade 6		HR 4 Grade 7	HR 5 Grade 7	HR 6 Grade 7	HR 7 Grade 8	HR 8 Grade 8
	Homeroom Teachers	Malament Duane	Sangalang McNamara	Weston Nicoletti		Rogers Dickhaut	Turet Nicodemus	Adams Rapacki	Arnold Sathyamoorthy	Subramanian Baafi
Homeroom	7:45–8:15	M, TH HR and OC; TU ADVISORY/COMM. BUILDING; WED, FR POWER								
Period 1	8:15–9:00	Language Arts Malament	Math McNamara	Reading Weston	8:15–9:15	W,Th,F–Chinese, M–Rapacki,	Science Nicodemus	History Rogers	Science Subramanian (M–Th); English–F	M1,W,F: PE Griffin; M2,T,Th– Drama–Turet
	9:00–9:15									
	9:15–9:30			M1,W,F: Art–Nicoletti; M2,Tu,TH: PE–Griffin						
Period 2	9:30–10:15	History Duane	Science Sangalang		9:15–10:15	Math Rapacki	M1,W,F:PE Griffin; M2,T,Th: Art–Nicoletti	English Dickhaut	English–Baafi M–Th; Science–F	Chinese Latimer
Break	10:15–10:35	AM Break								

Schedule (left grid)

Period 3	10:35–11:20	M1,W,F: Art–Nicoletti, M2,Tu,Th, PE–Griffin	Language Arts Malament	Math McNamara
	1120–11:35			
	11:35–11:50	Reading Watson		
Period 4	11:50–12:35		History Duane	Science Signaling
	12:35–1:05	Lunch	Lunch	Lunch
Period 5	1:05–2:05	Math McNamara	Reading Weston	Language Arts Malament
Period 6	2:04–2:20		M1,W,F: Art–Nicoletti; M2,Tu,Th: PE–Griffin	
	2:20–3:05	Science Sangalang	History Duane	History Duane
Tutoring	3:20–4:10	Tutoring		
Extended Day	4:10–5:00			
Dismissal	5:00	Dismissal		

Schedule (right grid)

Period 3	10:35–11:35	Science Nicodemus	History Rogers	W,Th,F: Chinese, M–Dickhaut, T–Rapacki	History Sathyamoorthy	Science Subramanian
Period 4	11:35–12:05	English Dickhaut	Math Rapacki	M1,W,F: PE–Griffin, M2,T,Th: Art–Nicoletti	Chinese Latimer	Lunch
	12:05–12:35			Lunch		
	12:35–1:05					Math Arnold
Period 5	1:05–2:05	History Rogers	English Dickhaut	Math Rapacki	M1,W,F: Drama–Turet; M2,T,Th: PE–Griffin	History Sathyamoorthy
Period 6	2:05–3:05	M1,W,F: PE–Griffin; M2,T,Th: Art–Nicoletti	M,T,F: Chinese; W: Rapacki; Th: Dickhaut	Science Nicodemus	Math Arnold	English Baafi
Tutoring	3:20–4:10	Extracurriculars and Tutoring				Early release for eligible students
Extended Day	4:10–5:00					Early release for eligible students
Dismissal	5:00	Dismissal				

learning time and developing intricate schedules to focus on their priorities, these schools effectively harness time to their advantage. These practices, combined with deliberate structuring of people and a nurturing culture, enable these charters to maximize time on task, channel precious resources into instruction and student support, and create academically focused environments.

Systems

How will 250 students change classes in a tight hallway in less than five minutes? How will the principal know who needs extra math tutoring? How will parents be informed that their child has detention? Facilitation of such school procedures requires the use of systems. The PELP Coherence Framework (Childress et al., 2007) defines systems as "processes and procedures through which work gets done." Whereas structures are frames for holding up the organization, systems are the ways in which the individuals within the organization function. More specifically, while the structures of advisory are that it meets on Tuesday at 7:45 AM and that twelve students are assigned to a particular teacher, the systems of advisory are the phone calls that teacher makes to the twelve students' parents and the activities that teacher conducts during advisory. Systems answer the *how* questions of school operations.

The purposeful, strategic decisions these five schools make regarding systems not only support their missions but also help define the culture of each school. That is, by contributing to how people experience life within the school, systems share a reciprocal relationship with the culture —simultaneously influencing what the culture becomes and reflecting the culture that already exists. An administrator at the Academy of the Pacific Rim explains:

> [Academy of the Pacific Rim] has been very thoughtful in developing systems. We spent a lot of time talking about teams, rituals, paying attention to detail. . . . I think doing that kind of work is tedious, frustrating sometimes, but it pays off because the highly consistent culture routine that you're able to develop out of that is so much more beneficial because then the kids walk in somewhere that's thoughtful. It helps create that academic tone.

Some of the more influential systems available to school personnel relate to internal accountability, which is the ways by which people with authority monitor the work and actions of those they oversee. The impact and effectiveness of internal accountability systems depend on the extent to which such systems cohere with staff members' individual sense of responsibility for their work *and* with the collective cultural expectations for how the school should function (Elmore, 2004). With rigid hiring processes focused on organizational fit and a penchant for homegrown leadership, as discussed in chapter 8, the individuals within each of these schools share an understanding of teachers' roles, of a vision for student outcomes, and of expectations for how work will be done. Thus, in considering how to hold teachers and students accountable, these schools design systems that reflect shared priorities, values, and assumptions. Taken together, accountability systems around instructional leadership, data-driven decisionmaking, and student management draw on common cultural elements in each school and thus have the coherence to increase the quality of the school's work and contribute to their success.

Breaking Down Classrooms Barriers

As noted above, these charter schools dedicate precious resources to positions of instructional leadership. Simply creating these positions, however, does not ensure that leaders will actually have an impact on the instructional core (Elmore, 2004; Miles & Frank, 2008). Instructional leaders also need procedures and tools to influence classroom practice. It is these procedures and tools— these systems—that enable leaders to hold teachers accountable for their work. In these schools, instructional leaders use what Spillane and Diamond (2007) refer to as boundary practices and boundary objects to reach across the leader-teacher divide to monitor classroom instruction. Boundary practices include things leaders do, such as observations and evaluations, while boundary objects include artifacts such as lesson plans, syllabi, and surveys. Spillane and Diamond argue that such practices and tools are the direct links between the work of instructional leaders and classroom instruction.

One boundary practice used across the schools is classroom observation. A teacher at Community Day reports that school leaders are "always in and out of the room." He explains: "She comes in a couple times a week and just sits down and watches what I'm doing. It's an informal thing where she just wants to know what's going on. She just kind of makes herself a presence. . . . Whenever they come in and observe, they tell you your strengths, any areas of need, or any suggestions." At Roxbury Prep, the codirector for curriculum and instruction visits between three and seven classes *every day*. As she describes, "I don't go for a long time. I go for five, ten, or twenty minutes. I sit in the back of the class with my laptop, and I take notes. Then I email teachers feedback that day." Some experienced teachers actually wish the codirector would visit more often. A five-year veteran teacher at Roxbury Prep reflected about a past codirector:

He was in my room probably every day for the first three-four months of teaching, which was really nerve-racking. But I owe so much of why I am the teacher that I am today to that. So obviously I get observed a lot less now . . . but it's also my fifth year and they have new teachers to worry about and second year teachers that need help. I would like to be observed more, because I think . . . I could be doing a lot better. I think that once you stop getting observed and you stop getting feedback, you kind of slip back.

A MATCH teacher shares a similar recollection: "In my first year here when [the former principal] was in my classroom a lot, we had a lot of conversations. . . . I was struggling. In my second year here, I had a sense that things were better because there were less conversations with him. So it was kind of awkward because the less I saw him, the better I knew I was doing." At MATCH and Roxbury Prep, the number of observations may reflect administrators' concern about the quality of a particular teacher's work, while observation is common at the other schools, representing the belief that all teachers can improve.

Further systematization of observation occurs through boundary objects, such as standardized feedback forms. Boston Collegiate's teacher-observation form (see figure 9.3) enables the middle and high school principals to assess the same elements of instruction during their weekly visits to nearly every classroom. Furthermore, the form—available to all teachers in *The Red Book*, the school's employee handbook—communicates Boston Collegiate's instructional values: student engagement, clear objectives, tight pacing, and academic rigor.

Other boundary objects—lesson plans and syllabi—also help administrators monitor instruction at the Academy of the Pacific Rim, Boston Collegiate, Community Day, and Roxbury Prep. At the Academy of the Pacific Rim and Roxbury Prep, for example, teachers submit their lesson plans or syllabi to their principal each week. A Roxbury Prep administrator explains the purpose of submitting this material:

> If there is something I'm concerned about—someone's pacing, for example, or if someone's having management issues—I'll look at the syllabus more closely and say, "Okay, what are they really planning, and is the issue a function of planning?" And rather than just going to their class and giving feedback, I'll say "Let's talk about tomorrow's lesson today and figure out how we can avoid some of the issues."

At Boston Collegiate and Community Day, this monitoring process is slightly different; Boston Collegiate principals focus on reviewing regular

FIGURE 9.3 Boston Collegiate Teacher Observation Form

Teacher:_____   Date:_____

Observer:_____   Class:_____

Yes	No	N/A	Students are engaged in academics for every minute of observation.
Yes	No	N/A	BBC is clearly posted and aim of class / learning objective is clear, measurable and achievable.
Yes	No	N/A	Lesson plan is tight, moving at a challenging pace, with neither time nor space for students to be off task.
Yes	No	N/A	Rigor of lesson is age-appropriate and indicative of high expectations for student achievement.
Yes	No	N/A	Teacher's resources and materials are organized and prepared.
Yes	No	N/A	Teacher varies lesson format and method of instruction (pair/group work, visual presentation, discussion, etc).
Yes	No	N/A	Students are working with clear directions and expectations.
Yes	No	N/A	Classroom procedures are clearly in place.
Yes	No	N/A	Teacher formally and/ or informally checks for student understanding. (Q&A, whole class response, pop quiz, extended student(s) response, connecting to guiding questions, etc.)
Yes	No	N/A	Teacher uses board to effectively support and clarify instruction.
Yes	No	N/A	By differentiating instruction, knowledge of students with IEPs and various learning styles is evident.
Yes	No	N/A	Teacher conducts smooth transitions between activities or parts of lesson.
Yes	No	N/A	Teacher provides students with clear, meaningful feedback to encourage continued work.
Yes	No	N/A	Teacher insists on student posture and students do not speak out or get out of seat without permission.
Yes	No	N/A	Disruptions to learning are not permitted. If a student is disrupting, they receive a consequence.
Yes	No	N/A	Students are able to follow lesson and speaker no matter where they are seated in room.
Yes	No	N/A	Students are participating respectfully and following speaker with eyes and attention.
Yes	No	N/A	Students appear interested and thoughtfully engaged in what they are learning.
Yes	No	N/A	Classroom is neat and walls reflect current curricular topics and outstanding student work.

lesson plans from teachers about whom they have concerns, whereas at Community Day, all teachers post their lesson plans on the school's shared computer drive, making instructional plans continually accessible to the school heads.

The coherence between teachers' values and school goals (which results from the hiring and induction processes discussed in chapter 8) enables teachers to accept this monitoring and feedback without a sense that they are being overly supervised. Furthermore, the strong cultures in these schools stress consistency and whole-school approaches to meeting goals. An administrator at MATCH explains:

> Teachers are asked to be a part of a team and therefore to give up some of the way they as an individual want to do things and join with their fellow teachers in observing some basic tenets. We try to create consistency in how we approach things. . . . When teachers choose to work here, obviously they know that they're signing up for that. Instead of having, like in most schools, 98 percent autonomy about how they run their class, they probably have 75 percent autonomy.

The competitive hiring environment also contributes to how teachers respond to feedback from instructional leaders. Having emerged from a selective and informed hiring process saturated with mission, culture, and philosophy, and in which they may have beaten out a stack of other applicants, many teachers respond with vigor and determination, seemingly wanting to meet the demands to which they committed in their interviews. Certainly, yearly contracts and administrators' freedom to fire underperforming teachers are also factors. An Academy of the Pacific Rim administrator explains the link between teacher improvement and firing:

> You set specific expectations of benchmarks—whether it's around lesson planning or management strategies. Then you try to make it work. And if it's that arduous, then it's really clear by the midyear performance review. We try to be really clear at that point to say, "Here's what needs to change in order for your contract to be renewed." And we tell people as quickly as we can[,] . . . "We're not going to renew your contract, you need to find another job."

Because shared values, clear expectations, and firm consequences are all part of the "cultural soup" in these schools, most teachers respond to instructional leadership practices and tools with the serious intent of using feedback to improve instruction.

To keep teachers informed of how their performance aligns with school expectations, all five schools also use formal evaluation systems. At Community Day, teachers receive written evaluations three times a year, the product of formal classroom observations and meetings between the teacher and school head, while MATCH teachers receive a midyear written evaluation that includes indicators from classroom observations, student evaluations, and data on the fulfillment of responsibilities, such as phone calls to parents and the number of demerits issued. At Boston Collegiate, midyear feedback reviews the teacher's success in meeting goals from the beginning of the year, as along with documentation of formal lesson observations conducted by the dean of curriculum. In formal meetings held at every school, instructional leaders drive discussions with teachers about their teaching as tracked through boundary practices and objects.

MATCH uses a novel boundary tool—a Zoomerang survey completed online each day by each tutor—to monitor the daily activity in the building. A tutor explains:

> You're supposed to write down the students that you worked with, the students that you didn't work with, what you did with that time specifically. So, even if I wasn't working with any of my students, like during my fifth and seventh periods on Mondays and Wednesdays, I have to give an account of the prep work I was doing—if it was calculus, if I was calling a parent, if I was having a meeting.

Administrators use the survey to keep close tabs on students with issues of concern. The tutor continues:

> I have to be very specific in terms of how I thought the student's mood was and also how productive I thought our tutorial was, and I have a space in which I can elaborate. So I can rank from 1–10 how productive our tutorial was and how the mood was, and I can give specific notes. "A certain student didn't go to bed last night so he was very distracted. Our productivity was very low because of this. A certain student was in a good mood."

Each morning, the MATCH Corp director reads the prior day's surveys from all forty-five tutors, allowing the survey to serve the same purpose as the other boundary practices and objects: to hold tutors formally accountable for using time efficiently in accordance with the expectations of the school.

These accountability systems for instructional leadership can allow the long arm of administration to reach into the classroom and directly influence classroom practice. These systems cohere with each school's culture and mission to target student outcomes. This coherence is critically important because, as Elmore (2004) notes, "Organizational coherence on basic aims and values, then, is a precondition for the exercise of any effective leadership around instructional improvement" (p. 63). Furthermore, because hiring and firing practices create like-minded groups of teachers working diligently to meet the expectations of the school, teachers generally embrace these systems.

Digging into Data

In addition to monitoring instructional inputs, these schools also hold teachers accountable for instructional outcomes through frequent, systematic assessment of student learning. In their guide to using assessment data to improve teaching and learning, Boudett, City, and Murnane (2005) outline several important steps in the effective use of data, including identifying needs revealed by data; examining current instruction in light of identified needs; modifying instruction to address needs; enacting and assessing altered instruction. These five schools use detailed, data-driven systems that reflect these steps to guide their efforts to improve instruction and student performance. As with feedback from instructional leaders, teachers respond to student performance data because data-driven instruction is a cultural norm. Moreover, teachers' individual sense of responsibility for student performance, the collective expectation that instruction will respond to data, and clear accountability to instructional leaders who monitor student data (Elmore, 2004) all align coherently and enable these charters to conform to the definition of a "good school" offered by Boudett, City, and Murnane (2005):

> A good school is not a collection of good teachers working independently, but a team of skilled educators working together to implement a coherent instructional plan, to identify the learning needs of every student, and to meet those needs. We believe that the process of learning from data contributes to building an effective school and to helping the school continue to improve its performance. (p. 2)

Accordingly, these schools engage in regular interim assessments, enabling them to routinely monitor students' progress toward learning standards. In addition to regular tests and quizzes, Roxbury Prep administers comprehensive exams three times a year, while Boston Collegiate and the Academy of the Pacific Rim supplement teacher-created assessments with an external, middle school six-week interim assessment program from the Massachusetts Public School Performance Project, which provides standardized assessments and immediate reports of the results. MATCH has a policy of

"Thursday assessments" and conducts monthly MCAS practice tests throughout the year. Four or five times a year, Community Day implements benchmark assessments at both the Lower and Upper schools that are designed by school personnel and which consist of MCAS-style multiple-choice and open-response items.

Administering and collecting data is one thing, but without careful analysis and interpretation, data is meaningless. Community Day provides perhaps the most formal system for data use in this sample of schools, employing an on-site data analyst who examines test results for each student in the school and presents these results to teachers in user-friendly "Blue Binders" to enable careful instructional planning for each student. Teachers use the Blue Binders to track students' subsequent performance on benchmark assessments throughout the year. Roxbury Prep teachers use Microsoft Excel spreadsheets to conduct item analyses of comprehensive exams, emphasizing long-term planning around emerging instructional needs. At Boston Collegiate and the Academy of the Pacific Rim, detailed six-week assessment reports break down the data by question and standard, enabling systematic evaluation of performance and identification of skills for further instruction. A math teacher at the Academy of the Pacific Rim explains the system and the all-important timeline for analyzing data:

> During that week we have the data, we're sitting with it, we're kind of looking over it, we're pulling out major trends, we're identifying students of concern. We're thinking through, "What are we going to reteach to the whole class? What are we going to focus on in Focus or tutoring?" And then usually we'll come back together a week later as a mini-department, grades 5–8. All the teachers will meet with the principal facilitating the conversation, and we will go over the data.

Policies for using assessment data also apply to teacher-designed formative assessments. Boston Collegiate's *Red Book,* for example, advises that

> data from assessments should drive daily lesson planning and curricular structure. Design assessments in such a way that they provide information on what concepts are being retained by whom. It is critical that we are always aware of what students know and what they are able to do.

The Red Book also outlines specific steps for connecting data analysis to instruction and suggests that teachers "analyze assessments to evaluate student understanding of specific frameworks, and plan subsequent units with this information in mind."

Academy of the Pacific Rim's *Instructional Guidebook* for teachers states similarly that

> teachers should use the data they intake from informal assessments to inform their teaching to ensure student understanding before formal assessments. If informal assessments indicate that students are struggling with certain content or skills, teachers should re-teach and/or spiral back to increase understanding.

By declaring these expectations in handbooks and working systematically with teachers to respond to data, these schools reinforce this collective expectation as an organizational norm. Given the power of data-driven practices to lead to more effective instruction (Boudett et al., 2005), these systems help students meet their learning goals.

Teachers in these schools also use assessments to monitor their *own* effectiveness. The data analyst at Community Day explains that generating data about student performance allows teachers to look at their craft and "maybe their strengths and weaknesses in certain areas of English or math. It gives them ideas on how to work on curriculum." Through the cyclical process of modifying instruction in response to data and then retesting students and modifying again, teachers internalize the connection between their instruction and learning outcomes. A MATCH teacher reflects:

> I feel like here was the first time I realized that assessments aren't my proof that a student actually earned a B. It's actually evidence for me to say, "Am I teaching Bs, or am I teaching As? . . . Looking at assessments was a lot of information for me, and that was a whole huge revelation. I realized that assessments aren't for giving kids grades. They're to give me information about how successful I'm being.

By systematically enabling these schools to track the effectiveness of their work and then reshape and reevaluate practice accordingly, data-driven instruction systems hold teachers accountable for working strategically toward school goals. Moreover, because these practices are often done collectively, they contribute to the transparency of teaching and increased performance across the school (Boudett et al., 2005; Elmore, 2004).

Setting Student Expectations

A third group of systems that enable classrooms to be places of intense productivity are the student management systems. Stressing that students themselves are accountable for creating and maintaining focused and productive learning environments, these schools use systems that encourage positive behaviors and address negative behaviors. Like the accountability systems for teachers, accountability systems for students rely on other organizational factors: alignment among students' sense of personal responsibility, students' collective expectations for how they will behave in school, and the actual accountability system itself. Student behavior systems are effective not only because school personnel enforce them, but also because students and families are well informed about the systems and commit to them upon enrollment.

All four secondary schools use schoolwide merit and demerit systems. At Boston Collegiate, the *Student and Family Handbook* explains that students can earn merits for good deeds such as "taking initiative, showing courtesy, or doing what's expected when others are not." Conversely, students earn demerits for infractions such as "an untucked shirt or minor uniform infraction, arriving late to school or class, or a minor classroom disruption." Beyond demerits, students earn immediate afterschool detention for "disrespecting a fellow student, inappropriate physical contact with a student or staff member, or being out of uniform." By committing to rewarded or punished behaviors in writing, these secondary schools clarify their expectations. A teacher at Roxbury Prep explains:

> I need to be comfortable knowing that if a student leaves my classroom and goes into a history class, the same high expectations in terms of academic achievement and behavior are kept. Now that may be executed in a different manner, but on a base level they know what is expected of them and they know what the consequences are.

These schoolwide expectations increase the likelihood that students will learn and meet behavioral expectations across locations and personnel.

All of the secondary schools outline their behavioral management systems in a written handbook for students and families. At MATCH, the 22-page Code of Conduct provides explicit rules in areas ranging from tardiness and absences to dress code and procedures for expulsion. Figure 9.4 shows two pages from the MATCH Code of Conduct, which illustrate the fine-grained, systematic detail and specify how students earn detention, how they should spend time during detention, and exactly what punishment will occur if students fail to meet these expectations.

By offering a written code or handbook that outlines rewards or sanctions, these secondary schools communicate their expectations clearly and unequivocally. However, as noted previously, having this information documented clearly is necessary but not sufficient. Rather, what proves critical are the

FIGURE 9.4   MATCH Code of Conduct Pages on Detention

DETENTIONS

All Demerits lead to detention: Students who accumulate 5 or more demerits in a week will have to serve detention. When it describes "demerits" below, it refers to both first AND second degree demerits:

Number of demerits	Consequence:
5 demerits	1 hour of detention
6 demerits	2 hours of detention
7 demerits	3 hours of detention
7 demerits	6 hours of detention
8 or more demerits	Immediate suspension, parent meeting and 6 hours of detention
10 or more demerits	Academic Violation and 6 hours of detention

If students begin to accumulate more hours of detention than can be served in the corresponding weekend, future hours will be tallied and students will be expected to complete all hours before being promoted to the next grade.

Expectations for Detention:
- Students serve detention in silence unless otherwise specified.
- Students are expected to read and/or do schoolwork and/or do community service around the school, such as cleaning or other chores.
- Students must refrain from any communication including passing notes.
- Students may not sleep.
- Students must bring all necessary work materials to detention.
- Laptops or any electric devices may not be used in detention.
- Tutoring cannot replace detention.
- Failure to observe any of the detention rules will result in additional or lengthened detention, parent conference, and/or suspension.
- Skipping detention carries the same consequences or skipping class or school. For example, a student who skips a detention gets 6 extra hours of detention and must have a parent conference before re-entering school.

How students know if they have detention:
1. The names of students with detention are posted by the main door every Friday morning before school begins.
2. Parents will be notified by their child's tutor on Thursday night if their child has detention.
3. It is always the student's responsibility to check the list every Friday morning!

Friday Detention:
- Runs from 1:00 pm – 4:00 pm depending on how many hours a student must serve.
- Students must arrive in MATCH School dress code.
- The Code of Conduct applies during detention and if a student misbehaves he/she will be given one warning and then asked to leave detention and given an Academic Violation. (consequences specified on page 16)

continued on next page

- All students who have Friday detention should arrive by 12:55 pm; they must be seated with something to read or do as homework in the Detention Room by 1:00 pm.
- If student is up to 10 minutes tardy to Friday Detention, the student must serve triple time (i.e. the 10 minutes they missed and 20 additional minutes for a grand total of 30 minutes). The student will also receive 2 demerits for being tardy.
- If student is later than 10 minutes, there are no exceptions or excuses, the students will not be admitted to detention, will be sent home and will receive an unexcused absence.

Saturday Detention:
- Saturday detention begins promptly at 9:00 am and runs until noon.
- Students must arrive in MATCH SCHOOL dress code.
- The Code of Conduct applies during detention and if a student misbehaves he/she will be given one warning and then asked to leave detention and given an Academic Violation. (consequences specified on page 16)
- If student is up to 10 minutes tardy to Saturday Detention, the student must serve triple time (i.e. the 10 minutes they missed and 20 additional minutes for a grand total of 30 minutes). The student will also receive 2 demerits for being tardy.
- If student is later than 10 minutes, there are no exceptions or excuses, the student will not be admitted to detention, will be sent home and will receive an unexcused absence.

---

collective coherence and accepted culture established in these schools around these systems.

Formal positive reinforcement is also intricately planned in all of the secondary schools. The extensive and elaborate classroom-management systems outlined in the school chapters, such as MAPP at Boston Collegiate and KG-PRIDE at the Academy of the Pacific Rim, are instrumental to the operations of these schools. From whole-class tidiness evaluations to commentary on the level of professionalism students exhibit, these character-development programs underscore comprehensive, schoolwide, nonacademic norms for the students in these schools. Similarly, Roxbury Prep rewards good deeds and positive acts with Creed Deeds, which function as school-based currency. On a larger scale, teachers at Roxbury Prep and the Academy of the Pacific Rim gives speeches about students who exemplify desired behavioral characteristics and publicly reward these students with schoolwide honors, such as the *Gambatte* award at the Academy or the Spirit Stick at Roxbury Prep. Similarly, MATCH presents a Student of the Month award in each grade during an assembly attended by the recipients' families. Through ever-present systems for highlighting positive acts, attitudes, and activities, these schools reinforce desired behaviors.

Community Day, the only elementary school in the study, relies on individual teachers to establish developmentally appropriate systems for addressing student behavior in their classrooms, paying close attention to the individual needs of particular students. Unlike the other schools in the study, Community Day does not have a schoolwide system. A classroom teacher at Community Day explains the management system that she and her coteacher use:

> We have a positive system in our classroom, where if students do something good, they earn a marble. We have a jar of fifty marbles and a jar that they're trying to fill up with the fifty marbles. If they do something good, we move the marble in there. If they do something bad, we don't take them out. When they fill up that jar they earn a party or something special—maybe ten extra minutes outside—something exciting for them.

By enabling individual teachers to establish systems for their classes, Community Day uses a more varied approach to monitor student behavior in their kindergarten through eighth-grade classrooms.

As with other accountability systems described in this chapter, the effectiveness of behavior management systems rests on coherence—not only among those who implement the systems but also between the systems and other aspects of school organization. Most important, families and, by proxy, their children actively embrace these academic and social norms. As noted in chapter 7, these schools explicitly describe what is expected of students during information sessions for prospective students and their families, which enables them to make a commitment to working within the school culture. As a MATCH parent acknowledges:

> Parents have to buy into the fact that if you want quality education, and if you want your kids to be challenged and whatever, it's going to be tough on them. It's going to be tough on you, and you have to back the system.

Like teachers who might feel privileged to be hired, parents and students often consider themselves blessed to have won a place at these schools through the lottery. Thus they feel they are among the chosen and are psychologically primed to buy into the culture, which helps cement a shared acceptance for how the school will operate. Tapping into these expectations, school leaders and teachers effectively enforce behavioral accountability systems and promote the academic environment needed to support high expectations for student achievement.

Lessons for Replication

Several elements described in this chapter that contribute to the success of these five schools are within the reach of traditional and charter school practitioners. As one considers the way these schools structure and organize the people who work in them, a particularly important lesson is that the manner in which administrative positions are structured lies well within the purview of any school leader. Perhaps the notion of creating an entirely new position that focuses on instructional leadership is beyond the financial resources of some schools, but it is worth noting that these five charter schools have done this without spending more per pupil than their host districts. A realignment of roles and responsibilities within a school can achieve a great deal.

Similarly, it may be that contractual issues as well as financial concerns limit the ability of a school to extend the length of the school day, but such limitations do not impact what can be done within the existing school day. Time allocations within the school day can focus directly on the results that a school wishes to accomplish without impacting contracts or financial limitations. As illustrated at the Academy of the Pacific Rim and MATCH, all subjects don't necessarily receive the same amount of instructional time. Such changes are possible. One useful question for all practitioner to ask whenever they are considering the adoption of a new initiative—whether a new schedule, an extracurricular activity, or a new program—is, "What does this new initiative have to do with our mission and our desired outcomes?" If the answer is "not much" or only a lukewarm connection, the activity should be dropped.

Other useful findings that can transfer include Boston Collegiate's observation protocol and other boundary tools in use in these five schools. Additionally, since we know that schools with strong internal accountability systems are more likely to respond effectively to external demands for performance (Elmore, 1995), efforts to connect individuals within a school around the work of the school will reap positive results. Communication about the work, as well as the sharing of values and beliefs as mentioned in chapter 7, are essential to a high-performing organization. Using data to inform curriculum and instruction decisions represents another accessible tool. The financial costs of externally created tests, as well as the internal costs of taking time away from instruction to assess student learning, deserve consideration but should be measured in contrast to the power of formative and summative assessments as school improvement tools (Boudett et al., 2005). Finally, the advantages of consistently employed student management systems far exceed the inconveniences of intricate design and consistent enforcement; such systems are worthy of all schools. For students, knowing and understanding clear behavioral expectations can create an important sense of security and personal control.

Conclusion

While the complete list of structures and systems used in these five schools extends well beyond the examples here, this chapter illustrates the schools' purposeful decisionmaking regarding daily operations and the coherence among various organizational elements. Throughout the interviews with key personnel, respondents repeatedly attributed their school's success to structured, systematic, and coherent work environments. These schools clearly structure people and time to focus on instruction and personalization, and they use accountability systems to monitor data-driven instruction and establish environments conducive to learning. In these ways, the operational rhythms of these schools extend beyond the predictable machinery of comfort and familiarity, and they actually harness a coherent alignment among structures, systems, and culture to aggressively and purposefully propel them toward meeting their missions.

CHAPTER TEN

CLASSROOM INSTRUCTION AND STUDENT OUTCOMES

Those wishing to identify charter school practices that lead to success on a variety of performance measures, including state-level high-stakes assessments, may be curious about what happens within the classrooms of these high-performing schools. Are there particular instructional approaches or structures being practiced in these classrooms that merit documentation and sharing? After all, what students actually do in the classroom has an impact on what they learn. Furthermore, in the context of the preceding chapters, it is reasonable to ask whether the coherence that figures so prominently in these schools' cultures and theories of action, across systems and structures, and in their policies for hiring and retaining staff prevails in the area of instruction. Does the culture of coherence in these schools penetrate the notoriously private world of teachers' classrooms?

To address these questions and provide important information about how these schools function inside the classroom, this chapter explores instructional practice in two ways. The first is to discuss structural elements and activities that help shape instructional practice within classrooms. Such elements include the format of lesson delivery, the parameters used to determine the content of lessons, the use of time, and the preparation for assessments. These elements define fixed and purposefully executed structures related to instruction in these schools. The second is to offer a glimpse of instructional practice inside the classrooms by presenting data from several representative classes. The

The primary authors for this chapter are Katherine K. Merseth and John Roberts.

data focuses on the level of cognitive demand present in the academic tasks teachers set for their students. Cognitive demand describes the "kind and level of thinking required of students in order to successfully engage and solve the task" (Stein, Smith, Henningsen, & Silver, 2000, p. 11).

These two perspectives provide an equivocal answer to the question of coherence posed above. The external structures influencing instructional practices are remarkably coherent across and within these schools, yet within the classroom, this coherence fades, giving way to variation in instruction as measured by academic tasks and related cognitive demand. The fact that variation exists in these schools is not a criticism—nearly every school struggles to some degree with variation across classrooms. What is noteworthy is that examining the variation between classes in these five schools has led to a powerful—and perhaps even counter-cultural—finding: *that common purposes, consistent structures, coherent school cultures, and deliberate planning appear to trump or at least mitigate the potential effects of variation in classroom instruction.*

Should practitioners worry about variation in academic tasks within a school? The answers vary and depend on context. Some scholars, including Richard Elmore, feel that variation is a critically important concern. He posits that "variability in instructional practice is the Achilles' heel of the [educational] enterprise" (personal communication, July 16, 2008). Others argue that efforts to create schoolwide coherence in instructional practice could curtail intellectual freedom or teacher professionalism. Still others suggest that it is important to get basic organizational structures in place before taking on the challenge of creating more uniform instructional practice. One school leader notes, for example, that his school doesn't have a particular philosophy of instruction:

> Our philosophy is [that] we have a greater school culture that allows each teacher the maximum opportunities for them to use that time well. Our culture allows fifty-six minutes of learning to really be fifty-six minutes. . . . It's not like we have unique, amazing ideas of how to teach math. . . . We don't have an overarching philosophy of "How to actually teach," "How to actually instruct." It's more of making sure that there is no time wasted. And how to use that time is up to you.

In several of the schools in this study, school leaders express concern about the variation in instruction and are working to employ a range of efforts to influence classroom practice. One in particular notes, "We need to continue the work on effective classroom instruction. . . . Perhaps the charter school field has not paid enough attention to that aspect of our mission." In response to this concern, this chapter concludes by offering several current strategies used by these schools as they work to tackle the vexing challenge of variation in instruction.

Skeptics might argue that discussions about variations in the level of cognitive demand are irrelevant in this context because these schools already have achieved strong academic performance on standardized assessments. After all, they might say, the students in these schools significantly outperform their peers attending the Boston and Lawrence public schools, as well as many of their peers elsewhere in the Massachusetts, so why does instructional variation matter? We believe that variation of instruction matters *precisely because* it is common in these schools and in traditional schools. It matters because many classroom experts believe that instruction is the core of schooling and therefore is a most important, indeed critical, aspect of schools (Elmore, 1992, 2004; National Research Council, 1999; Stigler & Hiebert, 1999). Furthermore, it matters as one contemplates the future demands likely to be placed on schools because it is likely they will be asked to move from state competency levels to more ambitious—and perhaps more challenging—outcomes. In this new environment, teaching that engages students in challenging cognitive tasks on a regular basis will be a requirement. Even today, several studies of high-performing urban schools, as well as essays on learning (e.g., Shulman, 2004, in his analysis of Bruner's 1966 work), suggest that classroom instruction that focuses on higher order thinking skills is important for developing both the academic knowledge for college readiness as well as lifelong learning habits (Cohen, McLaughlin, & Talbert, 1993; Neufeld & Roper, 2003).[1] This type of instruction in urban schools can be achieved, as evidenced by Darling-Hammond and her colleagues (Darling-Hammond, Ancess, & Ort, 2002), who describe the classrooms of successful inner-city schools in New York:

> The schools' curriculums focus on preparing students for the demands of college. Most of the assignments that we reviewed required the production of analytic work—research papers and projects, demonstrations and discussions of problems, experiments and data collection organized to answer open-ended questions. Worksheets and fill-in-the-blank tasks were rare. Extensive reading and writing were expected in all of the schools. Many classes required large end-of-course projects that included elaborate written documentation and were presented and defended orally. (p. 642)

And, finally, it is critical to address variation in instruction because extensive variation can create enormous difficulty for children moving from subject to subject or from teacher to teacher during the school day.

This chapter now turns to examine instructional practices in the classrooms of these schools, starting with the external structural elements that influence the execution of instruction. These elements are coherent and consistent across and within all of the study schools.

Structural Elements of Instructional Practice
The Blackboard Configuration

Across every classroom at nearly every level (with the possible exception of the Early Learning Center at Community Day), students in these five charter schools see a common blackboard configuration (BBC) at the beginning of every class period. All students find a "Do-Now," so named by educator Lorraine Monroe (c.f. Checkley, 2004), written either on the board or offered in a handout to students upon entering the classroom. The Do-Now is one element of the BBC that frames the instructional activities by reviewing previous material or introducing new content. In addition, the BBC provides the classroom's agenda and a posting of daily homework assignments. Starting classes with this immediate and often silent activity makes the transition from the hallways to classrooms explicit and unequivocal. The Do-Nows also communicate a sense of urgency that classroom time is sacred and not a minute will be wasted. The box on the next page provides an example of a BBC for an eleventh-grade history class.

The BBC is a structure that communicates the school's culture. A teacher makes this connection explicit:

> We start a class with a Do-Now that says, "We're gonna use every minute of that classroom time that we can. We're not going to do anything that's just going to fill up space." It comes up time and time again, in terms of, . . . "How are you articulating to your students, and even to yourselves, exactly what you want your students to be able to do to show mastery?" I think those things are . . . built into the culture, built into the structure of the school.

Use of the BBC is consistent across each school. A Roxbury Prep teacher comments that

> the things that are completely consistent are that every class where students walk in, they see the configuration of the board where you have a list of what the Aim is for the day and what the Do-Now activity is. . . . Every class is started with a silent Do-Now activity.

By using the BBC, these schools frame the structure, but not necessarily the content, of classroom lessons.

DO-NOW

Write the Date/Aim on your paper.
Complete the graphic organizer on the salmon-colored packet.

AIM
YWBAT [you will be able to] analyze the use of Christianity for abolitionist and anti-abolitionist arguments.

AGENDA
Do-Now (for a class-work grade—be brilliant!)
Notes: 2nd Great Awakening
Source: Stowe v. McCord

HOMEWORK
PPET #3 (SG 2.3 – last one)

Maximizing Time on Task

The BBC reflects a conscious effort to maximize students' time on task. Academic content dominates nearly every minute of every class period, with little class time allotted to conversation or activities outside the BBC agenda. Furthermore, observational data and teacher reports confirm that most teachers in the study spend little time disciplining students because of the coherent behavior-management systems, the consistent implementation of these systems, and the schools' seriousness of purpose. Taking classroom time to discipline students in many other schools is often the norm rather than the exception: a Metropolitan Life Foundation report (Markow, Fuath, & Gravitch, 2001) found, for example, that only one-quarter (24%) of secondary school students give an "A" to their teachers in maintaining discipline in the classroom (p. 22). Moreover, in the 2007 annual Phi Delta Kappan/Gallup Poll, discipline ranked as the second-largest problem facing schools overall, with 11 percent of the public stating that discipline was the biggest problem in schools today. Maintaining a well-disciplined classroom, then, can create a strain on teachers and a drain on what they are able to accomplish. Mary Kennedy (2005) observed that classroom interruptions make it difficult for teachers to return to the classroom lesson:

Whenever a distraction occurs, it is not only students who are distracted, but teachers as well. Teachers must make a complicated decision quickly, before they lose the momentum of their lesson altogether. And at the same time, they must regain their composure. (p. 80)

At the study schools, the consistent implementation of school behavior codes with strong, swift consequences means that interruptions and annoyances are rare. In fact, the founder of one school notes that the reduction of distractions is what enables students to learn:

While there are certainly teachers who manage in a traditional high-poverty school to create a functional, productive classroom, . . . the median teacher in those schools has a lot of interruptions and low-level distractions. . . . I describe that as a tax on learning. You need to, essentially, bring that tax down, . . . not through magical instruction or highly innovative ways of teaching literature . . . but through turning somersaults in interlocking ways that make the average classroom one where the kids' eyes are on the teacher.

Curricular Planning

In addition to the BBC that frames the learning experience and the urgency communicated by the school culture, consistency is created across these schools through important structural similarities in the way teachers align their lessons to the Massachusetts State Frameworks. Not surprisingly, all five schools work hard to match their curriculum to the state's expectations of what students know and are able to do. Roxbury Prep, for instance, requires the use of a "curriculum alignment template" to help ensure full coverage of the Massachusetts Learning Standards, while a teacher in another school describes the state standards as a "reference point" for organizing work with students. Aligning classroom plans with results on the Massachusetts Comprehensive Assessment System (MCAS) or other interim MCAS-like assessments is also critical to their success. A Community Day teacher states that

one of the things that is integral to our entire operation . . . is goal-setting and measuring whether we're getting to those goals. . . . We look at the MCAS high-stakes exam [and that] gives us a wealth of data. . . . We have translated much of that assessment data and results into classroom practice, [and] we analyze how individual students are doing, how groups of students are doing, what the test is telling us about whether we're being effective.

Summer planning also helps keep students and faculty on task. Teachers at Roxbury Prep meet for three weeks in the summer and plan the entire yearlong curriculum, sometimes down to daily lessons. This process achieves several goals. First, it serves as an informal pacing guide to ensure that teachers cover all the content required by the standards for a particular grade level. Thus, even though a particular group of students may not grasp the content in the allotted amount of time for the topic, having a yearlong curricular plan signals to teachers that they either need to address student confusion outside of class time or recoup time lost to reteaching the subject matter later in the year. Second, summer planning encourages coherence across the school that might be missing if teachers planned their lessons individually. Third, planning in the summer allows teachers to get ahead in their work for the year. As one teacher noted, "The whole idea behind the curriculum is that you plan it early, before the school year starts, and that you plan it all the way through so that when you come to planning a particular lesson for a particular day, you already have a sense as to what you are going to do."

Aligning lessons and curricula with the Massachusetts State Frameworks is an important strategy to ensure that students achieve proficiency on the state's high-stakes tests. Other researchers note the importance of aligning the curriculum with standards. For example, in a study of five small high schools in New York City, Darling-Hammond and colleagues (2002) identify "a carefully constructed curriculum aimed at specific proficiencies" as one of several factors influencing the schools' success.

Preparing for Assessments

A fourth common feature of these schools that contributes to strong state-level assessment scores is explicit, targeted preparation. These schools regularly expose students to publicly released MCAS items, while some teachers generate tests and quizzes in formats similar to standardized tests. For example, when asked why their students perform well on the MCAS, an administrator stated:

> I think that it's a lot of test prep. I think it's a lot of knowing the test and knowing what skills our kids need to be successful. . . . It's just knowing what the kids need, being prepared, and getting the resources to give them what they need. [If] the teachers know that open response is difficult for the school, they really tackle it in the summer and they come up with a handbook on strategies for open response. . . . I think that our school really analyzes their results and the questions and constantly looks at them.

In an advisory meeting at one of the middle schools, students heard months in advance that they would start preparing, heavily, for the MCAS. The teacher mentioned that students would see many more MCAS questions as Do-Nows and might even see a math Do-Now in their reading class. The school also created various competitions and rewards for classes or individuals, which recognized the best performance on standardized test questions. For example, every time a student answered a sample question correctly, a link was added to a chain; when the collective chain got long enough, the class would earn a prize. Tenth graders in several of these schools sit for practice exams that mimic both the MCAS and the SAT on one day each month, a significant allocation of the schools' time and resources. This targeted preparation for assessments means that students are familiar with both the format and the content of the exams long before they take them.

Typically, the five study schools outscore the Boston and Lawrence public schools on the MCAS and are competitive with schools statewide, placing them among the top schools in the state (see appendix 10.A for the 2007 MCAS results). It is impressive that nearly all of these students, many of whom arrive at these charter schools in the bottom quartile of state performers, rise to the "Proficient" and sometimes even the "Advanced" level during their years at these schools.

These charter schools emphasize and collect data on a variety of other tests as well, including the SAT (which purports to measure critical thinking skills needed for academic success in college); the SAT Subject Tests (formerly SAT II); the Secondary School Admissions Test; the Independent School Entrance Examination; and Advanced Placement exams, which measure the attainment of content knowledge.

On most of the subtests of the SAT taken in 2006, the mean scores at each of the three high schools in the study match or exceed those of students in the Boston Public Schools—an important milestone, since *all* charter school students take the SAT, while only slightly more than 60 percent of the Boston students do so, likely inflating the Boston mean score. (See appendix 10.B for 2006 data. Appendix 10.B also offers the mean SAT scores for the charter schools in 2007, but similar data are not available from the Boston Public Schools.) More comprehensive quantitative studies are also underway to examine the impact of attending a charter school on student enrollment and persistence in college, but results are not available at the time of publication (Castleman, 2008). Strong SAT performance is a focus of the high schools in this study because of their college-oriented missions and the reality that SAT scores are central to students' admission prospects and eligibility for scholarships. SAT scores also help direct students to the appropriate type of college.

Many of these schools employ techniques that could be helpful to other school leaders who are striving to improve standardized test scores. For example, an administrator describes the attention his school gives to translating data for teachers about MCAS results and the fact that teachers actually use this information in planning their instruction. The school provides an analysis of each student's performance on each area of the exam in what they call "Blue Binders":

> My feeling is [that] most of the teachers don't just get these [Blue Binders] and say, oh, that's nice. They really are using them throughout the year. Particularly the stuff with the [released MCAS items]. I say 90 percent of figuring out what's going on here is the fact that the state gives you the questions. They tell you everything about it so you can modify your teaching based on it.

One school leader at the secondary level describes activities related to SAT performance that were undertaken in collaboration with another charter school in the study:

> We have been working for some years on teaching our kids the skills they need to be successful on the SAT. . . . [For example,] many of us spent this past year on a task force specifically designed to rethink our high school program to be more like college and [to] more intentionally and effectively foster the thinking skills and independence our students need in college. Significant change came out of the task force: thematic English seminars modeled on college curriculum; a two-year AP U.S. history course for all students; major research capstone projects in each subject area.

Another school engages in different activities to help prepare students for the SAT, offering college-prep days multiple times a year. Students in grades 9–11 take mock versions of the SAT, and the data are used by teachers to create an instructional feedback loop to help them examine their curricula, lesson plans, and assessment formats (this is discussed more extensively in the school's chapter). The college-prep days, according to the school head, were

> the brainchild of our College Readiness Committee led by our high school principal. The committee has been meeting for two years and, in addition to studying the SAT, has developed a collegiate skills curriculum for grades 9–12 devoted to further emphasizing skills our students need in college, from research to public speaking to career discovery. The College Readiness Committee and the college-prep days grew directly out of feedback we have been receiving from our alumni and in response to the SAT scores of our students in our early years.

The ultimate aim of schools, of course, is to do much more than prepare their students for standardized tests such as the MCAS or SAT, or for any other exam. Ideally, schools enable students to learn more than what appears on a standardized test. Lengthy, targeted assessment preparation can lead to impressive MCAS or SAT scores, but if those impressive results do not have an impact elsewhere in students' lives, it is possible that students are learning how to take standardized tests without fully grasping the deeper concepts or lifelong learning skills.

Thus, several structural elements, such as the blackboard configuration, planning curriculum content to align with state standards, and explicit preparation for standardized assessments, are coherent across and within these schools and help define the execution of instruction in these schools. Looking more closely, what can be said about the work students complete within the classroom? Although offered the opportunity to do so, teachers and administrators did not comment as frequently about the specifics of internal classroom practices and student work as they did about the impact of the broader structural elements mentioned above. Thus, the research team returned to the schools to collect firsthand data on classroom interactions, conducting over 135 classroom observations (see appendix 10.C for methodological details). The next section describes the process of data collection and briefly offers representative descriptions of classrooms that are taken from different schools, levels, and subjects.

Academic Tasks and Cognitive Demand

It is a Herculean task to undertake a comprehensive discussion of all aspects of classroom instruction. At any given time, myriad features compete for consideration, including teacher skill, student agency, and school context. Furthermore, any attempt to examine all of the features comprising instruction would extend well beyond the scope of this chapter. Nevertheless, what happens within these charter classrooms offers an important window for practitioners and policymakers who want to understand the operation of these schools.

To arrive at a view of instruction, then, this chapter adopts a simple yet powerful approach as it explores one particular aspect of instructional practice—the discrete academic tasks that students undertake in their classes (Doyle, 1983, 1988). Several researchers, including Porter (2006), Stein et al. (2000), Hawkins (1974), and Hiebert and his colleagues (1997), justify this particular focus. For example, Hiebert et al. observe that "students learn from the kind of work they do in classrooms and the tasks they are asked to complete determines the kind of work they do. . . . The tasks make all the difference" (p. 17). This particular focus also strikes at the heart of instruction because it stresses what the student must do to comply with the teacher's direction about the content. In other words, academic tasks are "defined by the answers students are required to produce and the routes that can be used to obtain these answers" (Doyle, 1983, p. 161). Tasks are also an important indicator in that they influence students' perception of the subject, since their perceptions "are built from the kind of work they do, not from the exhortations of the teacher" (Hiebert et al., 1997, p. 18). Academic tasks, then, are what students actually experience inside the framework of blackboard configurations and lesson structures.

A further refinement of academic tasks is to consider the cognitive demand required by a particular task. Researchers classify the cognitive demand of student work using taxonomies that often include hierarchical levels of increasing cognitive difficulty. The familiar Bloom's Taxonomy features six cognitive processes that range from knowledge (information retrieval) to evaluation.[2] More recent work builds on Bloom's Taxonomy (Anderson & Krathwohl, 2001; Marzano & Kendall, 2007) and adds student agency and meta-cognitive procedures (c.f. Marzano & Kendall, 2007), as well as considering the hierarchical nature of these tasks (c.f. Furst, 1981; Seddon, 1978).

Accordingly, classroom observations become an important data source when the researchers try to untangle the use of time, tasks, and student experience in classrooms. Using a common observation protocol, researchers collected data in classrooms with a primary focus on two questions: "What are the students being asked to do? and "What is the level of cognitive demand of this task?" (see appendix 10.C for additional methodological details).

Classroom Examples

Recall the first grader at Community Day in chapter 1, who served as the Student of the Day. He opened class by posing several questions to his classmates: "What day is today?" "What day is tomorrow?" "Who lost a tooth?" According to the researcher, he carried out his duties "unabashedly, confidently posing these questions to his classmates and then choosing respondents and listening to their answers, rephrasing his queries in complete questions when prompted by the teacher." Though rehearsed, these were important questions in that classroom's routine, ones for which this particular student was assuming responsibility. The practice of asking one another questions and learning to listen and respond, as well as learning the days of the week, established important skills and norms for these six-year-olds. Cognitively they were relatively demanding, asking students to recall both the calendar and days of the week. Later in the day, the same students applied similar strategies as they talked with one another about number patterns and tried to predict sequences of numbers.

To provide a picture of the work going on in secondary classrooms, detailed descriptions of two middle school English classes, two high school mathematics classes, and two high school history classes appear below. The math examples come from two classrooms in the same school, while the English and history examples are classrooms from two different schools.

Middle School Language Arts Classrooms
The BBC for this sixth-grade English class greets students as they enter and instructs them to complete a Do-Now, which will be followed by "partner work." The AIM or objective for the day, written on the board, states: "I will make inferences based on quotes from the text."

After spending ten minutes working on the Do-Now, students work in pairs to complete a three-page handout titled, "Character Traits Discussion Quotes." This worksheet draws from a short story, *Beethoven Lives Upstairs,* by Barbara Nichol. The directions at the top of the worksheet give students the following instructions:

1. Please discuss and make inferences about the quotes below.
2. Take notes on the ideas that are discussed.
3. Remember, a large part of your grade will be based on how well you write your ideas.

The pages of the worksheet have two columns, with four rows on each page. The left side of each row gives quotations from the story, and the right side lists questions and space for students to answer them. Of the thirteen questions that make up the worksheet, twelve use the word "infer" in the question. For example:

Every morning at dawn Mr. Beethoven begins to make his dreadful noise upstairs. Loud poundings and howling come through the floor. They are like the sounds of an injured beast." Pg. 744	What can you infer about Beethoven's character from this quote?

After about forty minutes into this hour-long class period, the teacher draws the students' attention to the homework assignment:

READING OPEN RESPONSE HOMEWORK
10 Points

Sentence Starters:

Craziness means . . .

I believe Beethoven was crazy because . . .

I do not believe Beethoven was crazy because . . .

_____

I will grade you on grammar and your ideas.
- Indent your paragraph.
- Use correct end punctuation.
- Use correct capitalization.

Please answer both questions in your open response.
1. Was [sic] does it mean to be "crazy?"
2. Was Beethoven crazy?

A second middle school English class enters their classroom and sees a BBC configuration that outlines the agenda for the day. The first task is a quiz on the book, The Raider's Jacket. The quiz has seventeen questions, ten multiple choice and seven short response. Several selected items from the quiz are below:

4. Gary Soto's [use] of Spanish words is an example of which of the following literary devices?
    A. metaphor
    B. flashback
    C. diction
    D. onomatopoeia
11. Put the following events in order from 1–8 (1 point each)
    ____ Lorena buys a new Raiders Jacket
    ____ In French class, Lorena embarrasses herself while daydreaming.
    ____ Lorena leaves the jacket in biology
    ____ Eddie gives Lorena his jacket
    ____ Lorena stays home from school
    ____ Lorena and Guadalupe cry at the mall
    ____ Eddie and Frankie stomp on milk cartons while waiting for the bus
    ____ Lorena and Guadalupe run into Frankie and Eddie at the mall
17. What are the four steps fo r defining unfamiliar words? (You must write them in order!)
    (3 points each)

During the quiz, the teacher comments to the whole class, "I like the way most of you are crossing out the wrong answers" and "If you're managing your time wisely, you should be on section 2 or beyond."

A quick transition marks the change from the quiz to the teacher-directed portion of the lesson. The teacher says, "You have fifteen seconds to get [ready] and to get your agenda out. 15 . . . 14 . . . 13 . . . 12 . . . 11 . . . ." The students are looking at the teacher long before she reaches the end of her count. The teacher begins this portion of the lesson by writing the word "emulate" on the board, and then asks the class what the word means. There is some playful dialogue between the teachers and students, but the teacher does most of the talking during this portion of the discussion, which prefaces the next task: the students are to write a continuation of *The Raiders Jacket*. In discussing this task (see below), the teacher leads the students through several minutes of "writing notes" about similes and metaphors and probes the students about why Soto might use Spanish words in his story. Foreshadowing the assignment, the teacher states, "I want to make it very clear why we're doing this assignment. I want to be sure that you really get Gary Soto's writing style—that you can *emulate* it." After giving the students a few minutes to brainstorm individually about what might happen next in the story, the teacher asks for student volunteers. Perhaps 60 percent of the hands in the room go up. She explores some of these ideas with the class members before saying, "You get seven minutes to work on your homework."

Name_____   Date_____
English 7   Class Period_____

The Raiders Jacket by Gary Soto
Creative Writing Assignment
What happens next?

Directions: In the space provided here, write at least three more paragraphs of the story *The Raiders Jacket* by Gary Soto.

- Try to use his style of diction, and make sure that you have a humorous tone (attitude towards the subject).
- Think about what may have happened after the story. (We'll put our ideas in the brainstorm box!)
- You must use at least two kinds of figurative language. Have fun and be creative!

As the final minute of period approaches, the teacher begins another countdown from 15 . . . 14 . . . 13 . . . to get their attention for the last item of the day: the class's score on the student behavior system.

Cognitive Demand in Middle School Language Arts Classrooms

These two middle school language arts classes offer excellent examples of what students experience in these classrooms. In first example, the overarching classroom activity requires students to make inferences. The activity has several tasks that are associated with the teacher's requirement. For example, within the cognitive system, students must first be able to recall and recognize several discrete bits of information. They must draw from prior knowledge of the story, recall the definition of the word "infer," and then use that definition. These tasks represent the bulk of the cognitive demand in this portion of the lesson. In Bloom's Taxonomy (Bloom, Engelhart, Furst, Hill, & Krathwohl, 1956) they are classified as knowledge and comprehension. In Marzano and Kendall's Taxonomy (2007) they are classified as retrieval and comprehension. Students are not required to make decisions such as identifying appropriate quotes or critical details because the teacher has already selected the essential quotes. In fact, most students would be able to complete the worksheet without any previous knowledge of the story if they understood the general principle of making an inference, a task repeated twelve times in the worksheet.

In the second example, the lesson begins with a quiz. The first question requires students to use retrieval or knowledge-recall skills. Question 11 from the quiz asks students to order events in the story, a common format that teachers use to check for comprehension. However, the implementation of the task falls to the level of knowledge retrieval because of the use of prompts. In order to check for comprehension, the teacher would need to have students construct the order of events without prompts or ask them to delete events that are incorrectly ordered in a given sequence. The final example from the quiz requires students to recall the steps of a teacher-generated list. This task calls on students to use memorization skills to write the definition of a process for identifying unfamiliar words. Again, students are operating at the retrieval level of the cognitive system.

The homework assignments in both classes require the activation of several different levels of the cognitive system. In the first class, students are required to produce an "open response" to their choice of three sentence prompts, and therefore they must be able to retrieve prior information about the story and the teacher's required elements. They must demonstrate comprehension of the story by constructing a representation of the information through their own writing. Indeed, strong student responses would likely show knowledge utilization (Marzano & Kendall, 2007) or synthesis (Bloom et al., 1956) as students make decisions about what is and is not important information to include in their response. In the second classroom example, the homework similarly presents a higher cognitive task. Students must write several paragraphs in the "style" of Gary Soto as they "emulate" both his diction and tone. Students might construct an outline, design a concept map, or begin writing without any particular strategy at all. This assignment simultaneously activates several different levels of the cognitive system, which makes this task quite complex. Students must identify prior knowledge of the story that is important as they make decisions and *choose* which features of Soto's style they want to include and where. Again, strong responses would show knowledge utilization or synthesis.

Key commonalities across these classrooms include a progression from lower-level tasks in the class work to higher-level tasks in the homework assignments. Both classrooms also feature language that would be helpful in preparing for MCAS tests. For example, in the first classroom the homework assignment is called an open-response question, which is common wording in many state tests; in the second classroom, the teacher applauds students for "crossing out incorrect answers," a common test-taking strategy. Finally, both classrooms use the BBC to structure the lesson presentation, which represents an acute awareness of the use of time.

There are also subtle differences between these classrooms. While the first classroom's homework assignment gives students prompts that channel particular strands of thought and also reminds students about grammatically and stylistically correct writing, the second classroom's homework assignment features a more open-ended approach, suggesting that students write "at least" three paragraphs and use "at least" two kinds of figurative language. This teacher also emphasizes language choice, while the first assignment emphasizes grammar and the content prompts.

Two High School Math Classes

Moving to another level and another subject, a 56-minute precalculus class presents a different view of the tasks required of students. Like the vast majority of classrooms documented in this research, the class begins with a Do-Now and a BBC listing the class AIM:

- Review parts of a hyperbola
- Give an official definition of a hyperbola
- Graph a hyperbola

The Do-Now asks students to "find the equations for the asymptotes of the following hyperbolas."

$$\frac{(x-3)^2}{49} - \frac{(y+5)^2}{64} = 1$$

$$\frac{(y+2)^2}{4} - \frac{(x-3)^2}{81} = 1$$

After students worked individually and silently at their seats for six minutes completing the Do-Now, the teacher asks for answers. Several hands go up as he proceeds to integrate student responses into the answers he is writing on the overhead. Next to Problem 1, he makes the following note on the overhead: "X indicates a horizontal curve when it's first," while in his discussion of Problem 2 he writes that "it's vertical because Y comes first." No further explanation of this concept is offered and no student asks why this is true.

It takes the teacher approximately twenty minutes to write the solutions to both problems on the overhead and to graph the associated asymptotes. At this time, he tells the students that they will spend the remainder of the period working in groups of three on a similar set of questions (see the worksheet below) that the students receive in a handout. The teacher states, "This assignment will count as a quiz grade. I'll collect the notebook of one student from each group at the end of class and all the group members will be graded based on that notebook."

I. STANDARD FORM
   Rewrite the equations in standard form in your class notebook:
   $$25x^2 - 4y^2 - 50x + 16y - 91 = 0$$
   $$-36x^2 + 9y^2 - 288x - 900 = 0$$

II. GRAPH
   Graph the above hyperbolas in your notebook:

III. WRITE THE EQUATION
   Use the given information to write the equation of the hyperbola in standard form:

Vertices: $(-2, 0)$, $(-2, -8)$
Foci: $(-2, -4 + \sqrt{65})$, $(-2, -4 - \sqrt{65})$
Vertices: $(-2, 3)$, $(-8, 3)$
Foci: $(-5 + 3\sqrt{2}, 3)$, $(-5 - 3\sqrt{2}, 3)$

IV. GRAPH

Graph the above hyperbolas in your notebook.

Down the hall of the same school, a tenth-grade geometry class begins with a five-minute quiz. The first six of twelve questions appear below:

Use the diagram to describe the relationship
between the pair of angles. (Lesson 3.3)

1. <1 and <8   2. <4 and <6

3. <6 and <2   4. <2 and <7

5. <4 and <5   6. <3 and <6

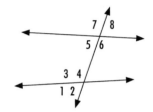

The teacher gives instructions as class begins: "You have five minutes for the Do-Now. Take your time. You may abbreviate." When the digital timer goes off five minutes later, the students trade papers with a classmate sitting nearby. The teacher asks, "Number 1 is . . . ?" Most of the students respond in unison.

After the Do-Nows have been graded and collected, the teacher begins the lesson.

"Can anyone tell me what a construction is?" Pausing briefly and hearing no answers, he answers his own question as he passes out a compass, colored pen, and unlined sheet of paper to each student. The teacher asks students to "hold your paper lengthwise" and "fold your paper this way." He then uses the compass to scribe a semicircle on the paper that intersects the fold in the middle of the paper. Unfolding the paper and connecting the points where the compass crossed the fold as "M" and "N" and the point where he placed the compass as "P," he states, "Here's my line segment." He tapes the resulting diagram on the board:

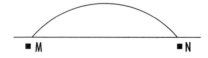

■ M   ■ N

■ P

The teacher asks students to use this construction to complete two additional assignments on their own: to construct a line OP that is perpendicular to line MN, and then to construct a line that is parallel to the line OP they constructed previously.

Cognitive Demand in High School Mathematics Classrooms

Analyzing the cognitive demand exhibited in these mathematics classrooms can take advantage of more recent and detailed work on levels of cognitive demand for mathematics (Stein et al., 2000; Porter, 2006). Andrew Porter (2007), for example, offers a useful heuristic of different levels in mathematics classrooms: memorize facts/definition/formulas; perform procedures; demonstrate understanding of mathematical ideas; conjecture/generalize/prove; and solve non-routine problems/make connections.

While the mathematical content in the first math classroom example class might seem challenging, the cognitive demand for students in these exercises resides more at the knowledge level than (Bloom et al., 1956) or perform procedures (Porter, 2007) than at any higher level. For example, the questions in Part I of the worksheet require students to remember the definition of "standard form" and to retrieve, from memory, an algorithmic procedure called completing the square to transform the equation. In the second set of exercises, the cognitive requirements to graph these hyperbola[3] lie in the application or procedures end of the spectrum, as the task requires students to choose values for "x" and "y" in order to sketch and apply the results to complete the graph. In other words, to complete the task successfully, students must activate knowledge of graphing techniques and apply this knowledge in a new situation.

To increase the cognitive demand from algorithmic and procedural exercises, the teacher might include pictures of graphs other than hyperbolas as a mix-and-match exercise, or give students a geometric picture and ask for the equation that represents the picture. This change could cause students to appraise and compare as well as discriminate and distinguish, and thus move the cognitive task toward demonstrating understanding of mathematical ideas (Porter, 2007). An alternative, still more cognitively challenging task would show incorrectly matched graphs and equations and ask the students to determine the errors and correct them.

Changing the worksheet in this way also increases the challenge because students need to move conceptually from one representational system (geometric) to another (algebraic). For students, having the fluid ability to move between geometric and algebraic representations suggests an in-depth understanding of conic sections.[4] Changes such as these could increase the cognitive demand for students to Marzano and Kendall's (2007) analysis, where "analysis involves five mental processes: matching, classifying, analyzing errors, generalizing and specifying" (p. 153).

In the second mathematics classroom where students are working in geometry, the quiz that opens the period directs students to "use the diagram to describe the relationship between the pair of angles in the following diagram." The directions are somewhat ambiguous, in that a student might answer that Angle 1 is less than Angle 8, or that Angle 4 appears in the diagram to be smaller than Angle 6. However, from a math-content perspective, it is more likely that the intention of the quiz was to assess students' memory of common mathematical terms given to angles formed by intersecting lines, such as corresponding angles, alternate interior angles, and so forth. If this was the intention, then the quiz represents cognitive tasks that reside primarily at the knowledge or memorization level, where memorization, recognition, and recall (Bloom et al., 1956; Porter, 2007) are the dominant modes of cognition.

In the construction tasks set by the teacher for this geometry classroom, the cognitive demand increases in interesting ways. For instance, the notion of a construction can be a purely mechanical, step-by-step procedure, where first one draws this arc and then one draws the next arc and so on. In the first exercise (to construct a line perpendicular to a given line), the teacher has initiated the first step, perhaps to help students who are drawing only on memorized steps of the construction. However, in order to fully comprehend the reasons that justify the steps, students must operate at several cognitive levels. Firs, being asked to complete these constructions themselves, the students must initiate the necessary steps, reasoning to themselves why certain steps are necessary and in what order, as well as consider the geometric properties created by a combination of constructions. Essentially, and perhaps at the higher level of cognitive demand, students must apply concepts of congruent triangles and proofs to be sure that the steps they are putting together will produce a perpendicular line. The thinking required to complete this task tends toward application (Bloom et al., 1956) or demonstrating understanding of mathematical ideas (Porter, 2007). Students must undertake many thinking tasks in order to be successful, including choosing, operating, appraising, differentiating, and creating.

The second exercise students must complete in the geometry classroom is far more complicated than the first construction, for two reasons. First, it depends on the successful completion of the first construction. A student challenged by the first construction will not be able to start the second construction. Another reason that this second construction is more cognitively challenging is that in order to create a parallel line, students must recognize several important geometric principles and apply them. One approach to completing this assignment (there are several, which also raises the level of challenge) requires the student to copy an angle from one part of the figure to another area on the page, which will allow for the creation of corresponding angles. The student next must realize the importance of a particular geometric theorem that states that when corresponding angles are formed by a transversal cutting two other lines, if the angles are congruent, then the lines will be parallel.

Students successfully completing this task must assemble or formulate a strategy that involves theorems about parallel lines. Pushing further, they must create a vision about where the new points will be located on the paper, and then execute a process by choosing particular moves with the compass to establish these points. In nearly all regards, this simple-sounding task of constructing a line parallel to a given line qualifies at the higher end of cognitive demand, possibly even solving non-routine problems and making connections (Porter, 2007). The final examples describe classroom instruction in two high school history classes from different schools in the study.

High School History Classrooms

Students in this first tenth-grade U.S. history class are studying the role of African Americans in the Revolutionary War. Sixteen of the nineteen students in the class are African American. The Do-Now for this class is similar to the worksheet (see below) that includes excerpts from the Constitution of the Commonwealth of Massachusetts and Part the First: A Declaration of the Rights of the Inhabitants of the Commonwealth of Massachusetts. Students are to complete a "SOAPS" analysis, which identifies the subject, occasion, audience, purpose, and speaker for the document excerpts.

HSS 10

Name:_____
Date:_____

Directions: Read and complete a SOAPS analysis for the following document.

CONSTITUTION OF THE COMMONWEALTH OF MASSACHUSETTS (1780)

...We, therefore, the people of Massachusetts, acknowledging, with grateful hearts, the goodness of the great Legislator of the universe, in affording us, in the course of His province, an opportunity, deliberately and peaceably, without fraud, violence or surprise, of entering into an original, explicit, and solemn compact with each other; and of forming a new constitution of civil government, for ourselves and posterity; and devoutly imploring His direction in so interesting a design, do agree upon, ordain and establish the following Declaration of Rights, and Frame of Government, as the Constitution of the Commonwealth of Massachusetts.

Part the First. A Declaration of the Rights of the Inhabitants of the Commonwealth of Massachusetts

Article I. All men are born free and equal, and have certain natural, essential, and unalienable rights; among which may be reckoned the right of enjoying and defending their lives and liberties; that of acquiring, possessing and protecting property; in fine, that of seeking and obtaining their safety and happiness.

> S: What is the Subject?
> O: What is the Occasion?
> A: Who is the Audience?
> P: What is the Purpose?
> S: Who is the Speaker?

What would you do if you were a slave during the American Revolution? Would you fight for the British or the Americans or neither?"

The teacher leads what he calls the "Answers to the Do-Now" section of the class. Only one or two students offer answers for the SOAPS analysis, and the students do not discuss them. However, the final question, which asks students to take a side in the war, causes the classroom to come alive with student interest; most students raise their hands now. Many respond to each other saying "I agree" or "exactly."

Following this discussion, the students watch a seven-minute video on slavery that addresses the role of African Americans during the Revolutionary War. The teacher asks students to take notes during the film on a sheet with two columns, labeled "The Revolution increased the liberty of African Americans" and "The Revolution did not increase the liberty of African Americans." The teacher reminds students to list evidence supporting the statement at the top of each column. The students appear to be engaged with the video and take notes when the narrator speaks. Immediately following the video, the teacher asks students to read a brief passage in their handout called "The Revolutionary War and African American Freedom." They work independently or with a partner to find additional evidence to add to the T-chart that they began during the video. Most students opt to work with a partner or small group to identify evidence in the reading. One student group of five in the corner of the room engages in a detailed and lively discussion of the ways in which inventions (such as the cotton gin) changed the economy in the South.

In the second example of a high school history class, students complete the Do-Now during the first five minutes of class. The AIM written just below the Do-Now sets the stage for the class:

"Analyze the use of Christianity for abolitionist and anti-abolitionist arguments."

After the Do-Now papers are returned to the teacher, the class conversation begins. The teacher asks, "What was your favorite quote or part from the text?" All the students track the teacher with their eyes, and a majority of the students participate in the conversation related to the AIM.

A few minutes later, the teacher gives each student a 3 x 5 note card, which assigns them to a particular student group. Groups 1 and 2 are to become "experts" on the argument by Harriet Beecher Stowe in an excerpt from *Uncle Tom's Cabin*. They are to "read, annotate, and dissect" the reading as a group so that they might "understand the argument," while Groups 3 and 4 are to read Louisa McCord's response to Stowe (McCord was "a member of South Carolina's slaveholding elite"). To guide their inquiry, the teacher gives each group the following worksheet:

SIDE 1: HARRIET BEECHER STOWE

1. Source information:
   Who is the author?
   What is the source of the document (i.e., book, letter, etc.)
   What year was the source published?
   Where was the document written?
2. How does Stowe define slavery? What characteristics does she attribute to slaves?
3. What religion does Stowe reference throughout the text? How does religion connect to slavery, according to Stowe?
4. For whom is Stowe writing this test? What message(s) does she want the audience to receive? What is her purpose in writing the text?

SIDE 2: LOUISA MCCORD

1. Source information:
   Who is the author?
   What is the source of the document (i.e., book, letter, etc.)

What year was the source published?

Where was the document written?

2. How does McCord define slavery? What characteristics does she attribute to slaves?

3. What religion does McCord reference throughout the text? How does religion connect to slavery, according to McCord?

4. For whom is McCord writing this test? What message(s) does she want the audience to receive? What is her purpose in writing the text?

The teacher walks around the classroom, talking with student groups. Sometimes she sits at a student desk and asks the small group questions or she calls on a member of the group to read the group's written responses. Some student groups work on the questions much of the class period. Others do not.

After about twenty minutes, the class gathers into two groups, with the Stowe and McCord camps now represented in groups of eight. The teacher states, "I want you to have a discussion about our AIM." After about ten minutes of fairly obvious statements, the teacher remarks to the whole class, "I hate to weigh in on this, because you definitely have to come up with your own interpretations, but, I think you're giving me sixth-grade answers. There's more to this than slavery is bad, all abolitionists are great."

Cognitive Demand in High School History Classrooms

In the first class, which is exploring the Constitution of the Commonwealth of Massachusetts, the SOAPS analysis requires students to classify pieces of information from the text as they match each piece to the prearranged categories, subject, occasion, audience, purpose, and speaker. The cognitive activities of classifying and matching belong to Marzano and Kendall's (2007) analysis or Bloom's (Bloom et al., 1956) application. In the task, the students receive both the method of analysis and five specific categories to scaffold their analysis. They do not create the categories.

The second task in this class requires students to gather evidence about whether the American Revolution increased the liberty of African Americans. Students must classify information as they record what they see and hear in the video and write them on the T-chart. While this task resembles the conditions for Marzano and Kendall's (2007) decisionmaking, which is emblematic of knowledge utilization, students are guided by preconditions for this decision that constrict the possible utilization of the knowledge. Because of this, the task may not entirely qualify for Marzano and Kendall's knowledge-utilization category. However, it is important to note that a few students have created important connections on their own, as evidenced by the student group that discusses the role of the cotton gin and how it connects to the role of African Americans in this period of history. The cognitive processing evident in making this connection is at a higher level and represents synthesis (Bloom et al., 1956) or analysis (Marzano & Kendall, 2007).

Students in the second history classroom are compiling information to answer the day's AIM, which is to determine the role of Christianity in abolitionist and anti-abolitionist arguments about slavery. They are completing many of the same cognitive tasks required in the SOAPS analysis in the first history class, but there is a feature of the groups in this classroom not present in the first. In this classroom, student groups must take on a particular point of view and argue on behalf of either Harriet Stowe or Louisa McCord. To complete this task, students need to provide explanations and arguments for why a particular position is more viable than another. This is a performance task, requiring synthesis skills and evaluation (Bloom et al., 1956), particularly as the teacher listens and probes the groups as they discuss their points. In addition, successful student responses show meta-cognitive and self-system thinking (Marzano & Kendall, 2007). These mental processes show how students monitor their own execution of the task and manage their own emotional responses while other students or the teacher challenge their thinking. Certainly, the students in the first history classroom might engage in similar tasks, but the teacher did not make this particular performance expectation explicit.

Looking across Classrooms

Drawing on these representative examples of classroom tasks, several general comments are apparent. First, across these schools, structural elements that guide instructed practices—the use of time for academic work, the uniform lesson structure of the BBC, the deliberate efforts to make students aware of the MCAS and its components, and the conscious strategy of aligning classroom content with the Massachusetts Curricular Framework—help drive academic achievement on standardized assessments. Furthermore, observations document that these charter classrooms are appropriately busy and active places. It is not uncommon to find multiple activities and strategies, such as small-group work, lectures, teacher demonstrations, and discussions, used within the same class period as teachers alternate their use of various instructional techniques.

Second, these examples, as well as the overall collection of classroom observation data, suggest variation in the level of cognitive demand required of students both across and within these schools. Certainly, all schools experience some degree of variation in instruction, since classrooms are unique units filled with children who differ developmentally. Teachers also may differ in important dimensions, such as background knowledge, teaching experience, and extent of pedagogical repertoire. And yet, as discussed in the previous chapter on "getting the right people," these schools work hard to find teachers who fit, so more coherence rather than less in terms of instructional practice would be expected.

There is no question that classrooms can be wild, unpredictable places affected by myriad contextual elements, including grade level, emotional maturity of students, and school and community contexts. Furthermore, as Sizer (1992) reminds educators in *Horace's Compromise*, negotiations between teachers and students around the work in classrooms are omnipresent, sometimes giving rise to "Treaties of Mediocrity." Cohen (1988), in his essay on the nature of teaching, also helps explain the level of variation in classrooms by identifying the necessary co-dependence between teacher and student. He describes teaching (along with psychotherapy) as an endeavor of "human improvement":

> In ... teaching and related practices, clients co-produce results. [The] students' ... will and skill are no less important than [the teachers']. No matter how hard practitioners try, or how artfully they work, they can produce no results alone. They can succeed only if their clients succeed. (p. 57)

Possible Explanations for Instructional Variation in Charter Classrooms

One general explanation for variations in classroom instruction is that instruction that incorporates problem-solving, decisionmaking, and creating and designing experiments is difficult to do and can create uncomfortable situations for teachers and students. Shulman (2004), for example, notes that

> classrooms and schools that are characterized by activity, reflection, and collaboration in learning communities are inherently uncertain, complex and demanding. Both learning and teaching in such settings entail high levels of risk and unpredictability for the participants. (p. 515)

Because these schools have an annual teacher turnover rate of approximately 15 percent to 25 percent, some teachers may not be comfortable embracing Shulman's "unpredictability" as they settle into their new positions. After all, few teachers want to appear ineffective in the eyes of a frequently present supervisor (described in chapter 9). Furthermore, unlike teacher-centered and -controlled instruction, setting students on more open-ended, self-motivated investigatory tasks can cause teachers to encounter material or information that may lie beyond their knowledge base or the pedagogical repertoire they have developed through teaching experience.

Another explanation for variation in these schools may rest, ironically, on the very elements that contribute to the externally defined structural coherence in these classrooms. For example, quantitative measurements of learning in open-ended, creative experiences can be difficult to come by. Thus, being unsure or unable to measure what students are learning in concrete terms might pose a challenge in these data-driven schools because of their tight curricular planning structures and close alignment to the Massachusetts Curricular Frameworks common to these schools. In these schools, many decisions about instruction derive directly from the data analysis of tasks that are likely to exist on standardized assessments. Furthermore, a pervasive use of worksheets and short Do-Nows could influence students' approach to thinking and knowledge (Doyle, 1983). Depending on the tasks required on the Do-Nows, for instance, this form of instruction—short answer, five-minute or less exercises, repeated application of procedures—combined with a sense of urgency may work against reflection and make accessing cognitive tasks such as arguing, defending, supporting, valuing, or evaluating more difficult to achieve.

Requiring more cognitively demanding tasks in classrooms also can create uncertainties that administrators find difficult to manage. Recall the analogy that these schools operate like finely tuned, carefully coordinated Swiss watches. Yet, open-ended experiments and activities can be unpredictable: they may be inconclusive, create chaos, and spawn unpredictable student behavior that lies outside existing norms or standards of decorum. This could create a tension for staff members who have come to appreciate the purposefully defined and consistently implemented behavioral norms. Open-ended classroom projects may take longer than originally planned, creating a dilemma for staff members who expect to adhere to year-long plans created in the summer.

There are also legitimate concerns both internally and externally to these schools about whether pushing for large amounts of academic work results in pushing kids out the door; unlike their peers in traditional schools, these charter students have the option to attend other schools. Pushing students hard is tricky. For example, teachers in one of the study schools reasonably ask, "How can I push more kids to do more challenging work without losing kids along the way?" These charter school students have peers in other urban schools who are not required to do as much work. One administrator characterizes this tension:

[As] the kids realize they are doing more and more than their friends in traditional high-poverty schools, it becomes increasingly difficult to motivate them. Essentially, from a kid's point of view, it's [something like], "I'm already doing work three times harder than my friend, and you're saying I should do work five times harder?"

Another important concern in this area relates to the natural tendency to conflate rigor with quantity of work. Students in these charter schools have a great deal of work, they are busy all day, and they have little time off-task. The fact that students in these schools are busy and engaged is undeniable, yet it is important to explore the level and rigor of their engagement.

In all schools, not just these five schools, there are other factors that work against increasing the level of cognitive tasks. For instance, many students have an initial propensity to resist the more challenging intellectual work involved in open-ended or independent tasks (Sizer, 1992). Cohen (1988) describes this tension well:

Problems of difficulty and dependence interact. When teachers devise very taxing lessons, they create opportunities for students to make large intellectual leaps forward, and thus hold out the promise of great success and satisfaction for all concerned. But such lessons also increase the probability that students will demur, avoid the challenge, asks for less demanding assignments, resist, or rebel. This would close off much chance of success for practitioners. (p. 482)

Finally, there are inherent pedagogical challenges in the kind of teaching that consistently engages high cognitive demand. Elmore's ongoing research, for example, suggests that "as a teacher increases the cognitive task level within a classroom, the presence of student variation in performance may increase as well" (R. Elmore, personal correspondence, July 2, 2008). In other words, as tasks become more challenging, greater variability in a group of students emerges. Hence, the drive to create higher cognitive demand can introduce a new type of pedagogical challenge for teachers.

Lessons for Replication

This book focuses on practices that help create high-performing schools and offers important lessons for policymaker and practitioners alike about what these schools are starting to do to address the tensions around variation within classrooms instruction. Many of the school leaders express a deep concern about variation in academic tasks. For example, one leader rhetorically asked, "Is there variability in the tasks required of students in our schools? You bet —but we're working on it." In another school, a leader noted that "far from avoiding the uncertainties and unpredictability that the more cognitively demanding tasks can create, we are deeply committed to supporting our teachers as they engage in this challenging form of teaching." Offering information about the ways these schools are beginning to address instructional variation is important to anyone seeking to provide a high-quality education to all children.

Several of these five schools see professional development as a way to support teachers in discussions about instruction. For example, one leader noted that the professional development work in her school was beginning to focus "specifically on the rigor and cognitive demand of our lessons." In another school, the staff spent several meetings during the last year talking about student engagement and exploring explicit questioning strategies to raise the cognitive demand in classrooms.

To support their teachers, administrators in several schools regularly observe them and then offer feedback on a variety of practices ranging from the BBC and discipline to pedagogy, using a common observation form. In adopting this approach, it is important that practitioners comment not only on structural, perhaps more easily observable, elements of the classroom but also on teachers' actions that affect the cognitive level. For example, administrators at one charter school rate their teachers on a checklist with descriptions such as, "Lesson plan is tight, moving at a challenging pace, with neither time nor space for students to be off-task" and "Disruptions to learning are not permitted. If a student is disrupting, he/she receives a consequence." On the form in use during the 2007-08 school year in this school, only one of the nineteen elements referred to the cognitive level of the work: "Rigor of lesson is age-appropriate and indicative of high expectations for student achievement." As evidence of the school's growing awareness around cognitive demand, a subsequent revision of this observation form for 2008-09 now asks the observer to indicate whether the students are asked to "Know and Comprehend; Apply and Analyze; or Synthesize and Evaluate," reflecting Bloom's Taxonomy (Bloom et al., 1956). Thus, an important lesson for those adopting a similarly rigorous observation regimen for teachers is to ensure that the observation attends not only to structural elements but to cognitive indicators as well.

Several of these schools have initiated other strategies to address instructional practice and begin the work of increasing the cognitive demand for students. For example, one school recently created a position of instructional coach and placed one of the school's stronger teachers in this role. The school leader says this person, who is familiar with the school's culture and norms of operation, now serves as "a full-time instructional coach for our middle school precisely for the purpose of further improving our instruction in the middle school." Finally, schools report an increase in long-term projects, lengthy research papers, science fairs, and senior capstone projects in every twelfth-grade class, as well as mandated requirements that in some instances include Advanced Placement courses.

Conclusion

Despite school leaders' awareness of instructional practice and significant efforts to address issues of instruction, substantial variation in cognitive demand exists in these charter school classrooms. Charter schools are thus no more immune to the challenges of instructional practice than traditional schools. However, the significant success that these charter schools enjoy on standardized measures, such as the MCAS, suggests that the combined impact of the purposeful alignment of school culture, structures, systems, and the right people may serve as an antibody that helps mitigate variation in the level of cognitive demand.

As state accountability and performance measures change and likely increase, so will the attention to what happens inside classrooms, since much of the responsibility to respond to broader and more comprehensive measures will fall to teachers with support from their administrators. It is clear, in both this chapter and chapter 9, that the ability of these schools to function as highly coherent, high-performing schools in the future will be only as great as the quality and level of instruction delivered by teachers in classrooms. The teachers in these five schools work extraordinarily hard and are exceptionally smart, passionate, caring, and thoughtful. Having already accomplished great things with their students and with a demonstrated commitment to continuous improvement, these schools and the teachers in them are well positioned to advance their instructional practices to levels rarely seen in K–12 education.

CHAPTER ELEVEN

STEPPING BACK AND LOOKING FORWARD

Katherine K. Merseth

This is a book about five urban charter schools in the Commonwealth of Massachusetts. The teachers, administrators, and staff at these schools eagerly embrace the enormous responsibility of educating more than 1,600 youngsters, every day of every school year, year after year. These are not ordinary public schools, nor are they ordinary public charter schools. These schools are special in their singular focus on purpose, their coherent employment of practices, and their enduring and infectious cultures. Relatively new as schools, they offer important insights for all schools, whether start-up charters or the oldest traditional schools in America. These schools work tirelessly to enable the children in their classrooms to achieve strong outcomes.

What Are the Lessons?

What are the key elements that enable these schools to move children, who often begin their academic work performing well below grade level, to levels of basic proficiency and higher on statewide performance measures just a few years later? What enables the secondary schools in this study to have a nearly 100 percent college-acceptance rate for their graduating seniors, when traditional schools in the same urban communities struggle to get just over 60 percent of their students to graduate from high school?[1] These schools are not just moving a handful of students along the grade-level conveyer belt toward high school and college access and academic attainment; they are moving *most* of their students along this path.

The previous chapters highlight several important, even critical, elements that make these institutions both outstanding schools and high-performing nonprofit organizations. These elements include:

- A clear sense of mission and a broadly shared institutional culture dedicated to the achievement of the school's mission
- A set of organizational structures and systems that support student learning
- A collection of purposefully chosen teachers and administrators who "fit" the organization's objectives and exhibit a passionate commitment to the school's goals
- A family network that is aware of and willing to carry out their responsibilities in support of their children
- A set of classroom procedures that maximizes time on task and tightly links content to the Massachusetts Curriculum Frameworks

The essential thread that runs through all of the chapters is the notion of coherence, without which these schools would be nothing more than a loose confederation of systems, people, and random objectives; the whole would be less than the sum of its parts. However, these five schools operate in a purposeful and deliberate manner—in a coherent manner—where little is uncertain and less is left to chance. Mission statements are clear and powerful, systems and structures are designed judiciously to serve these missions, and teachers are hired for their fit to the school culture and their willingness to accept and implement these systems. As new students and staff join the school community, intentional programs indoctrinate them into the culture of the school. Everyone in the school buildings embraces and internalizes the driving purpose of these schools. Without this degree of coherence, these schools would not qualify as high-performing nonprofit organizations. They would be merely ordinary, not extraordinary. When asked about the attributes that lead to her school's success, one leader summarized it well:

> I think what's most important is the consistency in expectation and the attitude with which we approach the work. Everybody's on the same page, we're all working toward this goal, and we're going to work really hard to get there. I feel like that's the most important thing. This is why, when I've tried to work with other schools to pick up a program here and put it over there, it's never really worked.

Stepping Back

Stepping back from these lessons, this final chapter invites readers to reflect with the authors, their colleagues in these schools, and other K–12 practitioners and policymakers about deeper issues that emerge from the study. Each of these schools is a success in its own right, and each has done more than has ever been asked of it. Yet, exploring deeper issues raised by the practices of these schools is important, because they provide a broader context and help inform those interested in replicating these practices.

One fundamental question for practitioners and policymakers interested in the practices of these successful schools is, "What *does* it take?" No success comes without a price—decisions and actions always involve trade-offs. Each school in this study wrestles with, and will continue to confront, such trade-offs. A useful approach for exploring the trade-offs that all school practitioners and policymakers must face is the concept of dilemmas. Long-time school practitioner and Stanford University emeritus professor Larry Cuban (2001) describes dilemmas as "messy, complicated, and conflict-filled situations that require undesirable choices between competing, highly prized values that cannot be simultaneously or fully satisfied" (p. 10). Dilemmas are never solved; rather, they are managed (Lampert, 1985). Furthermore, there are no "right answers" to dilemmas—no "correct" ways to manage them. Dilemmas invoke values—values that often conflict because individuals necessarily hold different worldviews.

Dilemmas are an inescapable reality of school management. Some involve resource allocation, such as whether to devote limited resources to a music program or to additional afterschool tutoring. Others are more fundamental, such as whether to employ a schoolwide "No Excuses" student behavior system or to leave teachers with greater discretion over the disciplinary procedures inside their classrooms. Another example might be whether a school should expect a newly married teacher with a newborn at home to work sixty-eighty hours per week and offer a personal cell-phone number to students on a "24/7" basis.

More emotionally charged dilemmas arise around the attitude a school takes toward its role in educating children. Some schools, for example, may view their role as identifying and addressing children's weaknesses—that is, they see the task of a school, particularly in an urban environment, as having to compensate for what the children do not have. Another school, however, may not choose to focus on children's academic weakness and instead will strive to identify children's particular strengths and assets and then build on these competencies. Another equally charged issue concerns student agency: how strongly do educators value student independence and agency across the age span of learners? Do they believe that students, particularly those who enter these schools well behind their peers, need relatively tight structures and engagement with basic academic tasks that stress memorization, factual recall, procedures, and drill? All of the schools in this study face these and other dilemmas in one way or another, and they manage them in ways that are in accord with the values and beliefs they bring to the enterprise.

In the current accountability environment, the schools in this study may feel they have little latitude in how to manage several of these dilemmas, especially those related to student outcome measures. Their approach to the Massachusetts Comprehensive Assessment System (MCAS) seems particularly necessary, because this is the measure by which Massachusetts schools are evaluated in the current era of accountability. It is not surprising that these five schools have taken a relatively similar test-aware approach to their work. However, by embracing such approaches, are these schools, and other like-minded charters, living up to their mandate to "renew public education" (Finn, Manno, & Vanourek, 2000; Hill, Pierce, & Guthrie, 1997)? Are they fundamentally changing American education, or are they (perhaps unwittingly) players in an educational testing system that some call a "sucker's game" (R. Elmore, personal communication, July 16, 2008)? As commendable as these schools are in creating options for students whose opportunities are often limited, could they do more? And is it reasonable to expect them to do more? Answers to these questions are elusive, but without raising the questions, we, as researchers, educators, and policymakers, run the risk of unintentionally perpetuating a system that does not serve all children well.

In this particular context, one such question, addressed to policymakers but useful for all practitioners to consider, is this: Is it proper for government to support schools that explicitly and exclusively focus on college and college success (T. Sizer and N. Sizer, personal communication, July 22, 2008)? Is this an appropriate use of public funds when the state constitution guarantees all students the right to a publicly funded education, even if they do not aspire to college? By developing a reputation for nonnegotiable academic standards, are these schools excluding certain students or segments of the population? What about those who aspire to a job or career that does not require a college education, whether as a mechanic or a musician? Should it be an obligation of charter schools to attend to these "other" students in the same spirit with which traditional public schools must serve all students? Responses to this basic dilemma will vary, yet it helps illustrate broader, more general issues related to the charter movement.

Looking Forward: What Matters?

These charter schools, like all schools, operate in an increasingly challenging environment of strict accountability with narrow measures imposed by policymakers. Clearly, no charter school whose charter is renewed every five years can afford to ignore state-established performance measures, such as the MCAS. Even so, with the focus in these study schools being expanded to include other tests, such as the Secondary School Admissions Test, the Independent School Entrance Examination, or the Scholastic Aptitude Test, questions about their intense focus on tests warrant consideration because, as Koretz (2008) notes:

> Careful testing can in fact give us tremendously valuable information about student achievement that we would otherwise lack . . . and it does rest on several generations of accumulated scientific research and development. But that is no reason to be uncritical of using information from tests. . . . Of the many complexities entailed by educational testing, the most fundamental, and the one that is ultimately the root of so many misunderstandings of test scores, is that test scores usually do not provide a direct and complete measure of educational achievement. (pp. 8–9)

If this era of accountability has restricted schools' flexibility in managing these dilemmas, are there changes that policymakers could implement to give schools greater freedom to define how they should be held accountable? What other outcome measures would be appropriate for children who will live their lives entirely in the twenty-first century? Following this question, an even more essential question looms: *For what purpose do we educate children?*

What Should Matter?

It is clear that important questions remain: What do we want from our schools? Is the purpose of K–12 schools to participate exclusively in the attainment efforts and measures to get students to the next educational level? Or, does society want schools and their children to meet even broader standards, such as social skills, civic capacity, lifelong learning, democratic citizenship, or being responsible parents? The agenda for schooling in America soon may change and move its focus off high-stakes testing to embrace different outcomes and new measures. For example, Nancy Walser (2008) offers a comprehensive list of "Skills for a New Century," which includes some or all of the following:

Critical Thinking	Self-Direction
Problem-Solving	Leadership
Collaboration	Adaptability
Written and Oral Communication	Responsibility
Creativity	Global Awareness

Or, as Stacey Childress asks (personal communication, April 4, 2008), will it be possible for schools to "offer academics, enrichment, and socioemotional growth all at once? . . . [After all,] proficiency levels on state and norm-referenced tests are only the first step in a very long journey."

These five charter schools are increasingly aware of the tension between test preparation and broader goals. In order to accelerate the shift toward broader skills than those measured by standardized tests, we offer a refinement of the Charter School Coherence Model (CSCM). The new model incorporates the fundamental success elements discussed in chapter 6, but now puts a greater focus onto instruction than emerged in the previous model. The new model, the Charter School Coherence Model around Instruction (CSCMI), suggests what will be necessary for the future success of these schools (see figure 11.1)

This new model makes instruction an integral focus for the people, structures, and systems of the organization within the context of culture. Instruction, in this model, links directly to student outcomes and represents the next level of work.

Several schools in this study already are engaging in this next level of work around instruction. As one school leader notes, "In fact, ten years into the work, our structures and systems are well-oiled and working, fortunately. The 'next level of work' is what we are doing now." To advance this focus, these schools will need to become "ambidextrous" (O'Reilly & Tushman, 2004). That is, while they continue their current work meeting state performance standards, they need to be simultaneously thinking, planning, and strategizing about how to impact the instruction in their schools and where to set their next goals. There is no better time, as Peter Drucker (1990) notes, to undertake future planning than when you are successful: "When you are successful is the very time to ask, 'Can't we do better?'" (p. 67).

Given their nimbleness, coherence, and ability to dedicate themselves to a clear purpose, if these schools decide they want to respond to this next level of work it is likely they will succeed. The task will not be easy, but these schools

FIGURE 11.1   Charter School Coherence Model around Instruction (CSCMI)

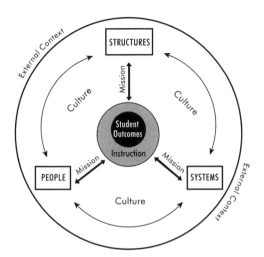

have never avoided challenging tasks. In fact, they embrace them. These charter schools excel at taking youngsters who are traditionally left behind and helping them learn at basic proficiency levels. In several more years, we will know whether these schools are successful not only in getting their students into college, but also in preparing them to *succeed* in college, and beyond. Furthermore, we also may know what these schools will do with students who do not want to go to college. At that point, these extraordinary schools may revisit the educational questions raised earlier: Who should we educate? How should we educate? For what purpose do we educate?

Perhaps their next level of work will not involve tests, standards, and narrow measures, but something more simple, yet profound:

> The entire object of true education is to make people not merely do the right things, but enjoy them; not merely industrious, but to love industry; not merely learned, but to love knowledge; not merely pure, but to love purity; not merely just, but to hunger and thirst after justice.
>
> —*John Ruskin (1819–1900), British critic, author, and poet*

Given the extraordinary capacity of these five charter schools, there is little doubt that if these schools and others like them make a commitment to a broader goal of education, such as outlined by Ruskin, their students will receive handsome rewards in the future.

Appendices

APPENDIX I.A

Inside Urban Charter Schools: Promising Practices and Strategies in Five High-Performing Schools is part of a larger work, *Keeping the Promise: The Massachusetts Charter School Dissemination and Replication Project*, which seeks to distinguish elements in high-performing charter schools that serve large numbers of students at educational risk. The U.S. Department of Education Charter Schools Program award 84.282N sponsors the work of *Keeping the Promise*. However, the contents of this book do not necessarily represent the policy of the Department of Education and do not represent endorsement by the federal government.

Data Collection

Investigating the practices that seem to contribute to the "success" of these five schools required several strategies for collecting data.

The primary source of information was on-site, semistructured interviews with teachers and administrators in these five schools. Over ninety interviews were conducted between 2007 and 2008, generally with either one researcher and one school staff member or two researchers and one school staff member. Interviewees were promised that their names would not appear in the book and, where possible, their identities would be disguised. Questions, drafted in advance of most interviews, ensured continuity across the schools, but researchers had the discretion to follow their interviewees when the conversation left the script. Most interviews were approximately one hour long. Every interview was recorded, using audio recorders, and transcribed, using a professional transcription service. The researchers then imported the transcripts into NVivo, a coding software program for qualitative research, for additional analysis (see below).

A second, important source of information was in-school observations. Each student researcher was the primary investigator at one of the five schools and spent considerable time on site. Other researchers on the team also purposefully visited sites other than their own. Research assistants became a consistent, familiar presence in the schools, sitting in classrooms, observing hallway interactions, and fully engaging in school (and afterschool) activities. The team created observation protocols to promote consistency across schools. In all, researchers spent over fifty days in the schools, amassing binders full of notes, class materials, and other data.

The researchers also conducted parent focus groups, where parents of current students were asked to describe their impressions of the school. These conversations also were recorded and transcribed. Focus groups lasted for at least one hour, and the number of parent participants at a particular school ranged from three to eleven. Schools were responsible for identifying, inviting, and communicating with potential participants, compromising the likelihood that each group's views accurately reflected those of the school community more generally.

Finally, the researchers used a variety of reports, handbooks, websites, and other documents to gather information about the schools. This included both school-developed materials (e.g., annual reports) and externally developed materials (e.g., Massachusetts Department of Education site visit renewal reports). References to these sources appear throughout the book.

One important data source that was not made available to the researchers included direct contact or permission to interview students. This was a decision made by the funder, the U.S. Department of Education. Thus, the impressions of student experiences at these schools are not directly confirmed through student interviews, even though they are firmly grounded in classroom observations, parent focus groups, and other data.

Data Analysis

Data analysis began with importing interview and focus group transcripts into NVivo and identifying a set of codes to use in categorizing information about school organization and practice. The primary codes included such topics as leadership; hiring; culture; structures and systems; teachers; curriculum and pedagogy; students, parents, and community; professional development; relationships; and finance. After coding data into these broad categories, a second round of coding further "fractured" the information into discrete topics for analysis (Maxwell, 2005). When this organizational stage of transcript review was complete, themes from literature about successful schools (Strauss &

Corbin, 1990) were reviewed, noting which comments and attributions were central to identifying characteristics underlying success. These represented "etic codes," which were then used in a third round of transcript coding within each subcategorical bin. Etic coding applied existing theory to determine whether and how the data aligned with the research on effective schooling. This data—as well as other information collected from observations, document reviews, focus groups, and so on—became the subject of weekly two-hour meetings with the research team over the course of the two-year project, ensuring careful scrutiny and analyses of the data.

Threats to Validity

Possible researcher bias, in which the researchers' identities, perspectives, and past experiences influence data collection and interpretation of findings, is a potential threat to the validity of this work (Maxwell, 2005). To address this possible threat, the principal investigator deliberately selected a team of research assistants with varied but substantial backgrounds in schools and education more broadly. Nothing presented herein represents the perspective of any single individual. Rather, all findings presented in this book are the result of extensive analysis, debate, and reflection among the six members of the research team and thus are informed by a variety of viewpoints and background knowledge. In addition, members of the research team acknowledged any potential biases brought from their prior experiences and attempted to minimize their impact by routinely recognizing and questioning these biases during analysis.

APPENDIX 2.A

Results Meeting Protocol

1. Identify Roles [5 minutes]
   - (timer, facilitator, electronic recorder, visual recorder)

2. Presentation by Case Study Writer [10 minutes]
   - Identify the skill and standard
   - Share what students need to know and be able to do to master this skill/standard
   - Share test question at issue and related relevant questions
   - Share data related to test question and related questions
   - Share what has been tried, what has worked, and what students are struggling with

3. Clarifying Questions from Group Members [5 minutes]

4. Brainstorm Solutions [15 minutes]
   - Be specific
   - 30 seconds per group member per solution
   - No judgment, commentary on any idea yet
   - Members may pass, but the group needs to continue brainstorming for 15 minutes
   - Visual recorder writes ideas on board; electronic recorder types

5. Group Identifies Top 3-5 Solutions and Fleshes Out These Ideas [10 minutes]

6. Group Summarizes Results and Develops Action Plan [10 minutes]
   - Electronic recorder creates notes summarizing the case study, action plan, and most important findings that can be emailed to group

APPENDIX 10.A

2007 Tenth-Grade MCAS Results, Percentage Scoring in Each Performance Category

Name	Subject Test	Advanced	Proficient	Needs Improvement	Failing	Total # Tested
Academy of the Pacific Rim	Math	72	19	6	3	36
Boston Collegiate	Math	55	34	10	0	29
MATCH	Math	76	24	0	0	46
Boston Public Schools	Math	33	22	27	18	3,951
Massachusetts	Math	42	27	22	9	72,471
Academy of the Pacific Rim	ELA	11	58	26	5	38
Boston Collegiate	ELA	14	69	14	3	29
MATCH	ELA	11	72	17	0	46
Boston Public Schools	ELA	11	39	37	13	4,044
Massachusetts	ELA	22	49	24	6	71,692

2007 Eighth-Grade MCAS Results, Percentage Scoring in Each Performance Category

Name	Subject Test	Advanced	Proficient	Needs Improvement	Failing	Total # Tested
Academy of the Pacific Rim	Math	8	48	34	9	64
Boston Collegiate	Math	14	61	21	4	57
Lawrence Community Day	Math	35	58	8	0	26
Roxbury Prep	Math	49	45	6	0	49
Boston Public Schools	Math	7	20	31	42	4,211
Massachusetts	Math	17	28	30	25	74,319
Academy of the Pacific Rim	ELA	0	77	23	0	62
Boston Collegiate	ELA	16	74	11	0	57
Lawrence Community Day	ELA	15	81	4	0	26
Roxbury Prep	ELA	12	80	8	0	49
Boston Public Schools	ELA	4	51	30	14	4,208
Massachusetts	ELA	12	63	18	6	74,433
Academy of the Pacific Rim	Science	0	13	61	27	64
Boston Collegiate	Science	2	40	49	9	57
Lawrence Community Day	Science	12	62	27	0	26
Roxbury Prep	Science	6	43	47	4	49
Boston Public Schools	Science	0	8	38	54	4,207
Massachusetts	Science	3	30	44	24	74,257

APPENDIX 10.B

Mean SAT 2006 School Year Results for Charter Schools and Boston Public Schools (Range 200—800)

	Reading	Writing	Mathematics	Participation Rate
Academy of the Pacific Rim*	436	424	451	~100%
Boston Collegiate**	470		490	~100%
MATCH***	420	430	490	~100%
Boston Public Schools****	434	431	451	61%
Standard deviation (U.S.)	113	109	115	

Data Source: 2006–07 School Annual Reports[1] and Boston Public Schools Office of Communication
Source: APR 2006–07 Annual Report
**Source:* BCCS 2006–07 Annual Report
***Source:* MATCH 2006–07 Annual Report
****Source:* BPS Research Brief: SAT Results

Mean SAT 2007 School Year Results for Charter Schools (Boston Public Schools data unavailable)

	Reading	Writing	Mathematics	Participation Rate
Academy of the Pacific Rim	450	466	482	~100%
Boston Collegiate	476	480	488	~100%
MATCH	476	459	512	~100%

Data Source: College Entrance Examination Board[2]

APPENDIX 10.C

Observation Methodology

Building on the information presented in the appendix to the Introduction about the study's methodology, additional details surrounding the observational data used in this chapter are important.

As noted previously, the primary set of codes used to categorize data gathered from teacher and administrator interviews and parent focus groups included the following topics: leadership; hiring; culture; structures and systems; teachers; curriculum and pedagogy; students, parents, and community; professional development; relationships; and finance. After coding data into these broad categories, a second round of coding distributed this data into discrete topics for analysis (Maxwell, 2005). Upon completion and review of this process, the research team noted that the category of curriculum and pedagogy was underrepresented with respect to the other categories. Furthermore, the existing data in this category referred more significantly to curriculum and structural features of the classroom than to pedagogy or to the "instructional core." The research team takes the meaning of instructional core to be:

> The instructional core is defined by the relationship of the student and the teacher in the presence of content. In this model, it is possible to talk about the knowledge and skill of the teacher in relation to the content, the knowledge and skill of the teacher in relation to the student's mastery of the content, and the ways in which the content is refracted through the understanding of the teacher and the student. (Elmore, 2004, p. 222)

Because of the lack of data around teacher pedagogy and the instructional core, the team made a commitment to return to the school sites and conduct classroom observations using an observation protocol. In addition, the primary researcher at each school site shadowed one student for an entire day, which afforded more opportunities to gather data about instructional activities in the classrooms. The work of Hawkins (1974), Doyle (1983, 1988), and Elmore (personal communication, February, 2007) grounded the design of the observation protocol. The protocol has three guiding questions:

1. What do I see the students doing?
2. What do I see the teacher doing?
3. How do I classify the cognitive demand of the task the student is required to do?

Certainly, this protocol might have focused on other aspects of instruction and student engagement. Questions around teacher pedagogy, for example, might ask: Is the teacher standing in front of the room lecturing, or is she organizing students into small groups to collaboratively complete a worksheet? Is he walking around providing assistance to students as they write an essay? Is she showing a video? These are important questions to ask about instruction, but such descriptions of teachers' actions do not by themselves expose what learners actually have to do to meet the demands of the class. In another example, collaborative groups might be the latest trend in classroom practice, but students could be working in collaborative groups to answer factual recall questions from a textbook, or they could be working in collaborative groups to transfer the lessons learned in the Cold War into a political strategy for a new nation. In other words, any modality of teaching can draw upon a spectrum of cognitive demand for students. Therefore, one approach to quickly and efficiently represent a view of classroom instruction is to ask, What do we see students doing?

Each of the five researchers was given primary responsibility for classroom observations in one of the five schools. Researchers visited a total of eighty-nine different classrooms at least once, totaling twenty-two full days of classroom observations. We also shadowed five students, one at each site, picked at random, for one full school day. In addition, each researcher completed validity checks by visiting two of the other school sites that were not their primary research site; we completed a total of forty-nine secondary observations for these validity checks.

These observations occurred during the fall of 2007 and the winter of 2008. Once again, it is important to note that the researchers were restricted by the U.S. Department of Education from interviewing or contacting individual students for data collection purposes.

Data Analysis

Team members began by reviewing observation notes, classroom artifacts, student handouts, and other classroom materials collected during the observations. Analysis and discussion of the data occurred during the weekly team meetings in the spring of 2008. Given the length limitations of the chapter, as well as literature suggesting that a focus on academic tasks affords a powerful lens into how students experience classroom instruction, the team focused primarily on the specific academic tasks the students were required to complete.

We further narrowed our focus to English, math, and history classrooms for two reasons: (1) across all grades in these five schools, a heavy emphasis on English and math instruction comprises the bulk of the mandatory state testing in Massachusetts; (2) mandatory testing in U.S. history will begin for tenth graders in 2010, thus the schools are developing curriculum and strategies to prepare students for this exam. Although science and technology exams are now mandatory for high school students in the class of 2010, schools have a choice around whether to test students in biology, chemistry, introductory physics, or technology/engineering. Accordingly, the schools take distinct approaches to science curriculum and instruction that make discussions of classroom instruction more difficult in this subject area.

Next, we selected three pairs of classrooms. The pairs consisted of the following:

1. Two middle school English classrooms, from different schools in the study
2. Two high school mathematics classrooms, from one school in the study
3. Two high school history classrooms, from different schools in the study

These pairs reflect an iterative process by the research team to highlight both the similarities and the variation resulting from the review of many hours of classroom instruction. There were strong similarities across classrooms in terms of how lessons were structured and organized around the Do-Nows and aligned to specific Aims that reflected the Massachusetts Content Frameworks. But, important differences remained in terms of what teachers required students to do within these similar frameworks. Thus, selecting the classroom pairs permits an illustration of the structural similarities while permitting a deeper examination of the differences in what students are required to do in different classrooms. Pairs 1 and 3 showcase similarities and differences across schools, while Pair 2 illustrates similarities and differences within one school. The patterns revealed in these pairs reoccur frequently across the entire dataset.

In order to provide a common measure for what students are required to do in these six classrooms, two members of the research team (Merseth and Roberts) drew from the work around academic tasks (Doyle, 1983) and taxonomies of cognitive demand (Bloom et al., 1956; Marzano & Kendall, 2007).

Threats to Validity

The appendix to the Introduction addresses the potential threats to validity and the steps taken to guard against the introduction of bias. A further strategy to protect against bias in the analysis of the classroom observation data included the assignment of a senior researcher (Merseth) with over forty years of experience working in a wide range of schools and classrooms, both nationally and internationally, and a research assistant (Roberts) with training in classroom observations and experience both as a teacher and as an administrator in charter schools.

Notes

Introduction

1. A students who leaves a school and enrolls in another school before October 1 of the following school year is not counted as a dropout against the school the student has left.

2. The authors identified several specific concerns about these measures, including a fundamental concern that the lone student performance criterion for selection was MCAS results for 2006. State test scores offer but one measure of student learning and represent an imperfect reflection of academic quality.

   A second concern was the arbitrariness of a school being located in a Massachusetts district that falls within the top 10 percent of state districts with the highest proportions of children in poverty, according to the 2003 U.S. Census. Why not 20 percent or 5 percent? And why was only one year's worth of census data used to identify districts. Different years produce different communities that meet the 10 percent cutoff. For example, using 2002 data would include Somerville and Quincy but exclude Taunton and Westfield, while the 2004 data adds Monroe and Oak Bluffs and removes Easthampton and Ware. A better method would be a three-year average.

   Third, a major concern was that only charter schools *located* in the top 10 percent communities were considered for selection even though a school in a community not in the top 10 percent could very easily have high levels of students in poverty. For instance, a charter school in Somerville would likely draw many students from Cambridge, Everett, and even the Boston Public Schools, yet according to this method would not be included. Conversely, charter schools *located* in a high-poverty district, such as several in this study, may not have the same concentrations of low-income youth as the geographic district. For example, the low-income student population for the Boston Public Schools was reported as 71 percent, whereas the same measure for the Boston-based Academy of the Pacific Rim and Boston Collegiate Charter School was 51 percent and 42 percent, respectively. An additional concern focuses on the use of actual census-defined poverty rates to identify high-need communities for the first criterion and a different measure of free and reduced-price lunch eligibility in fourth criterion. This means that different criteria use different indicators of poverty in the selection process.

   A final but important concern relates to the fourth criterion, Adequate Yearly Progress (AYP) with respect to NCLB. The only subgroup reviewed in this regard was low-income students and not other important subgroups such as special education and English-language learner students. There were significant differences with these particular subgroups and the district in which these schools are located.

Clearly one cannot rule out that differences in student population due to self-selection may explain some portion of the differences in performance at these schools, rather than factors that are attributable to the schools themselves. Without specifically considering other subgroups and conducting a controlled study for those who wished to attend these schools and were not selected, any analysis of a "high-performing" charter school will necessarily be incomplete and subject to methodological criticism.

Chapter One

1. Researchers conducted a focus group with parents at each school. School administrators invited parents to participate. As is true for any voluntary focus group, it is possible that the parents assembled may not be a truly representative sample of the opinions of all parents at the school.
2. These measures of individual growth and student goals are computer generated through a software program developed by the data manager.
3. At the ELC and in the first and second grades, the Dynamic Indicators of Basic Early Literacy Skills, or DIBELS, is used as the benchmark assessment and is administered every other week.

Chapter Three

1. Teacher pay at Boston Collegiate is competitive with the Boston Public Schools in teachers' first few years, but salary increases do not keep pace with BPS in subsequent years.

Chapter Five

1. This section is adapted in part from MATCH's facilities history, available at www.matchschool.org.
2. This 22-page document is available at http://www.matchschool.org/publications/Code.pdf.
3. This may be a result of hiring young, talented people who fit the culture, and is a trade-off that the school is willing to accept. School documents specifically welcome new teachers who believe they may leave teaching at the five-year mark. The school documents also say that they are willing to "customize" a work schedule for "lifers" who want to stay in the profession and at the school for many years. Information available at http://www.matchschool.org/publications/Teacher%20Success.pdf.

Chapter 7

1. See http://www.schoolculture.net/.
2. See, for example, http://www.keystoneaccountability.org/node/115.

Chapter 8

1. When asked to explain the spike in teacher attrition at MATCH in 2005–06, the founder stated that it "was just random chance. One had her husband relocate and followed him there. One became a full-time mom and has not worked since. One followed the 'Teach For America' profile of three years with TFA, then three years with a charter, then try something new, and so on."

Chapter 10

1. Lee Shulman, retired president of the Carnegie Foundation for the Advancement of Teaching and Professor Emeritus at Stanford University, discusses his interpretation of Jerome Bruner's Principles of Learning in "Teacher Portfolios," an essay in his book *Wisdom of Practice: Essays on Teaching, Learning, and Learning to Teach* (2004). In this essay, Shulman outlines five principles of "Effective and Enduring Learning for Students and Their Teachers." These five principles are:
   - *The principle of activity*—"Students who are the learners in these settings are remarkably active most of the time."
   - *The principle of meta cognition*—"Successful students . . . are thinking about what they are doing and why."
   - *The principle of collaboration*—"Collaboration is a marriage of insufficiencies. . . . There are difficult intellectual and professional challenges that are nearly impossible to accomplish alone but are readily addressed in the company of others."
   - *The principle of passion*—"Authentic and enduring learning occurs when teachers and students share a passion for the material, are emotionally committed to the ideas, processes, and activities, and see the work as connected to present and future goals."
   - *The principle of learning communities*—"Students and teachers both require a school and community culture that supports and rewards . . . risk taking." (pp. 513–515, italics added)
2. Bloom's Taxonomy refers to six major categories or cognitive levels of knowledge or intellectual skills. From the simplest behavior to the most complex, they include:
   - Knowledge (retrieval of information)
   - Comprehension (understanding meaning, instructions, or problems)
   - Application (use of a concept in a new situation)
   - Analysis (separation of concepts into constituent parts to understand structure)
   - Synthesis (rearrange or combine parts to create new meaning)
   - Evaluation (justify the value of information through comparison or contrast)
   (Bloom, Engelhart, Furst, Hill, & Krathwohl, 1956)
3. A hyperbola is a geometric curve resulting from the cut of a right circular cone by a plane parallel to the axis of the cone. It is one of the conic sections and has a particular algebraic form.

4. Conic sections are geometric curves that come from the intersection of a plane and a cone. Examples include ellipses, hyperbolas, circles, and parabolas; they also may be represented algebraically.

Chapter 11

1. The Massachusetts Department of Education reported graduation rate for urban schools for the 2006 graduating cohort was 62.3 percent; information available at http://www.doe.mass.edu/infoservices/reports/gradrates/06state.html.

Appendix 10.2

1. Academy of the Pacific Rim: 2006-07 APR Annual Report, available at http://www.doe.mass.edu/charter/reports/2007/annual/default.html; Boston Collegiate: 2006-07 BCCS Annual Report, available at http://www.bostoncollegiate.org/pdf/BCCS-Annual%20Report-2006-07.pdf; MATCH: 2006-07 MATCH Annual Report, available at http://www.matchschool.org/publications/2007%20Annual%20Report.pdf.
2. College Board Massachusetts Public Schools Summary of High School SAT Reasoning Tests, available at http://www.boston.com/news/daily/28/sat.pdf.

References

Academy of the Pacific Rim. (2007). *Academy of the Pacific Rim annual report, 2006–2007.* Hyde Park, MA: Academy of the Pacific Rim. Retrieved October 20, 2007, from http://www.doe.mass.edu/charter/reports/2007/annual/0412.pdf

Achievement First. (2008). *The achievement first model.* Retrieved July 12, 2008, from http://www.achievementfirst.org/af/index.php?option=com_content&task=view&id=19&Itemid=34

Anderson, L. W., & Krathwohl, D. R. (Eds.). (2001). *A taxonomy for learning, teaching, and assessing: A revision of Bloom's taxonomy of educational objectives.* New York: Longman.

Argyris, C., & Schön, D. (1974). *Theory in practice: Increasing professional effectiveness.* San Francisco: Jossey-Bass.

Barth, R. (1990). *Improving schools from within: Teachers, parents, and principals can make the difference.* San Francisco: Jossey-Bass.

Bauch, P., & Goldring, E. (1995). Parent involvement and school responsiveness: Facilitating the home-school connection in schools of choice. *Educational Evaluation and Policy Analysis, 17,* 1–21.

Birkeland, S., & Curtis, R. (2006). *Ensuring the support and development of new teachers in the Boston public schools.* Boston: Boston Public Schools.

Bloom, B. S., Engelhart, M. D., Furst, E. J., Hill, W. H., & Krathwohl, D. R. (Eds.). (1956). *Taxonomy of educational objectives: The classification of educational goals. Handbook I: Cognitive domain.* New York: David Kay.

Bosetti, L. (2001). The Alberta charter school experience. In C. R. Hepburn (Ed.), *Can the market save our schools?* (pp. 101–120). Vancouver, BC: Fraser Institute.

Boudett, K. P., City, E. A., & Murnane, R. J. (2005). *Data wise: A step-by-step guide to using assessment results to improve teaching and learning.* Cambridge, MA: Harvard Education Press.

Boyer, E. (1994). Blending the neighborhood school tradition with "choice within schools." In S. Hakim, P. Seidenstat, & G. Bowman (Eds.), *Privatizing education and educational choice: Concepts, plans, and experiences* (pp. 137–145). Westport, CT: Praeger.

Bradach, J. (1996). *Organizational alignment: The 7S model.* Boston: Harvard Business School.

Bryk, A., Lee, V., & Smith, J. (1990). High school organization and its effects on teachers and students: An interpretive summary of the research. In W. H. Clune & J. F. Witte (Eds.), *Choice and control in American education* (Vol. 1, pp. 135–226). London: Falmer.

Buddin, R., & Zimmer, R. (2005). Student achievement in charter schools: A complex picture. *Journal of Policy Analysis and Management, 24,* 351–371.

Campbell, C. (2007). Building a pipeline of new school leaders. In R. Lake (Ed.), *Hopes, fears and reality: A balanced look at charter schools in 2007* (pp. 29–42). Seattle: National Charter School Research Project.

Carnoy, M., Jacobsen, R. Mishel, L., & Rothstein, R. (2005). *The charter school dust-up: Examining the evidence on enrollment and achievement.* New York: Teachers College Press.

Carter, S. C. (2000). *No excuses: Lessons from 21 high-performing, high-poverty schools.* Washington, DC: Heritage Foundation.

Castleman, B. (2008). *Considering college outcomes in the charter school achievement debate: The effect of attending a charter school on student enrollment and persistence in college.* A proposal submitted to the American Education Research Association for presentation at the 2009 Annual Conference, San Diego, CA.

Checkley, K. (2004). A is for audacity: Lesson in leadership from Lorraine Monroe. *Educational Leadership, 61*(7)(April), 70–72.

Childress, S. (2004). *Note on strategy in public education.* Boston: Harvard Business School Press.

Childress, S., Elmore, R., Grossman, A., & Johnson, S. M. (Eds.). (2007). *Managing school districts for high performance: Cases in public education leadership.* Cambridge, MA: Harvard Education Press.

Childress, S., Elmore, R., Grossman, A., & King, C. (2007). *Note on the PELP coherence framework.* Boston: Harvard Business School.

Christensen, C. (2006). *The innovator's dilemma: The revolutionary book that will change the way you do business.* New York: Collins Business Essentials.

Churchill, N., & Lewis, V. (1983). The five stages of small business growth. *Harvard Business Review, 61*(3), 30–50.

Cohen, D. (1988). Teaching practice: Plus que ça change. In P. W. Jackson (Ed.), *Change in continuing to educational change: Perspectives on research and practice* (pp. 27–54). Berkeley, CA: McCutchan.

Cohen, D., McLaughlin, M. W., & Talbert, J. E. (Eds.). (1993). *Teaching for understanding: Challenges for policy and practice.* San Francisco: Jossey-Bass.

Colby, S., Stone, N., & Carttar, P. (2004, Fall). Zeroing in on impact. *Stanford Social Innovation Review.*

Coleman, J. S., Campbell, E., Hobson, C., McPartland, J., Mood, A., Weinfeld, F., et al. (1966). *Equality of education opportunity.* Washington, DC: U.S. Government Printing Office.

Collins, J. (2005). *Good to great and the social sectors: A monograph to accompany good to great.* Boulder, CO: James Collins.

Connell, J. P. (1990). Context, self, and action: A motivational analysis of self-system processes across the life-span. In D. Cicchetti (Ed.), *The self in transition: Infancy to childhood* (pp. 61–97). Chicago: University of Chicago Press.

Cuban, L. (2001). *How can I fix it? Finding solutions and managing dilemmas, an educator's road map*. New York: Teachers College Press.

Darling-Hammond, L. (2004). Keeping good teachers: Why it matters, what leaders can do. *Educational Leadership, 60*(8), 6-13.

Darling-Hammond, L., Ancess, J., & Ort, S. W. (2002). Reinventing high school: Outcomes of the coalition campus project. *American Educational Research Journal, 39*, 639–673.

Deming, W. E. (2000). *The new economies for industry, government, education* (2nd ed.). Cambridge, MA: MIT Press.

Doyle, W. (1983). Academic work. *Review of Educational Research, 53*, 159–199.

Doyle, W. (1988). Work in mathematics classes: The context of students' thinking during instruction. *Educational Psychologist, 23*, 167–180.

Drucker, P. F. (1980). *Managing in turbulent times*. New York: Harper & Row.

Drucker, P. F. (1985). *Innovation and entrepreneurship: Practice and principles)*. New York: Harper & Row.

Drucker, P. F. (1989). *The new realities: In government and politics, in economics and business, in society and world view*. New York: Harper & Row.

Drucker, P. F. (1990). *Managing the non-profit organization: Practices and principles*. New York: Harper Collins.

Drucker, P. F. (2006). What executives should remember. *Harvard Business Review, February, 84*, 144–152.

Eccles, J. S., Midgley, C., Wigfield, A., Miller Buchanan, C., Reuman, D., Flanagan, C., et al. (1993). Development during adolescence: The impact of stage-environment fit on young adolescents' experiences in schools and in families. *American Psychologist, 48*, 90–101.

Edmonds, R. R., & Frederiksen, J. R. (1979). *Search for effective schools: The identification and analysis of city schools that are instructionally effective for poor children*. Cambridge, MA: Harvard University. (ERIC Document Reproduction Service No. ED170396)

Education Trust. (2005). *Gaining traction, gaining ground: How some schools accelerate learning for struggling students*. Washington DC: Author. Retrieved March 10, 2008, from http://www.ecs.org/html/offsite.asp?document=+http%3A%2F%2Fwww2%2Eedtrust%2Eorg%2FNR%2Frdonlyres%2F6226B581%2D83C3%2D4447%2D9CE7%2D31C5694B9EF6%2F0%2FGainingTractionGainingGround%2Epdf

Education Trust. (2007). *Dispelling the myth online*. Retrieved August 12, 2008, from http://www2.edtrust.org/edtrust/dtm/

Elmore, R. (1992). Why restructuring alone won't improve teaching. *Educational Leadership, 49*(7), 44.

Elmore, R. F. (1995). Teaching, learning and school organization: Principles of practice and the regularities of schooling. *Educational Administration Quarterly, 31*, 355–374.

Elmore, R. F. (Ed.). (2004). *School reform from the inside out: Policy, practice, and performance.* Cambridge, MA: Harvard Education Press.

Ericson, J., & Silverman, D. (2001). *Challenge and opportunity: The impact of charter schools on school districts.* Washington, DC: U.S. Department of Education. Retrieved February 10, 2008, from http://www.ed.gov/rschstat/eval/choice/district_impact.pdf

Filby, N. (2006). *Charter high schools closing the achievement gap.* Washington DC: U.S. Department of Education.

Fine, M. (1991). *Framing dropouts: Notes on the politics of an urban public high school.* Albany: State University of New York Press.

Finn, C. E., Manno, B. V., & Vanourek, G. (2000). *Charter schools in action: Renewing public education.* Princeton, NJ: Princeton University Press.

Fullan, M., & Stiegelbauer, S. M. (1991). *The new meaning of educational change* (2nd ed.). New York: Teachers College Press.

Furst, E. J. (1981). Bloom's taxonomy of educational objectives for the cognitive domain: Philosophical and educational issues. *Review of Educational Research, 51,* 441–453.

Gill, B., Timpane, M., Ross, K., Brewer, D., & Booker, K. (2007). *Rhetoric versus reality: What we know and what we need to know about vouchers and charter schools.* Santa Monica, CA: Rand.

Graham, P. (1984). Schools: Cacophony about practice, silence about purpose. *Daedalus, 113*(4), 27–57.

Graham, P. A. (2005). *Schooling America: How the public schools meet the nation's changing needs.* New York: Oxford University Press.

Hawkins, D. (1974). *The informed vision: Essays on learning and human nature.* New York: Agathon Press.

Henderson, A., & Berla, N. (1994). *A new generation of evidence: The family is critical to student achievement.* Washington, DC: National Committee for Citizens in Education.

Henig, J. R., Holyoke, T. T., Brown, H., & Lacireno-Paquet, N. (2005). The influence of founder type on charter school structures and operations. *American Journal of Education, 111,* 487–522.

Hiebert, J., Carpenter, T., Fennema, E., Fuson, K., Wearne, D., Murray, H., et al. (1997). *Making sense: Teaching and learning mathematics with understanding.* Portsmouth, NH: Heinemann.

Hill, P., Lake, R., Celio, M., Campbell, C., Herdman, P., & Bulkley, K. (2001). *A study of charter school accountability.* Washington, DC: U.S. Department. of Education, Office of Educational Research and Improvement. Retrieved March 10, 2008, from http://www.ed.gov/pubs/chartacct/

Hill, P. T., Pierce, L. C., & Guthrie, J. W. (1997). *Reinventing public education: How contracting can transform America's schools.* Chicago: University of Chicago Press.

Hollander, E. P. (1978). *Leadership dynamics: A practical guide to effective relationships.* New York: Free Press.

Ingersoll, R. (2001). Teacher turnover and teacher shortages: An organizational analysis. *American Educational Research Journal, 38,* 499–534.

Ingersoll, R. (2002). The teacher shortage: A case of wrong diagnosis and wrong prescription. *NASSP Bulletin, 86*(631), 16–31.

Ingersoll, R. (2004). *Why do high-poverty schools have difficulty staffing their classrooms with qualified teachers?* [A joint initiative of the Center for American Progress and the Institute for America's Future. Renewing Our Schools, Securing Our Future]. November 19, 2004. Washington, DC: Center for American Progress.

Jencks, A. (1972). The Coleman report and conventional wisdom. In F. Mosteller & D. Moynihan (Eds.), *On equality of education opportunity* (pp. 69–115). New York: Random House.

Jenks, C., Smith, M., Acland, H., Bane, M. J., Cohen,, D., Gintis, H., et al.. (1973). *Inequality: A reassessment of the effect of family and schooling in America.* New York: Harper & Row.

Kanter, R. M. (1983). *The change masters: Innovation for productivity in the American corporation.* New York: Simon and Schuster.

Kaplan, R., & Leonard, H. (2005). *Aligning mission, support and capacity in public sector programs (draft).* Cambridge, MA: Harvard University Press.

Kennedy, M. (2005). *Inside teaching.* Cambridge, MA: Harvard University Press.

KIPP Foundation. (2007). *About KIPP: Five pillars.* Retrieved July 12, 2008, from http://www.kipp.org/01/fivepillars.cfm

Koretz, D. (2008). *Measuring up: What educational testing really tells us.* Cambridge, MA: Harvard University Press.

Lake, R. J., & Hill, P. T. (Eds.). (2005). *Hopes, fears, and reality: A balanced look at American charter schools in 2005.* Seattle: National Charter School Research Project. Retrieved February 13, 2008, from http://www.crpe.org/cs/crpe/view/csr_pubs/3

Lake, R. J., & Hill, P. (Eds.). (2006). *Hopes, fears, & reality: A balanced look at American charter schools in 2006.* Seattle: National Charter School Research Project. Retrieved February 13, 2008, from http://www.crpe.org/cs/crpe/view/csr_pubs/8

Lake, R. J. (Ed.). (2007). *Hopes, fears, & reality: A balanced look at American charter schools in 2007.* Seattle: National Charter School Research Project. Retrieved February 13, 2008, from http://www.ncsrp.org/cs/csr/view/csr_pubs/17

Lampert, M. (1985). How do teachers manage to teach? Perspectives on problems of practice. *Harvard Education Review, 55,* 178–194.

Lee, V., Smith, J., & Croninger, R. (1995). Another look at high school restructuring: More evidence that it improves student achievement and more insight into why. Issues in restructuring schools. *Newsletter of the Center on Organization and Restructuring of Schools.* University of Wisconsin, Madison.

Lee, V. E., & Ready, D. D. (2007). *Schools within schools: Possibilities and pitfalls of high school reform.* New York: Teachers College Press.

Lee, V. E., & Smith, J. B. (1995). Effects of high school restructuring and size on early gains in achievement and engagement. *Sociology of Education, 68,* 241–270.

Leschly, S. (2007). *Reform in large urban districts.* Unpublished manuscript.

Letts, C., Grossman, A., & Ryan, W. (1999). *High performance nonprofit organizations: Managing upstream for greater impact.* New York: John Wiley.

Lieberman, A. (1988). *Building a professional culture in schools.* New York: Teachers College Press.

Lieberman, A. (Ed.). (1995). *The work of restructuring schools: Building from the ground up.* New York: Teachers College Press.

Lightfoot, S. L. (1983). *The good high school.* New York: Basic Books.

Little, J. (1993). Teacher's professional development in a climate of educational reform. *Educational Evaluation and Policy Analysis, 15,* 129–151.

Lubienski, C., & Lubienski, S. T. (2006). *Charter, private, public schools and academic achievement: New evidence from NAEP mathematics data.* New York: National Center for the Study of Privatization in Education.

March, J. G., & Olsen, J. P. (1976). *Ambiguity and choice in organizations.* Bergen, Norway: Universitetsforlaget.

Markow, D., Fuath, S., & Gravitch, D. (2001). *The MetLife survey of the American teacher 2001: Key elements of quality schools.* Washington, DC: Metropolitan Life Foundation.

Marzano, R. J., & Kendall, J. S. (2007). *The new taxonomy of educational objectives* (2nd ed.). Thousand Oaks, CA: Corwin Press.

Massachusetts Department of Education. (1997). Regulation 603 CMR 27.00. Retrieved March 12, 2008, from http://www.doe.mass.edu/lawsregs/603cmr27.html

MATCH Charter Public High School. (2001). *MATCH annual report, 2000–2001.* Boston: MATCH Charter Public High School.

Maxwell, J. A. (Ed.). (2005). *Qualitative research design: An interactive approach* (2nd ed.). Thousand Oaks, CA: Sage.

Meyer, J., & Rowan, B. (1978). The structure of educational organizations. In J. Meyer & R. Scott (Eds.), *Environments and organizations: Theoretical perspectives* (pp. 78–109). San Francisco: Jossey-Bass.

Meyerson, D. (2008). *Rocking the boat: How to inspire change within your organization.* Boston: Harvard Business School Press.

Miles, K. (2001). *Rethinking school resources* [District Issues Brief]. Arlington, VA: New American Schools. Retrieved June 10, 2008, from http://www.educationresourcestrategies.org/documents/rethinking-resources.pdf

Miles, K., & Darling-Hammond, L. (1998). Rethinking the allocation of teaching resources: Some lessons from high-performing schools. *Educational Evaluation and Policy Analysis, 20,* 9–29.

Miles, K. H., & Frank, S. (2008). *The strategic school: Making the most of people, time and money.* Watertown, MA: Education Resource Strategies.

Miron, G., & Applegate, B. (2007). *Teacher attrition in charter schools.* Retrieved July 3, 2008, from http://epsl.asu.edu/epru/documents/EPSL-0705-234-EPRU.pdf

Mosteller, F., & Moynihan, D. (1972). *On equality of education opportunity.* New York: Random House.

Murnane, R. J., & Phillips, B. R. (1981). What do effective teachers of inner-city children have in common? *Social Science Research, 10,* 83–100.

Nadler, D., & Tushman, M. (1977). A diagnostic model for organizational behavior. In J. R. Hackman, E. Lawler & L. Porter (Eds.), *Perspectives on behavior in organizations* (pp. 85–98). New York: McGraw-Hill.

Nadler, D. A., & Tushman, M. L. (1980). A model for diagnosing organizational behavior. *Organizational Dynamics, 9*(2), 35–51.

National Center for Education Statistics. (2007). *Table 95: Public elementary schools, by grade span, average school size, and state or jurisdiction: 2005-06.* Retrieved March 10, 2008, from http://nces.ed.gov/programs/digest/d07/tables/dt07_095.asp

National Commission on Teaching and America's Future. (2003). *No dream denied: A pledge to America's children. Summary report.* Washington, DC: National Commission on Teaching and America's Future.

National Research Council, Committee on Science Education K–12 and Mathematical Sciences Education Board. (1999). *Global perspectives for local action: Using TIMMS to improve math and science education.* Washington, DC: National Academies Press.

Nelson, C., & Miron, G. (2005). *Exploring the correlates of academic success in Pennsylvania charter schools.* National Center for the Study of Privatization in Education.

Neufeld, B., & Roper, D. (2003). *Coaching as a strategy for instructional capacity development: Promises and practicalities.* Cambridge, MA: Education Matters.

Oliver Wyman Group. (2003). *The congruence model: A roadmap for understanding organizational performance.* Retrieved March 4, 2008, from http://www.oliverwyman.com/ow/pdf_files/Congruence_Model_INS.pdf

O'Reilly, C. A., III, & Tushman, M. L. (2004). The ambidextrous organization. *Harvard Business Review, 82*(4), 74–81.

Oster, S. (1995). *Strategic management for nonprofit organizations: Theory and cases.* New York: Oxford University Press.

Osterman, K. F. (2000). Students need for belonging in the school community. *Review of Educational Research, 70,* 323–367.

Peterson, K. (2002). Positive or negative. *Journal of Staff Development, 23*(2), 10–15.

Peterson, K., & Deal, T. (1999). *Shaping school culture: The heart of leadership.* San Francisco: Jossey-Bass.

Peterson, K., & Deal, T. (2002). *Shaping school culture fieldbook.* San Francisco: Jossey-Bass.

Porter, M. E. (1980). *Competitive strategy.* New York: Free Press.

Porter, M. E. (1996). What is strategy? *Harvard Business Review, 74*(6), 61–78.

Porter, A. (2006). Curriculum assessment. In J. L. Green, G. Camille, & P. B. Elmore (Eds.), *Handbook of complementary methods in education research* (pp. 141–159). Washington, DC: American Educational Research Association.

Porter, A. (2007). *The effect of a professional development intervention in middle school mathematics and sciences: Using alignment as a dependent variable* [PowerPoint slides]. Retrieved on September 20, 2008, from http://www.ccsso.org/content/pdfs/AlignmentAnalysisAsVariable_Porter.pdf, slide 12.

Public Agenda Foundation. (1996). *First things first: What Americans expect from the public schools*. New York: Public Agenda Foundation.

Purkey, S., & Smith, M. (1985). School reform: The district policy implications of the effective schools literature. *The Elementary School Journal, 85,* 352–389.

Reeves, D. (2000). *High performance in high poverty schools: 90/90/90 and beyond*. Retrieved March 30, 2008, from http://www.sabine.k12.la.us/online/leadershipacademy/high%20performance%2090%2090%2090%20and%20beyond.pdf

Richardson, J. (2001). School culture survey. *Tools For Schools, 4*(5).

Rockoff, J. (2004). The impact of individual teachers on student achievement: Evidence from panel data. *American Economic Review, 94,* 247–252.

Rose, L. C., & Gallup, A. M. (2007). The 39th annual Phi Delta Kappa/Gallup poll of the public's attitudes toward the public schools. *Phi Delta Kappan, 89,* 33–45.

Rothstein, R. (2004). *Class and schools: Using social, economic and educational reform to close the black-white achievement gap*. New York: Teachers College.

RPP International. (2000). *The state of charter schools 2000: National study of charter schools* [Fourth-Year Report]. Washington, DC: U.S. Department of Education, Office of Educational Research and Improvement.

Rutter, M., Maughan, B., Mortimore, P., & Ouston, J. (1979). *Fifteen thousand hours: Secondary schools and the effects on children*. Cambridge, MA: Harvard University Press.

Sarason, S. (1971). *The culture of the school and the problem of change*. Boston: Allyn & Bacon.

Schein, E. (1985). *Organizational culture and leadership*. San Francisco: Jossey-Bass.

Seddon, G. M. (1978). The properties of Bloom's taxonomy of educational objectives for the cognitive domain. *Review of Educational Research, 48,* 303–323.

Sizer, T. (1992). *Horace's compromise*. Boston: Houghton Mifflin.

Shulman, L. S. (2004). *The wisdom of practice: Essays on teaching, learning and learning to teach*. San Francisco: Jossey-Bass.

Smith, T. M., & Ingersoll, R. M. (2004). What are the effects of induction and mentoring on beginning teacher turnover? *American Educational Research Journal, 41,* 681–701.

Spillane, J., & Diamond, J. B. (Eds.). (2007). *Distributed leadership in practice*. New York: Teachers College Press.

Stein, M., Smith, M., Henningsen, M., & Silver, E. (2000). *Implementing standards-based mathematics instruction: A casebook for professional development*. New York: Teachers College Press.

Stigler, J., & Hiebert, J. (1999). *The teaching gap: Best ideas from the world's teachers for improving education in the classroom*. San Francisco: Jossey-Bass.

Strauss, A., & Corbin, J. (1990). *Basics of qualitative research*. Newbury Park, CA: Sage.

Terry, R. W. (1993). *Authentic leadership: Courage in action*. San Francisco: Jossey-Bass.

Tschannen-Moran, M., Parish, J., & DiPaola, M. (2006). School climate: The interplay between interpersonal relationships and student achievement. *Journal of School Leadership, 16,* 386–415.

Tushman, M. L., & O'Reilly, C. A. (2002). *Winning through innovation: A practical guide to leading organizational change and renewal.* Boston: Harvard Business School Press.

Tyack, D. B., & Cuban, L. (1995). *Tinkering toward utopia: A century of public school reform.* Cambridge, MA: Harvard University Press.

UCLA Charter School Study. (1998). *Beyond the rhetoric of charter school reform: A study of ten California school districts.* Los Angeles: University of California, Los Angeles.

U.S. Census Bureau. (2006). *Lawrence, Massachusetts* [2006 American Community Survey data profile highlights]. Available at U.S. Census Bureau website http://factfinder.census.gov/

U.S. Department of Education,. (2004). *Innovations in education: Successful charter schools.* Washington, DC: U.S. Department of Education, Department of Innovation and Improvement. Retrieved October 10, 2007, from http://www.ed.gov/admins/comm/choice/charter/index.html

Valenzuela, A. (1999). *Subtractive schooling: U.S. Mexican youth and the politics of caring.* Albany: State University of New York Press.

Wagner, C., & Masden-Copas, P. (2002). An audit of the culture starts with two handy tools. *Journal of Staff Development, 23*(3), 42–53.

Walser, N. (2008, September-October). Teaching 21st century skills. What does it look like in practice? *Harvard Education Letter, 24*(5), pp. 1–3.

Waterman R. H., Jr., Peters, T. J., & Phillips, J. R. (1980). Structure is not organization. *Business Horizons, 23*(3), 14–26.

Zimmer, R., & Buddin, R. (2007). Getting inside the black box: Examining how the operation of charter schools affects performance. *Peabody Journal of Education, 82*(2-3), 231–273.

Zollers, N. J., & Ramanathan, A. K. (1998). For-profit charter schools and students with disabilities: The sordid side of the business of schooling. *Phi Delta Kappan, 80,* 297-304.

About the Authors

Dr. Katherine K. Merseth, the principal investigator of this study, has over forty years of experience in instruction, administration, and research in public education in the United States and internationally. She taught math in traditional public middle and high schools for ten years, has provided instruction in math pedagogy, and is the director of the Harvard Graduate School of Education (HGSE) Teacher Education Program, which she founded in 1984. Merseth holds a master's degree in mathematics from Boston College, and both a master of arts in teaching and a doctorate in education administration, planning, and social policy from HGSE.

Kristy Cooper is a National Board Certified teacher who taught elementary school for six years in traditional public schools. She is an editorial board member of the *Harvard Educational Review,* holds a master's degree in education from the University of California, Los Angeles, and a master's degree in education policy and management from the Harvard Graduate School of Education. Cooper is in her fourth year of doctoral studies in education policy, leadership, and instructional practice at HGSE.

John Roberts worked as a teacher in a traditional public high school for four years and as principal of a charter school for three years. He holds a master's degree in administration, planning, and social policy from the Harvard Graduate School of Education and works as a consultant for a charter school in Lowell, Massachusetts. He is in his third year of the doctoral degree program in education policy, leadership, and instructional practice at HGSE.

Mara Casey Tieken has three years of experience teaching in a traditional public elementary school and one year teaching preschool as a Harris Fellow at the Yale Child Study Center. She is the cochair of the *Harvard Educational Review* editorial board, holds a master's degree in education from the Harvard Graduate School of Education, and is entering her fourth year as a doctoral student in the culture, communities, and education concentration at HGSE.

Jon Valant has four years of experience working at charter schools, one year as a tutor and afterschool coordinator and three years as a data analyst and curriculum developer. He holds a master's degree in public policy from Harvard University's John F. Kennedy School of Government. Valant currently consults with various charter management organizations and is a first-year doctoral student in administration and policy analysis at the Stanford University Graduate School of Education.

Chris Wynne's teaching experience includes three years in a traditional public middle school and four years in a charter middle and high school. He is an editorial board member of the *Harvard Educational Review* and holds a master's degree in human development and psychology from the Harvard Graduate School of Education. Wynne is currently a fourth-year doctoral student in the education policy, leadership, and instructional practice concentration at HGSE.

Index